CREDIT
DERIVATIVES
&
THE
MANAGEMENT
OF RISK

INCLUDING MODELS FOR
CREDIT RISK

RELATED BOOKS BY THE AUTHOR

CREDIT
DERIVATIVES
&
THE
MANAGEMENT
OF RISK

INCLUDING MODELS FOR
CREDIT RISK

DIMITRIS N. CHORAFAS

NEW YORK INSTITUTE OF FINANCE

NEW YORK • TORONTO • SYDNEY • TOKYO • SINGAPORE

Library of Congress Cataloging-in-Publication Data

Chorafas, Dimitris N.
    Credit derivatives and the management of risk / Dimitris N. Chorafas.
       p. cm.
    Includes bibliographical references and index.
    ISBN 0-7352-0104-8 (cloth)
    1. Credit derivatives. I. Title.
    HG6024.A3C488 2000
    332.63'2—dc21
                                           99-23606
                                              CIP

Printed in the United States of America

10 9 8 7 6 5 4 3 2 1

This publication is designed to provide accurate and authoritative information in regard to the subject matter covered. It is sold with the understanding that the publisher is not engaged in rendering legal, accounting, or other professional services. If legal advice or other expert assistance is required, the services of a competent professional person should be sought.

—From a Declaration of Principles jointly adopted
by a Committee of the American Bar Association
and a Committee of Publishers and Associations

ISBN 0-7352-0104-8

ATTENTION: CORPORATIONS AND SCHOOLS

Prentice Hall books are available at quantity discounts with bulk purchase for educational, business, or sales promotional use. For information, please write to: Prentice Hall Special Sales, 240 Frisch Court, Paramus, New Jersey 07652. Please supply: title of book, ISBN, quantity, how the book will be used, date needed.

 NEW YORK INSTITUTE OF FINANCE

On the World Wide Web at http://www.phdirect.com

NYIF and NEW YORK INSTITUTE OF FINANCE are trademarks of Executive Tax Reports, Inc., used under license by Prentice Hall Direct, Inc.

Contents

PART ONE
UNDERSTANDING THE MANAGERIAL BASIS AND CONSEQUENCES OF CREDIT DERIVATIVES

Chapter 1
CREDIT DERIVATIVES AND THEIR IMPACT ON THE FINANCIAL INDUSTRY

Chapter 2
ASSETS, LIABILITIES, THE TRADING BOOK, AND THE BANKING BOOK   31

Chapter 3
INFORMATION REQUIREMENTS FOR ISSUERS AND USERS OF CREDIT DERIVATIVES   53

Chapter 4
CREDIT DERIVATIVES, TRANSPARENCY, AND COLLATERALIZATION   71

Chapter 5
FUND MANAGERS AND CREDIT DERIVATIVES MARKETS   89

PART TWO
CREDIT DERIVATIVES INSTRUMENTS AND THEIR UNDERLIERS

Chapter 6
ASSET SWAPS, TOTAL RETURN SWAPS, AND DEFAULT SWAPS
111

Chapter 7
CREDIT-LINKED INSTRUMENTS, STRUCTURED NOTES, AND CREDIT-ENHANCED VENTURES
131

Chapter 8

CREDIT SPREADS, CREDIT OPTIONS, AND DEBT OPTIONS

Chapter 9

CREDIT DERIVATIVES AND CATASTROPHE INSURANCE

Chapter 10

NEW DERIVATIVES INSTRUMENTS, HEDGING POLICIES, AND CREDIT RATING AGENCIES

PART THREE
MODELS FOR THE EVALUATION AND MANAGEMENT OF CREDIT RISK

Chapter 11
THE ART OF MODELING CREDIT RISK AND ITS ANALYTICS   201

Chapter 12
BUILDING IMPROVED VERSIONS OF ACRA AND OTHER CREDIT MODELS   219

Chapter 13

Chapter 14

Chapter 15

Chapter 16
ROCKET SCIENTISTS   293

INDEX

Foreword

"That was the day Smiley went on the attack."
John LeCarré

In every market, business, or life there comes a time when it is necessary to move from being observers of events to being managers of those events. This is what's happening today in the management of credit risk.

Credit risk is the oldest form of risk in the financial markets. Credit can be defined as "nothing but the expectation of a sum of money within some limited time." Then credit risk is the chance that this expectation will not be met. The business of taking credit risk began when banks were organized in Florence 700 years ago. Since then banking institutions have been society's primary lenders, and managing credit risk formed the core of their expertise. For most of their history, banks made a loan and waited for it to be repaid or hoped that it would be repaid. At a recent moment in history things changed. Managing credit risk became something essential to ensure success in financial service.

Financial institutions are undergoing phenomenal change. However, in functional terms, financial service really has not changed at all. Financial service has always been a place to put your savings, a place to keep liquid assets, a place to borrow money to purchase a home, car, or business, a place to invest for retirement or send a child to school, a way of sharing life's risk. These functions have been a constant in every generation. But who provides these services has changed dramatically. The traditional providers have been banks and insurance companies. Today they are competing with a variety of new entrants—specialty finance and insurance companies, pension and mutual fund operators—all who have made great inroads into the market share of their more established competitors. As a consequence, the traditional players—particularly the bankers—are looking to manage themselves more effectively. No longer do they have a buy-and-hold mentality. Today's modern bankers look to make a loan, warehouse it for a time, and send it off into the capital markets. In order to do that successfully, they need to become more sophisticated about the assets that they have created. What are the probabilities of default? What is the likelihood that a loan might deteriorate or improve during its life? What are the pricing consequences? They must learn how to slice and dice the assets for different investor needs. They have to recognize that investors generally manage risk through diversification so they have to create diversified pools where the assets exhibit low correlations to each other. In this new world, technology and analytical tools are enormously important.

Meaningful changes are only possible when we have new tools to facilitate the change. The eighties were a decade when the focus was on market and interest rate rise. The successful management of these risks was only possible when sophisticated new options models were developed. Similarly, the taming of credit risk will only happen when new reliable tools are developed to help do this job. New analytical tools to measure, manage, and control credit risk are created and promoted just about every day, making the present a very exciting time for credit professionals. But revolutions are also times of enormous uncertainty. How reliable are the new tools? How firm is the science underlying their development? Do the new techniques truly enhance an institution's ability to manage credit risk? Do they expose an institution to new forms of risk?

Credit derivatives will be a powerful tool and catalyst in this analytical revolution. When we buy an asset or make a loan with a plan to hold on to it until it matures or is used up, generally we don't worry too much about pricing changes that might occur in the interim. However, when we buy it with a plan to sell that asset before maturity, then price and changes in its value over time become much more important. This is why secondary markets, syndication of risk, and financial guarantee insurance have become significant activities in the past 20 years. It is also the reason that credit derivatives have become the latest market rage. One of the important reasons for changes in market value in a debt security is a change in the economic fortunes of the issuer. The market is constantly valuing and revaluing these instruments against other alternative investments. As more financial institutions mark-to-market their credit portfolios, the need for hedging these risks grows. As these same organizations become more skilled at risk management, they inevitably incorporate portfolio diversification techniques into their system, and the need for hedging credit risk grows. And, finally, as they fully understand the nature of the concentration of counterparty risk that is a result of our modern consolidating financial market, the need for hedging credit risk grows.

Dr. Chorafas has tackled these subjects and more in *Credit Derivatives and the Management of Risk*. This comprehensive review provides perspective, asks important questions, and points us in the direction of where this important market and the tools that underpin it are headed.

This book is recommended reading for all those interested in these subjects.

Preface

Sir Francis Bacon (1561–1626) once stated that three things made his world different from that of the ancient Greeks and Romans: the printing press, the compass, and gunpowder. He did not mention the water pump yet it was critical to the advancement of agriculture and commerce.

Taking a similar approach to present-day finance, senior executives who contributed to the research that led to this book were asked to name the top three factors that three centuries down the line might distinguish, for our successors, the world in which we are living. In the majority of cases, the answers have been

- Deregulation and globalization of banking,
- Derivative financial instruments, and
- Networks, computers, and software.

But like the 17th century's top list, this three-bullet description is incomplete, since it makes no reference to *models, simulation,* and *cyberspace.* Yet, inventiveness in finance by way of derivatives, which has become the moving gear of a modern economy, is not possible without advanced mathematical tools.

Rapid innovation and *risk management* underpin the financial industry's new strides and they characterize the way tier-1 banks operate. While the clout of old financial products is fading, credit derivatives and other leveraged instruments alter the financial landscape and fill it with many unknowns. Due to this fact, regulators maintain a healthy skepticism toward the new instruments while they try to understand their mechanics and assess their further-out risks.

Whether from the Basle Committee of Banking Supervision, the Financial Accounting Standards Board (FASB) in the United States, the Accounting Standards Board (ASB) in the UK, or any other authority, the new accounting standards and regulations address the growing levels of exposure in finance, and aim to make reporting more transparent. Nobody has all the answers. As an old Spanish proverb warns, "Traveler, there are no roads. Roads are made by walking."

This book is written for practitioners in investment banking and commercial banking as well as for supervisors. Typically, its reader wishes to update his or her skills in terms of new financial instruments and their impact on the bottom line—most specifically, *credit derivatives* and *models* as well as the business opportunities associated with them.

The book is divided into three parts. Part One addresses the dynamics of credit derivatives, focusing on the managerial basis and the most likely consequences in terms of profits and losses. Chapter 1 defines credit derivatives and looks into their impact on the financial industry. Because credit derivatives are essentially debit derivatives, Chapter 2 takes a look at assets, liabilities, the trading book, and the banking book.

The focus of Chapter 3 is information requirements of issuers and users of credit derivatives. This is a vital issue, yet little attention has been paid to it so far. Chapter 4 treats two subjects: the need for transparency and the risks of collateralization. Chapter 5 explores new markets for credit derivatives including retirement plans and private banking.

Part Two is dedicated to the instruments of credit derivatives and their underliers. Chapter 6 handles asset swaps, total return swaps, and default swaps. The theme of Chapter 7 is credit-linked instruments, structured notes, and credit-enhanced ventures. Chapter 8 looks at credit spreads, credit options, and debt options.

While the instruments treated in Chapters 6 through 8 are those most people today believe constitute the credit derivatives landscape, other more imaginative financial products are waiting in the wings. This is the case with securitization of catastrophe insurance, for both natural and man-made large accidents, as presented in Chapter 9. Chapter 10 goes a step further, addressing hurricane derivatives and energy derivatives. As the reader will appreciate in the text, all of them have as underlying factors credit risk and its securitization.

Part Three provides the third pillar of the credit derivatives edifice: the contribution expected from technology and models. After an introduction to the modeling of credit risk in Chapter 11, Chapter 12 follows up with an analysis of the Actuarial Credit Risk Accounting (ACRA) system—its strengths, its weaknesses, and the supplements that it needs. Chapter 13 does the same for RiskMetrics, CreditMetrics, and CreditRisk+.

Using the same frame of reference of describing and evaluating existing credit risk models that can be bought off-the-shelf, Chapter 14 discusses the Risk Adjusted Return on Capital (RAROC), CreditPortfolioView, and the Loan Analysis System (LAS). The theme of Chapter 15 is a model that in a matter of just three years has been accepted by practically every institution, value at risk (VAR). It is reviewed from the perspective of satisfying both managerial and regulatory requirements.

But who is going to build all these models, upgrade them, maintain them, and fine-tune them? The answer is the rocket scientists, the subject of Chapter 16. Rocket scientists are expected to develop new products, simulate them on high-speed computers, and experiment with the models they build. They must also be wizards at improving existing models. The chapter examines two cases where improvements are needed: ACRA and CreditMetrics.

Chapter 16 also brings the reader's attention to the need for rigorous risk management. Risk management poses a massive technology problem made more complex by the fact that most institutions still have legacy systems that use various types of basic software that don't talk to one another. Quite often, even at the same site, a bank's trading and position keeping systems are based on different technologies. This is highly counterproductive.

Information on the trader, the instrument, the counterparty, and the trading unit should be fully integrated in order to evaluate and control risk. Senior managers should be linked to one another through *interactive computational finance*—which means ad hoc in real time. Only then sophisticated instruments like credit derivatives can be handled effectively, and only then the work by rocket scientists makes sense.

I am indebted to a long list of knowledgeable people and organizations for their contribution to the research that made this book possible. Thanks also go to several senior executives and experts for constructive criticism during the preparation of the manuscript. The complete list of the 124 senior executives and 70 organizations participating in this research is shown in the Acknowledgments.

Let me take this opportunity to thank Ellen Schneid Coleman for suggesting this project and seeing it all the way to publication, and Bruce Sylvester and Sharon L. Gonzalez for the editing work. To Eva-Maria Binder goes the credit for compiling the research results, typing the text, and preparing the camera-ready artwork and index.

Dr. Dimitris N. Chorafas
Valmer and Vitznau

Acknowledgments

(Countries are listed in alphabetical order.)

The following organizations through their senior executives and system specialists participated in the recent research projects that led to the contents of this book and its documentation.

AUSTRIA

National Bank of Austria

Dr. Martin Ohms
Finance Market Analysis Department

3, Otto Wagner Platz
Postfach 61
A-1011 Vienna

Association of Austrian Banks and Bankers

Dr. Fritz Diwok
Secretary General

11, Boersengasse
1013 Vienna

Bank Austria

Dr. Peter Fischer
Senior General Manager, Treasury Division

Peter Gabriel
Deputy General Manager, Trading

2, Am Hof
1010 Vienna

Creditanstalt

Dr. Wolfgang Lichtl
Market Risk Management

Julius Tandler Platz 3
A-1090 Vienna

Wiener Betriebs and Baugesellschaft mbH

Dr. Josef Fritz
General Manager

1, Anschützstrasse
1153 Vienna

FRANCE

Banque de France

Pierre Jaillet
Director, Monetary Studies and Statistics

Yvan Oronnal
Manager, Monetary Analyses and Statistics

G. Tournemire
Analyst, Monetary Studies

39, rue Croix des Petits Champs
75001 Paris

*Secretariat Général de la Commission Bancaire
—Banque de France*

Didier Peny
Head of Big Banks and International Banks Department

Michel Martino
International Affairs

Benjamin Sahel
Market Risk Control

73, rue de Richelieu
75002 Paris

Ministry of Finance and the Economy,
Conseil National de la Comptabilité

Alain Le Bars
Director International Relations and Cooperation

6, rue Louise Weiss
75703 Paris Cedex 13

GERMANY

Deutsche Bundesbank

Hans-Dietrich Peters
Director

Hans Werner Voth
Director

Wilhelm-Epstein Strasse 14
60431 Frankfurt-am-Main

Federal Banking Supervisory Office

Hans-Joachim Dohr
Director Dept. I

Jochen Kayser
Risk Model Examination

Ludger Hanenberg
Internal Controls

71-101 Gardeschützenweg
12203 Berlin

European Central Bank

Mauro Grande
Director

29 Kaiserstrasse
29th Floor
60216 Frankfurt-am-Main

Deutsches Aktieninstitut

Dr. Rüdiger Von Rosen
President

Biebergasse 6 bis 10
60313 Frankfurt-am-Main

Commerzbank

Peter Bürger
Senior Vice President, Strategy and Controlling

Markus Rumpel
Senior Vice President, Credit Risk Management

Kaiserplatz
60261 Frankfurt-am-Main

Deutsche Bank

Professor Manfred Timmermann
Head of Controlling

Hans Voit
Head of Process Management, Controlling Department

12, Taunusanlage
60325 Frankfurt

Dresdner Bank

Dr. Marita Balks
Investment Bank, Risk Control

Dr. Hermann Haaf
Mathematical Models for Risk Control

Claas Carsten Kohl
Financial Engineer

1, Jürgen Ponto Platz
60301 Frankfurt

GMD First—Research Institute for Computer Architecture, Software Technology and Graphics

Prof. Dr. Ing. Wolfgang K. Giloi
General Manager

5, Rudower Chaussee
D-1199 Berlin

HUNGARY

Hungarian Banking and Capital Market Supervision

Dr. Janos Kun
Head, Department of Regulation and Analyses

Dr. Erika Vörös
Senior Economist, Department of Regulation and Analyses

Dr. Géza Nyiry
Head, Section of Information Audit

Csalogany u. 9-11
H-1027 Budapest

Hungarian Academy of Sciences

Prof. Dr. Tibor Vamos
Chairman, Computer and Automation Research Institute

Nador U. 7
1051 Budapest

ITALY

Banca d'Italia

Eugene Gaiotti
Research Department, Monetary and Financial Division

Ing. Dario Focarelli
Research Department

91, via Nazionale
00184 Rome

Instituto Bancario San Paolo di Torino

Dr. Paolo Chiulenti
Director of Budgeting

Roberta Costa
Director of Private Banking

Pino Ravelli
Director Bergamo Region

27, via G. Camozzi
24121 Bergamo

LUXEMBOURG

Banque Générale de Luxembourg

Prof. Dr. Yves Wagner
Director of Asset and Risk Management

Hans Jörg Paris
International Risk Manager
27, avenue Monterey
L-2951 Luxembourg

POLAND

Securities and Exchange Commission

Beata Stelmach
Secretary of the Polish
1, Pl Powstancow Warszawy
00-950 Warsaw

SWEDEN

Skandinaviska Enskilda Banken

Bernt Gyllenswärd
Head of Group Audit
Box 16067
10322 Stockholm

Irdem AB

Gian Medri
Former Director of Research at Nordbanken
19, Flintlasvagen
S-19154 Sollentuna

SWITZERLAND

Swiss National Bank

Dr. Werner Hermann
Head of International Monetary Relations

Dr. Christian Walter
Representative to the Basle Committee

Robert Fluri
Assistant Director, Statistics Section
15 Börsenstrasse
8021 Zurich

Federal Banking Commission

Dr. Susanne Brandenberger
Risk Management

Renate Lischer
Representative to Risk Management Subgroup, Basle Committee

Marktgasse 37
3001 Bern

Bank for International Settlements

Mr. Claude Sivy
Head of Internal Audit

Herbie Poenisch
Senior Economist, Monetary and Economic Department

2, Centralplatz
4002 Basle

Bank Leu AG

Dr. Urs Morgenthaler
Member of Management
Director of Risk Control

32, Bahnhofstrasse
8022 Zurich

Bank J. Vontobel and Vontobel Holding

Heinz Frauchiger
Chief, Internal Audit Department

Tödistrasse 23
CH-8022 Zurich

Union Bank of Switzerland

Dr. Heinrich Steinmann
Member of the Executive Board (Retired)

45, Bahnhofstrasse
8021 Zurich

The Geneva Association

Dr. Orio Giarini
Secretary General and Director

18, Chemin Rieu
1208 Geneva

Prudential-Bache Securities

Yvonne Stucki-Vast
Senior Vice President
17, Bellerivestrasse
8034 Zurich

UNITED KINGDOM

Bank of England and Financial Services Authority

Richard Britton
Head, Prudential Supervision Department
Threadneedle Street
London EC2R 8AH

British Bankers Association

Paul Chisnall, Assistant Director
Pinners Hall
105-108 Old Broad Street
London EC2N 1EX

Accounting Standards Board

A.V.C. Cook, Technical Director

Sandra Thompson, Project Director
Holborn Hall
100 Gray's Inn Road
London WC1X 8AL

Barclays Bank Plc

Brandon Davies
Treasurer, Global Corporate Banking

Alan Brown
Director, Group Risk
54 Lombard Street
London EC3P 3AH

ABN-AMRO Investment Bank N.V.

David Woods
Chief Operations Officer, Global Equity Directorate
199 Bishopsgate
London EC2M 3TY

Bankgesellschaft Berlin

Stephen F. Myers
Head of Market Risk

1 Crown Court
Cheapside, London EC2V 6JP

Standard & Poor's

David T. Beers
Managing Director, Sovereign Ratings

Garden House
18 Finsbury Circus
London EC2M 7BP

Moody's Investor Services

Samuel S. Theodore
Managing Director, European Banks

David Frohriep
Communications Manager, Europe

2 Minster Court
Mincing Lange
London EC3R 7XB

Fitch IBCA

Charles Prescott
Group Managing Director, Banks

David Andrews
Managing Director, Financial Institutions

Travor Pitman
Managing Director, Corporations

Richard Fox
Director, International Public Finance

Eldon House
2 Eldon Street
London EC2M 7UA

Merrill Lynch International

Erik Banks
Managing Director of Risk Management

Ropemaker Place
London EC2Y 9LY

The Auditing Practices Board

Jonathan E.C. Grant
Technical Director

Steve Leonard
Internal Controls Project Manager

P.O. Box 433
Moorgate Place
London EC2P 2BJ

International Accounting Standards Committee

Ms. Liesel Knorr
Technical Director

166 Fleet Street
London EC4A 2DY

City University Business School

Professor Elias Dinenis
Head, Department of Investment, Risk Management & Insurance

Frobisher Crescent
Barbican Centre
London EC2Y 8BH

Dr. Giovanni Barone-Adesi
Professor of Finance

Faculty of Business
University of Alberta
3-20H Faculty of Business
Edmonton, Alberta
Canada T6G 2R6

UNITED STATES

Federal Reserve System, Board of Governors

David L. Robinson
Deputy Director, Chief Federal Reserve Examiner

Alan H. Osterholm, CIA, CISA
Manager, Financial Examinations Section

Paul W. Bettge
Assistant Director, Division of Reserve Bank Operations

Gregory E. Eller
Supervisory Financial Analyst, Banking

Gregory L. Evans
Manager, Financial Accounting

Martha Stallard
Financial Accounting, Reserve Bank Operations

> 20th and Constitution, NW
> Washington, DC 20551

Federal Reserve Bank of Boston

William McDonough
Executive Vice President

James T. Nolan
Assistant Vice President

> P.O. Box 2076
> 600 Atlantic Avenue
> Boston, MA 02106-2076

Federal Reserve Bank of San Francisco

Nigel R. Ogilvie, CFA
Supervising Financial Analyst, Emerging Issues

> 101 Market Street
> San Francisco, CA 94105

Seattle Branch, Federal Reserve Bank of San Francisco

Jimmy F. Kamada
Assistant Vice President

Gale P. Ansell
Assistant Vice President, Business Development

> 1015 2nd Avenue
> Seattle, WA 98122-3567

Office of the Comptroller of the Currency (OCC)

Bill Morris
National Bank Examiner/Policy Analyst,
Core Policy Development Division

Gene Green
Deputy Chief Accountant
Office of the Chief Accountant
250 E Street, SW
7th Floor
Washington, DC 20024

Federal Deposit Insurance Corporation (FDIC)

Curtis Wong
Capital Markets, Examination Support

Tanya Smith
Examination Specialist, International Branch

Doris L. Marsh
Examination Specialist, Policy Branch
550 17th Street, NW
Washington, DC 20006

Office of Thrift Supervision (OTS)

Timothy J. Stier
Chief Accountant
1700 G Street, NW
Washington, DC 20552

Securities and Exchange Commission, Washington, DC

Robert Uhl
Professional Accounting Fellow

Pascal Desroches
Professional Accounting Fellow

John W. Albert
Associate Chief Accountant

Scott Bayless
Associate Chief Accountant
Office of the Chief Accountant
Securities and Exchange Commission
450 Fifth Street, NW
Washington, DC 20549

Securities and Exchange Commission, New York

Robert A. Sollazzo
Associate Regional Director

7 World Trade Center
12th Floor
New York, NY 10048

Securities and Exchange Commission, Boston

Edward A. Ryan, Jr.
Assistant District Administrator (Regulations)

Boston District Office
73 Tremont Street, 6th Floor
Boston, MA 02108-3912

International Monetary Fund

Alain Coune
Assistant Director, Office of Internal Audit and Inspection

700 19th Street, NW
Washington, DC 20431

Financial Accounting Standards Board

Halsey G. Bullen
Project Manager

Jeannot Blanchet
Project Manager

Teri L. List
Practice Fellow

401 Merritt
Norwalk, CT 06856

Citibank

Daniel Schutzer
Vice President, Director of Advanced Technology

909 Third Avenue
New York, NY 10022

Prudential-Bache Securities

Bella Loykhter
Senior Vice President, Information Technology

Kenneth Musco
First Vice President and Director,
Management Internal Control

Neil S. Lerner
Vice President, Management Internal Control

1 New York Plaza
New York, NY 10292-2017

Merrill Lynch

John J. Fosina
Director, Planning and Analysis

Corporate and Institutional Client Group
World Financial Center, North Tower
New York, NY 10281-1316

International Swaps and Derivatives Association (ISDA)

Susan Hinko
Director of Policy

600 Fifth Avenue, 27th Floor
Rockefeller Center
New York, NY 10020-2302

Standard & Poor's

Clifford Griep
Managing Director

25 Broadway
New York, NY 10004-1064

Moody's Investor Services

Lea Carty
Director, Corporates

99 Church Street
New York, NY 10022

State Street Bank and Trust

James J. Barr
Executive Vice President, U.S. Financial Assets Services

225 Franklin Street
Boston, MA 02105-1992

MBIA Insurance Corporation

John B. Caouette
President, Structured Finance Division

885 Third Avenue, No. 14
New York, NY 10022

Global Association of Risk Professionals (GARP)

Lev Borodovski
Executive Director, GARP, and Director of Risk Management
Credit Suisse First Boston (CSFB), New York

Yong Li
Director of Education, GARP, and Vice President
Lehman Brothers, New York

Dr. Frank Leiber
Research Director and Assistant Director of Computational Finance
Cornell University, Theory Center, New York

Roy Nawal
Director of Risk Forums, GARP

980 Broadway, Suite 242
Thornwood, NY 10594

Group of Thirty

John Walsh
Director

1990 M Street, NW
Suite 450
Washington, DC 20036

Edward Jones

Ann Ficken (Mrs.)
Director, Internal Audit

201 Progress Parkway
Maryland Heights, MO 63043-3042

Teachers Insurance and Annuity Association/College Retirement Equities Fund (TIAA/CREF)

Charles S. Dvorkin
Vice President and Chief Technology Officer

Harry D. Perrin
Assistant Vice President, Information Technology

730 Third Avenue
New York, NY 10017-3206

Massachusetts Institute of Technology

Ms. Peggy Carney
Administrator, Graduate Office

Michael Coen, PhD Candidate,
ARPA Intelligent Environment Project

Department of Electrical Engineering and Computer Science
Building 38, Room 444
50 Vassar Street
Cambridge, MA 02139

School of Engineering and Applied Science, University of California, Los Angeles

Dean A.R. Frank Wazzan
School of Engineering and Applied Science

Prof. Richard Muntz
Chair, Computer Science Department

Prof. Dr. Leonard Kleinrock
Telecommunications and Networks

Westwood Village
Los Angeles, CA 90024

University of Maryland

Prof. Howard Frank
Dean, The Robert H. Smith School of Business

Prof. Lemma W. Senbert
Chair, Finance Department

Prof. Haluk Unal
Associate Professor of Finance

Van Munching Hall
College Park, MD 20742-1815

PART

ONE

Understanding the Managerial Basis and Consequences of Credit Derivatives

CHAPTER 1

Credit Derivatives and Their Impact on the Financial Industry

1. INTRODUCTION

Credit derivatives are credit risk and default migration instruments. Their predecessors have been all types of bonds and syndicated bank loans. Many financial analysts consider credit derivatives to be financial operations whose time has come. Others believe that credit derivatives are a push product banks must aggressively sell, because vanilla-ice-cream lending is never going to return to the profitability of the 1960s and 1970s.

Still other analysts think that the Latin American debt crisis of the early 1980s, the Texas and New England real estate bubbles of the late 1980s and early 1990s, the Asian and Russian debt meltdowns of 1997-98 have shown that lending is now as risky as trading. Therefore, they look at credit derivatives as the instruments that let banks pass off to other parties the risk of default on some of their loans, while offering investors a higher premium for the synergy of market risk and credit risk.

Some financial analysts believe that credit derivatives are really a very old product reborn. The old product is no other than that underpinning credit risk: default likelihood. All self-respecting credit institutions are trying to come up with a dependable method for calculating the risk of default by the counterparty.

3

By contrast, other financial analysts are of the opinion that the market for credit derivatives and alternative credit insurance mechanisms is new. It is also globalized (see Chapter 2). The market for securities backed by commercial paper is still developing, suggest Caouette, Altman, and Narayanan. [1] Some specialists consider it the latest approach to credit risk management. There exist several types of credit derivatives in the market (as explained in Part Two). The more popular are asset swaps, total return swaps, default swaps, and credit-linked notes.

No matter how one looks at credit derivatives in terms of purpose and market potential, there is no question that they are sophisticated, but also hyped, risk management tools. Their effect is not one of weeding credit risk out of the banking industry, but of moving the credit risk of sellers to the buyers who may be

- Other banks,
- Institutional investors,
- Nonbanks, and other companies.

Today credit derivatives transactions range from $10 to $50 million with maturity between 1 and 10 years. During this timeframe events alternatively occur or do not take place that command the cash flow from writer to buyer. We will talk more about this issue in section 3, in conjunction with the concept of *credit volatility* brought to the forefront by the securitization of corporates.

Credit volatility is important because one problem with selling to investors sophisticated novel financial instruments is that this requires accurate pricing methods. One of the advantages of this same activity is that it will lead to proper pricing over time. The complexity of pricing financial products increases in proportion to their novelty. Lack of information and tools handicaps this process (see Chapter 3).

2. BANKERS AND ANALYSTS TAKE A CAREFUL LOOK AT CREDIT DERIVATIVES

"One of the effects of credit derivatives," said Brandon Davies, treasurer, Global Corporate Banking, Barclays Bank, "will be to con-

---

[1] J.B. Caouette, E.I. Altman, and P. Narayanan. *Managing Credit Risk,* John Wiley, New York, 1998.

centrate counterparty risk. While assets are dispersed, derivatives risk will be in the hands of very few market participants, and this will pose an important issue for regulators." Both intended and unitended consequences must be thoroughly studied:

- To which extent will credit derivatives allow that counterparty risk becomes concentrated?
- How will investors and regulators evaluate credit derivatives risk versus loans risk which is more dispersed?

"Credit Derivatives," suggested John Walsh, director of the Group of 30, "will drive the whole reevaluation of capital standards and lead to rethinking credit risk." John Caouette, president of the Structured Finance Division, MBIA, took an equally broad view of the field when he stated that "Derivatives at large have revolutionized everything." But then he added that one problem with banking is the flaws in credit risk management.

To appreciate this statement one must bring into perspective the fact that *structured financial transactions* are usually derivative financial instruments that pool assets and transfer all or part of the originator's credit risk to new investors. Instruments are structured because they are designed in a way to answer customization requirements of the buyers.

- These sometimes call for unbundling credit risk and market risk, leading to *credit volatility* (see section 3).
- In other cases, what the buyers want is to recombine credit risk and market risk in novel ways.

A critical element in unbundling as well as in assembling risk factors by design rather than as a matter of chance is the segmentation of risk. Equally crucial to structured financing is the segmentation of projected cash flows and their allocation into fairly homogeneous risk buckets.

These activities must be executed in a dependable way to assure one of the advantages of structured solutions. Namely that they make possible to finance both strong credits and risky ones. *If* a pool of assets and liabilities is statistically valid, say composed of 50 items or so, *then* it can be subdivided in a way to observe different criteria—helping to create a valid segmentation pattern.

The tools and methods of structured finance such as the separation of the holder of a loan from its originator, pooling, the distinction between senior and junior (or subordinated) structures, and the eventual inclusion of guarantors,

- Transform the risk and return profile of underlying instruments,
- Make feasible modeling and the use of market response for price discovery, and
- Generalize cross-border debit financing, bypassing classical narrow barriers.

The traditional, time-honored policy of commercial bankers has been that "I lend to the people I know, in places I know." This leads to focalized credit risks—a historical lending policy that contributes to long-term volatility. "To manage it," John Caouette suggested, "banks need to diversify and credit derivatives may allow them to do just that."

The careful reader will observe that there is a difference of opinion between the treasurer Brandon Davies and the insurer John Caouette. One thinks that credit derivatives will concentrate credit risk; the other agrees that there will be some early concentration but eventually they will diversify it. Differences of opinion are healthy, because in the last analysis that's what makes the market.

- Davies believes that credit derivatives contribute to the concentration of risk, because the main clients will be institutional investors, insurance companies, and the big banks.
- Caouette thinks that credit derivatives will eventually diversify the risk which has been classically concentrated, because retail banks who mainly lend to their neighborhood now will have an opportunity to hedge that risk.

The two opinions can also be seen as converging. What gets diversified is the origination of credit risk, which moves from the local neighborhood to a global basis. What will be concentrated is position risk in the portfolio of investors who have significant exposure in credit derivatives. This position risk is a function of the quality of the issuer. We will talk more about this in Chapter 2, when we discuss the banking book and trading book.

No doubt, institutional investors would like to be well informed about the creditworthiness of the debtors behind the securitized corporate loans. Independent rating agencies can serve this purpose. Alert investors also appreciate that the creditworthiness of the debtor and the interest rate of the debt instrument are closely related. Information, therefore, will be at a premium (see Chapter 4 on transparency).

- Information on credit risk becomes more ample by making the contents of the bank's loans book a tradable commodity.
- Banks need to promote transparency in order to capitalize on new instruments and their globalization.

Figures 1.1 and 1.2 explain this transition. Classical commercial banking has been a closed system and institutions kept the information in their loans portfolio close to their chests. As Figure 1.1 shows, the content of the loans book was a matter concerning only two parties: the bank and the borrower.

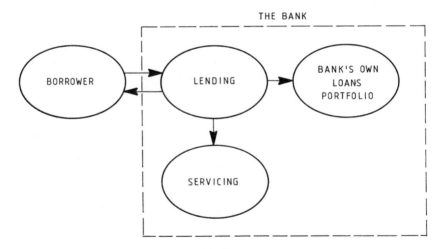

FIGURE 1.1 TRADITIONAL COMMERCIAL BANKING HAS BEEN A CLOSED SYSTEM.

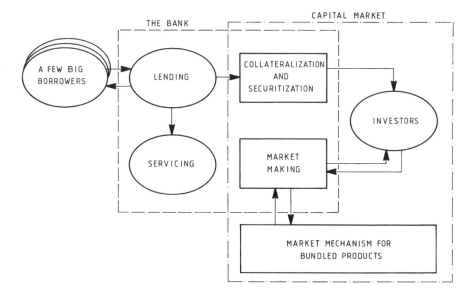

FIGURE 1.2 COLLATERALIZATION AND SYNDICATION OF LOANS CREATED A NEW OWNER WHO IS VERY DEMANDING.

This changed in the 1970s with the syndication of loans. The banks in the syndicate wanted to know more about the borrower, but this was still an oligarchic approach as the number of members in the syndicate was small. The big change really came with collateralized debt obligations offered to the capital market—a process shown in Figure 1.2 (see also the explanation in section 4).

Inquisitive investors pose questions about the type of assets that have been securitized. But as long as this concerned mortgages, the information the bank provided could be limited to some new metrics, like option-adjusted spread (OAS). Mortgages are fairly well-known instruments and, though conditions vary from one deal to another, there are not exotic clauses or covenants. Also, the pool of mortgages benefits from the law of large numbers.

With corporate loans, these arguments turn on their head. Uncertainties embedded in major loans dictate the use of a refined risk measurement system using a rigorous process of assessment and control. (See Part Three on models.) The auditors' responsibilities, too, have changed. To investors, credit exposure with corporate credit risk is a much more serious concern than that associated with mortgage-backed financing.

Nor is the issuing bank free from worries. Theoretically, with credit derivatives credit risk ceases to be an issue for bankers as exposure is transferred to investors. Practically this forgets the fact that there are many legal, regulatory, and operational obstacles to limit the promises of an ideal transfer of credit exposure, while new risks are being created, like credit volatility.

3. CREDIT DERIVATIVES AND THE CONCEPT OF CREDIT VOLATILITY

Sections 1 and 2 have defined credit derivatives as financial instruments making it possible to trade credit risk separate from other types of risk, by appropriately designing and packaging the product. The growth of the credit derivatives market depends on the ability to find counterparties willing and able to assume the unbundled credit risk in exchange for a cash flow.

A simple form of a bilateral credit derivatives deal is that of two parties agreeing to exchange predetermined cash flows associated to a given credit event over a defined maturity. Such an event might be associated, for instance, to a default or downgrade in rating—but this does not always need to be the case.

- The credit derivatives mechanism provides default protection to the originator who is the risk seller.

Also known as *protection writer,* the originator essentially shorts a loan or pool of loans in his books. He does so by tailoring the instrument used in the transaction.

- But the seller also offers compensation to the buyer for agreeing to the transfer of credit risk to *his* books.

The problem is that the fine print of the risks embedded in credit derivatives is not visible to outsiders—even if the nature of these risks is known to them in order of magnitude, which is not necessarily the case. It is always difficult to assess an institution's credit risk if it is being based only on disclosures showing up in annual reports and similar statements. But it becomes nearly impossible to do so with pools of assets and liabilities if one is not an insider. As a result, credit derivatives can pose a significant default risk to investors.

Statistics on worldwide defaults in 1998 provide a good documentation on what is meant by this exposure. In 1998, 126 issuers defaulted on $29.6 billion long-term corporate and sovereign debt. The three largest events have been:

- 54 defaults on $8.9 billion by East Asia companies, including crony capitalism deals,
- 52 defaults on $8.8 billion of publicly held long-term corporate debt in the United States, and
- Russia's massive $9.7 billion default in August 1998.

Moody's suggests that these figures mark an 80 percent increase in issuer terms and an 11 percent increase in dollar amount from 1997.[2] But 1998 has also seen other significant statistics. Standard & Poor's reports that its downgrades of corporate debt exceeded upgrades by a margin of 2:1. There were 510 downgrades versus 259 upgrades. More detailed figures are shown in Table 1.1.

The concept of *credit volatility* underpins these upgrades and downgrades, respectively diminishing or increasing the amount of credit risk taken by investors. As it is to be expected, in the securitization of loans of some industries is embedded much more risk than in the loans of other industries. For instance, in Table 1.1, 66 percent of the upgrades and 63 percent of the downgrades have been in manufacturing (Industrials). Based on statistics released by the Bundesbank in January 1999, Table 1.2 shows that 46.6 percent of insolvent enterprises in Germany were in manufacturing, followed by wholesale/retail and construction.

---

[2] Global Credit Research Special Comment, Moody's Investors Services, New York, 1999.

Table 1.1 Changes in Corporate Ratings in 1998
by Standard & Poor's

	Number of Changes	Debt in $ Billions	Average Debt Per Entity in $ Millions
Banking			
Upgrades	35	75.1	2.146
Downgrades	55	100.0	1.818
Other Financial			
Upgrades	24	14.7	.298
Downgrades	67	27.5	.410
Industrials			
Upgrades	179	179.5	1.003
Downgrades	325	194.9	.600
Telecommunications			
Upgrades	13	18.2	1.400
Downgrades	35	32.8	.937
Utilities			
Upgrades	18	21.1	1.172
Downgrades	31	90.5	2.919

These statistics should make investors aware of the fact that through credit derivatives they take credit exposure to parties with whom they never entered into formal credit relationships. This introduces new unknowns into the credit risk equation. Default by a counterparty with a substantial aggregate exposure that has been repackaged through credit derivatives could have far-reaching consequences, including a chain reaction affecting investors in the four corners of the globe.

There is, however, a silver lining in this warning. The good news is that, quite likely, credit derivatives have the potential of providing a better insight into credit risk and its *volatility*. Therefore, they are

Table 1.2 Percent of Insolvent Enterprises by Industry—Germany, January 1999

Manufacturing	46.6%
Wholesale/Retail	27.0%
Construction	16.8%
Services, Professions	5.6%
Agriculture	1.0%
Other	3.0%

a mechanism for price discovery of credit risk—even if by being off-balance sheet instruments with which regulators still have thin experience, they may increase systemic risk.

Cognizant financial analysts consider credit volatility to be more opaque than market volatility. First, because market volatility is better established in the conscience of bankers, traders, investors, and regulators: There are ways and means to measure it, and educated guesses can be done on the correlation between liquidity and market volatility. Second, because established exchanges help in discovery of market volatility.

- Credit volatility, which amounts to the impairment of creditworthiness of an obligor or group of obligors, also correlates with liquidity.
- But this has not yet been adequately researched in terms of its extent and its impact. Metrics are also missing, the nearest proxy to it being credit rating.

Credit volatility is an important factor in pricing credit derivatives, because like options, forwards, and swaps, these are both financial contracts and means of actuating a pricing mechanism that is credit-sensitive. The study of credit sensitivity often involves the obligor's credit history, payments track, and rating history. Usually in a transition matrix, credit ratings tend to move south.

Improvements in rating are possible, but such events are less frequent than downgraders, as it has been shown in the 1998 statistics presented in Table 1.1.

To further appreciate the concept of *credit volatility* we should recall that, as with any other derivative instrument, the price of credit derivatives is derived from an underlying price of an asset, such as a loan or pool of loans. What the bank does is to swap the default risk in that pool for the promise of a partial or full payout if the asset(s) default(s). In that sense, credit derivatives might also be seen as a credit insurance scheme, in a way similar to loan guarantees. A major change in intermediation comes from the fact that

- Using its established branch office network, the bank retaining the assets in its loans book becomes the originator and servicer of loans.
- But if its policy is to dispose of these loans by securitizing them, then it only temporarily (until the loans are sold to the capital market) stays on as the investor.

Banks securitizing their corporates appreciate that, in the general case, not every loan entering into a pool will be ultimately paid, though the exact proportion of defaults varies significantly with company rating. In fact there is more than one sort of risk assumed by people and companies by purchasing asset-based securities. The four most important are:

1. Counterparty risk—this is the most evident.
2. Collateral value risk—exactly what the collateral, if any, will be worth in the future.
3. Collateral illiquidity risk—which may not be compensated by the haircut.
4. Legal risk—particularly present with global asset pools.

Some of these risks might be counterbalanced through credit insurance and other means of hedging. This is advisable also for other reasons than pure credit risk, for instance, when companies do cross-border business with customers they don't know well, or don't trust 100 percent; when country risk is significant; and when political instability makes necessary some rigorous means of protection.

In conclusion, the risk present in the securitization of corporates may have many reasons and the nemesis of credit derivatives is, indeed, credit volatility. While the existence of credit volatility has been embedded in instruments like standby letters of credit and loan guarantees, which date back to the time of the Medici, only very recently has it come up as a self-standing notion to which investors will be well advised to pay due attention.

4. A CREDIT DERIVATIVES DEAL: A SIMPLE EXAMPLE

Part Two addresses the different types of credit derivatives, their market, and what they mean to investors. But just as a starter, let me take a very simple example that explains the message already presented in Figure 1.2. It can be kept in perspective until we discuss more complex deals.

Say that a bank takes the loans it has given to five of its clients, all companies with yearly sales in the $1 billion to $5 billion bracket. They are known in the market, but they don't have the same rating by independent agencies (see Chapter 10).

- The better two are AA and AA-, and the bank decides to compute prime rate plus 70 basis points.
- Of the other three, one is BB and two are BB-. The bank calculates prime rate plus 200 basis points.

The total amount of loans to be securitized is $500 million. What the bank wants to do is to take this pool of business loans and issue zero coupon bonds. In doing so, it puts itself during the life of the zero coupon, which it sets at five years, as a guarantor. Therefore, as the last paragraph of section 2 hinted, the issuer is assuming different risks, bankruptcy of the customer and early prepayment being among them.

This is information known to the investor interested in the instrument. The investor also appreciates that with the zero coupon the bank substitutes for the customers. But to know the risks it takes, the investor must examine the fine print of some other references concerning the companies in the pool:

- The asset structure of each of the bank's five client firms,
- The volatility of the assets characterizing each of these firms, and
- The earning flow and cash flow of each firm, individually.

Because the bank (which acts as underwriter for the credit derivatives) must give a guarantee, it has to price the credit risk as well as the interest rate risk to the maturity of the zero coupon bonds. Both senior and junior debt face arrival risk at the same time, the five years, but differ in expected recovery.

To carry out this deal in an able manner, the bank's management must be aware of the basic issues involved in underpinning credit derivatives and in making them appealing to the market. This goes beyond the skills of how to make a synthetic instrument. Supervisory guidance helps because it prescribes the internal accounting procedures: how to combine two or more exposures and how to report to the examiners.

The management of the bank, however, appreciates that while the supervisors will be there if something goes wrong, there is no assurance that investors will come and they will put the money on the table. To do so, the credit derivatives products must be familiar to them, the pricing must be consistent, and they must be able to see some good profits.

"I am skeptical about credit derivatives," said the director of rating of financial institutions at one of the major independent rating agencies. "The supply of credit protection for banks exceeds demand." This executive added that he also sees some major challenges associated to credit derivatives:

- Not so many people understand the advantages of credit protection,

- The cost of hedging credit risk is generally considered to be high, and
- The market has not yet been tested in the downside.

Many commercial and investment bankers talk of the 1997 NatWest case with the securitization of $5 billion of its loans, however there are also other examples of *management intent*. For instance, the 1997 Annual Report of Germany's Commerzbank explained as follows the institution's involvement in credit derivatives: "In order to finance our medium- to long-term lending, we made use of the healthy state of the market to issue securitized liabilities on a larger scale."

During 1997, Commerzbank's outstanding volume of bonds, notes, and other securitized liabilities grew by more than DM 40 billion (about $23.5 billion) to DM 190 billion ($112 billion), a 26.8 percent increase. Two of Commerzbank's affiliates, Hypothekenbank in Essen and Rheintyp, were especially active issuing jumbo and global obligations (Pfandbriefe), in addition to more traditional obligations and public-sector bonds.

But while commercial banks are interested in securitization, investors will not rush to buy a credit derivative product that makes payments based on the performance of some credit-sensitive assets and liabilities because they are conscious of credit volatility even if they don't use this term. Credit performance is measured by yield or price spreads relative to

- Benchmarks,
- Credit scores, and
- Default status.

These factors can be measured and therefore priced. As we shall see in Part Three, a model can help us determine the amount of risk involved in the deal, leading to the pricing of that risk through return on capital adjusted for performance. This must be done in a way that both the bank and the investor profit.

The pros think that credit derivatives will encourage more participants into the market of high-yield debt and credit enhancement products. But these are highly risk-sensitive domains. More risks will come from the fact that new market players in credit derivatives don't have the credit culture possessed by banks.

Entrants and possible entrants into the credit derivatives market include broker–dealers, insurance companies, pension funds, hedge funds, and other institutional investors. More examples are given in Chapter 5. They all search to alter their returns by absorbing or reducing the credit exposure of loans. But in my research I have found that only a few players know how to handle this new type of risk.

5. WHAT CAN BE LEARNED FROM OTHER EXPERIENCES IN SECURITIZATION?

To appreciate the thinking that characterizes the development of pools of loans, it is proper to recall the origins of securitization and the lessons learned from other instruments. While securitization started in the 1920s with real estate assets, the ways and means for doing a neat pooling job developed 50 years later. Baskets for mortgage-backed financing (MBF) loans, for instance, have been around since the 1970s. All carry basis risk.

Basis risk is the relationship in exposure between the underlying asset and the reference asset. Usually the reference asset is a public-traded security. Basic risk comes from the fact that the reference asset will not track the real risk against which it is hedged. As such, it is of major concern to everybody—from writers to investors and regulators.

One of the lessons taught by mortgage-backed financing is that the institutional investors who buy the bonds are demanding. They will not put up their cash until the underwriter gives them the option-adjusted spread, whose computation requires Monte Carlo simulation. Other instruments, like the securitization of credit cards and small loans, have their own requirement in terms of preparatory analysis and the study of the behavior of packaged loans.

Mortgages, credit card receivables, auto loans, and corporate loans have as a common background credit risk. They also share among themselves the fact that, until recently, more or less all the

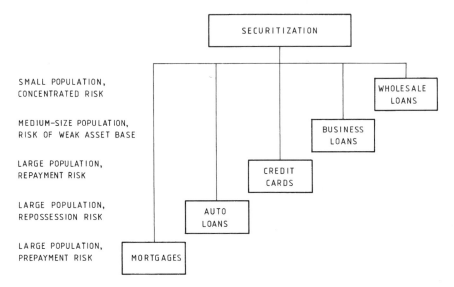

FIGURE 1.3 A BANKER'S VIEWPOINT OF CREDIT DERIVATIVES—FROM MORTGAGES TO WHOLESALE LOANS

risk of personal and commercial lending was borne by the banking industry—which is now transferring it to investors.

Figure 1.3 generalizes the use of the term *credit derivatives* to include five classes, each with its own specific risk associated to the counterparties (see also in section 8 the relative importance in the U.S. market of each class of securitized instruments). Rating of the pool of counterparties is critical to all five categories included in this figure.

With large populations, grading along a certain variable, such as creditworthiness, tends to follow a normal distribution. This is not true with business loans and most particularly with wholesale loans (see Chapter 11). Because grading is crucial to all products containing credit risk, it must be done most carefully counterparty by counterparty for big loans, and through statistical sampling for smaller ones, taking into account

- Rating by independent agencies,
- The bank's own credit risk evaluation,

- Whether interest rates are fixed or variable,
- Maturity or duration of the loan(s),
- Type and amount of loans as well as covenants,
- Valuation of available collateral,
- Repayment and other conditions (if any),
- Administrative expenses, and so on.

Pooling must be done in a way producing a homogeneous background in regard to the critical variables, so that the package is manageable and the bonds can be rationally priced. This means that to work in a sound manner with credit derivatives, we must know very well not only the loans portfolio and the market, but also modeling and experimentation.

Rating by independent agencies is not always forthcoming for all companies and their loans in the pool. Sometimes the estimates the banks are doing through guesswork or models are off the mark. Both the examiners of rating agencies and government supervisors are quite concerned about single risk weightings like those done by banks with the Korean and Indonesian loans.

That's why knowledgeable bankers say that the Asian meltdown will have a negative impact on the credit derivatives market, unless serious guarantees are given from now on. To overcome market resistance, a French bank brought to the market securitized loans from East Europe with the credit risk guaranteed by the French government. In this case, the taxpayer comes to the rescue.

Another problem with derivatives of corporate loans is sample size. Because of (1) small samples of corporate loans included in a pool and (2) the fact that small samples are not statistically dependable, banks should use the chi-square distribution rather than the normal distribution (see Chapter 12). Sound statistical solutions are at a premium because, as some bankers were to suggest, the financial industry is heading into a time when the securitization rules will be tailored to the customer's demand.

At the same time, because the market gets increasingly sophisticated, the dynamics of economic thinking shift. Cognizant bankers now believe that this shift includes a change in the way prudential capital is calculated—an important issue in years to come. As long as the 8 percent capital adequacy ratio remains, the credit derivatives market and the distinction banks make between entrepreneurial and economic capital are ways of bypassing the requirements reflected in the 1988 Capital Accord by the Basle Committee on Banking Supervision. Regulators, too, are now going beyond the common denominator because they recognize that in some cases this can be counterproductive. Commercial bankers are looking forward to the new discussion paper by the Basle Committee, nicknamed 2000+, which revamps the basis of capital requirements.

Regulators have another reason to be concerned about credit derivatives and the drive by commercial bankers to optimize regulatory capital through collateralization and securitization. They think that credit derivatives might lead banks toward lower-quality assets. Therefore, they watch carefully how the chips fall in the credit derivatives market and what may be the effect on the commercial banks' portfolios.

6. ARE CREDIT DERIVATIVES LOWERING THE QUALITY OF A BANK'S PORTFOLIO?

"As a portfolio manager you often don't tend to sell things that are good," said John Caouette during our meeting in New York. "The problem is that risk studies connected to credit derivatives are still works in progress and we have not made breakthroughs in correlations," suggested another knowledgeable banker. "In this period of transitions it is going to be jury time—and what I can negotiate with the client," said Caouette.

A way to improve the grade of securitized corporates is to bring in an insurer, as happens today with municipals. The haircut in interest rate may be worth the resulting improvement in pricing. It may also increase the appeal of corporate loans to institutional investors and other market players.

Another concern to bankers is the current uneven progress in regard to the marketability of credit derivatives. "There are people who lead the charge, and others who can't follow," said a New York investment banker. The problem that he sees is that ambivalence by some commercial and investment banks does not help in building market confidence.

The leverage factor also plays a role, increasing the buyer's worry about credit risk. One of the potential exposures with credit derivatives is that issuers may falter in the way they package their products and approach the market. "Derivatives are wonderful if they are well managed. In the hands of the wrong people they can be dangerous," a Wall Street expert was to suggest.

Regulators, too, would like to take a closer look on how products are packaged. If low-risk loans are put into credit derivatives in order to improve the appeal of the instrument to the market, then the 8 percent capital requirements for the loans remaining in the bank's banking book may no longer be enough. Some supervisors think that commercial banks should study the impact of securitized corporate loans on a case-by-case basis. The only general rule is that

- Credit derivatives will require much more than the minuscule capital needed for other derivative instruments.
- The exception to this rule is if pools have weights. For instance, the pool consisting of sovereigns might not need extra reserves.

A number of bankers studying the pluses and minuses of credit derivatives think that they may lead to disintermediation in regard to some of their best customers. They are particularly sensitive to this issue because commercial banks have already lost some of their best customers for loans as big industrial companies hire an investment bank and issue commercial paper at better terms than they would obtain from a commercial bank.

Both regulators and rating agencies think that credit derivatives can make traditional balance sheet analysis obsolete. Classical risks associated with loans are sold off, but new ones are introduced that are more difficult to track because experience with them will take years to build up.

"We are skeptical of the securitization of revolving issues like credit cards, because they may come back and hit the books," said a central banker. Another cognizant regulator mentioned that credit derivatives will be a complex issue to control, because a lot of them will involve a secondary market deal.

Proponents of credit derivatives don't worry about these arguments because they think that they will be taken care of through restructuring of the balance sheet. Indeed, they favor this type of transaction from a capital efficiency viewpoint. They also point to two events coming up in the same time frame as the introduction of credit derivatives:

- The European Monetary Union (EMU) and
- The restructuring of the whole Japanese banking sector.

These executives see both the Euro and Japanese restructuring as necessarily leading toward a broader type of securitization. Some bankers believe that these two processes will have global implications, resulting in greater scrutiny of equity and assets. Japanese banks, for instance, will need to do substantial securitizations of assets to shrink their balance sheets.

Even the concepts classically associated with equity and assets may change, some knowledgeable people who participated in my research suggested. For instance, the value of equity can be modeled as assets plus interest rates because, as one banker phrased his thoughts, "Equity is an option in the firm's assets."

7. CREDIT DERIVATIVES ARE ESSENTIALLY DEBIT DERIVATIVES

Credit derivatives can be thought of as one-period reference loans that have only two possible payoffs: borrower default and nondefault. Theoretically at least, we can price these binomial risks by choosing the associated reference loan's two payoff values.

In the general case, this approach is feasible if we take care that the mean and variance of the payoffs match the statistics of a multinomial loan's payoff distribution. Rocket scientists (see Chapter 16) are using this two-payoff approach as a proxy for the N-payoff prices of multinomial risk. Analysts who have followed this method suggest that it produces a good approximation. A better accuracy can be obtained by decomposing the derivatives instruments into

- An element reflecting the creditworthiness of borrowers,

- A component independent of the borrowers but dependent on assets, and
- A systematic component tied to economic factors simultaneously affecting borrowers and asset values.

Part of the risk of any financial instrument arises from the fact that sellers and buyers have conflicting interests in terms of pricing. If the price is relatively high relative to the yield of the fixed-income security, in order to cover the writer's potential exposure, it will not sell. If it is aggressively (low) priced to sell, it may leave its writer significantly exposed to market gyrations.

Because pricing is very important, and "how to do it" is not a strong point with credit derivatives, many of the bond experts surveyed by *Business Week* in December 1998 were relatively cool to asset-backed securities.[3] Particularly, mortgages were singled out. While the reason for this has been the relatively low yields and ongoing prepayment risks connected to securities mortgages, as homeowners refinance, other experts took a similar attitude toward credit derivatives because of credit volatility.

Nobody should say: "This would not happen to me." Russia couldn't default. It did. Brazil could not do anything wrong. The real crashed. The Nikkei was supposed to rally. It didn't. According to the Nobel Prize winners of Long-Term Capital Management (LTCM), spreads were supposed to narrow. They widened. To the opinion of other experts, inflation was supposed to jump. It disappeared.

- These are not the days one can depend too much on prognostication, and
- Novelties both in instruments and in companies carry with them some big surprises (see Chapter 2 on LTCM).
- Even a change in company management increases the risk, until the new executives find their balance.

---

[3] *Business Week,* December 28, 1998.

An article in *Business Week*[4] made this point while discussing the palace revolution at Goldman Sachs, as an example of the split between the company's trading and investment banking divisions. The former CEO, Jon S. Corzine, is a trader. Henry Paulson and John Thornton, who took over, are investment bankers. A big chunk of Goldman's earnings came from proprietary trading. "There has been a hedge fund in the center of Goldman Sachs," an analyst suggested. Therefore, the investment bankers were presented with two choices: to change the institution's fund culture or to adapt to it, passing through a period of turbulence.

Whichever strategy Goldman or any other institution choses, it will not escape the challenge of "right pricing" of debit derivatives. Benchmarks help. In the industrialized countries the credit quality of a banking system is often measured by calculating the spread between Treasury bills and time deposits in the banks of the system. This is known as the TED spread. The one prevailing between U.S. Treasury bill futures and Eurodollar futures has been used as proof that this relationship is not constant. Beyond the $100,000 guaranteed by the Federal Deposit Insurance Corporation (FDIC), many investors choose the greater security of the U.S. government rather than of commercial banks and other retail financial institutions. Other investors, however, appreciate that they can make money by taking credit risk.

The preference toward the security some sovereign lending offers tends to drive down the yield on government securities, relative to the yield of bank deposits. Just the same, when they borrow money, banks with AAA ratings pay less interest than banks with an AA or A rating—but the most important indicator for the financial markets is the TED spread.

In regard to creditworthiness, any rational pricing approach would account for the fact that in an industrial society dominated by debits, the credits and debits of some of the companies and some of the people are sustained by the credits and debits of other companies and other people.

---

[4] January 25, 1999.

- Financial operations come to a halt if market confidence bends or disappears, even in one part of this debit/credit cycle.
- At the same time not all companies and not all people have high ratings, a factor that is much more important when the sample is small.

Contrarians to the massive and leveraged trading of debt remind us of 1929, when the world's debt was stratospheric but there was general euphoria. At that time, Paul Warburg (the man who at the beginning of the century had drawn up the charter of the Federal Reserve System) was the only major banker expecting a crisis. In his judgment,

- When money runs on the short term much more than the long term, the whole economy is in peril.
- Eventually, aggravated by speculation, the debt economy will not survive. The debts have to be paid either by the debtors or by the lenders.

In a meltdown, the debtors cannot pay with their assets because these assets are heavily leveraged. Also, the value of these assets may have significantly diminished as market prices are falling. Yet, the pricing of instruments is necessarily based on the current value of assets, by marking them to market (fair value). We account for what might happen thereafter by factoring in risks.

Frequently, the solution that we follow is based on risk factors and their volatility. A portfolio is idealized as being formed of statistically identical copies of a risk factor. As the number of these copies goes to infinity, the asymptotic portfolio payoff variance is determined by its systematic component at the transaction level. It is appropriate to align the total variances only

- If the risks within each portfolio are mutually independent and
- If there is no systematic component of variance.

When pricing financial instruments we should appreciate that under the conditions described by these two bullets the risks are diversifiable, and arbitrage theory suggests that they would command no risk premium. But that's theory. Practical solutions for risk evaluation and pricing reflect the characteristics of the different kinds of derivatives and the way bankers, treasurers, and investors look at risk and return.

8. FACTORS THAT MAY IMPACT MARKET GROWTH

The market for securitized corporate loans has been moving rather slowly. Credit cards and home mortgages hold the upper ground in securitization respectively with 34.7 percent and 30.6 percent of the total. Autos follow with about 20 percent. Only during the last few years have large banks been truly interested in credit derivatives operations, which, as we saw in this chapter, they view as an opportunity to boost trading and manage their own credit risks.

But even if until recently the securitization of corporate loans, emerging market loans, and other issues were mainly just talked about, the market for credit derivatives grew significantly in 1998, and several experts expect that it might double in size in 1999. A survey by the British Bankers Association found that (1) the global market for credit derivatives grew to $170 billion at the end of 1997 from an estimated $40 billion to $50 billion in 1996 and (2) many banks expect the total outstanding value of credit derivatives to reach $740 billion by 2000.

Data from U.S. regulators show that the volume of credit derivatives handled by commercial banks in America alone leapt from $97.1 billion at the end of December 1997 to $148.4 billion at the end of March 1998. While, however, this increase is impressive, nobody is really sure that the curve will not bend.

Events that happen only once sometimes bias the statistics. As investment bankers suggest, much of the growth during 1997 has come from trade in emerging market paper, and most of this can be attributed to the effects of the Asian crisis, which has caused heavy losses for many banks and fund managers.

- According to some estimates, roughly 25 percent of the notional value of credit derivatives is linked to emerging market bonds, and
- The share of emerging market derivatives is even higher if measured by the number of transactions being executed and by the size of these markets.

Quite often, investors fail to keep under perspective the economic size of the so-called "emerging markets," including Russia. Paul Volcker, the former chairman of the Federal Reserve, points out that the entire banking system of many an emerging country is no bigger than a typical regional bank in the United States or Europe. That's precisely the size now considered too small for global financial markets.

For many emerging economies, the small size of its financial market means that interest rate and exchange rate volatility will be a structural problem, not a temporary one, and it will haunt them for many years to come. If a hedge fund decided to play in the stock exchange of an emerging market, or buy and sell its assets, or if a couple of mutual funds decided to make a serious investment, the country's exchange rate could rocket. This will start an unsustainable boom in real estate and banking, causing havoc for exporters. The opposite: A currency collapse will take place the moment the financial invaders go home—as shown in Thailand, Indonesia, South Korea, Russia, and Brazil.

Let's face it. Emerging markets are light-weighters in a global economy that is unforgiving. To capsulize, here are the heavy weights who should command the primary attention of investors and institutions interest in credit derivatives, and in any other modern, geared financial instrument:

- United States, with 27 percent of global gross domestic product (GDP)
- European Union, with 31 percent of global GDP
- Japan, with 16.5 percent of global GDP

Then come the "others," for the most part grouped together on a regional basis: Asia-Pacific countries, with 11 percent of global GDP; Latin American countries, with 6 percent of global GDP; Russia, with less than 2 percent of global GDP; all other emerging or submerging economies, with less than 7 percent of global GDP.

Another factor that may come into the credit derivatives market during the next few years and alter its pattern is the trend in the insurance industry to tap the vast capital markets for reinsurance reasons (see Chapter 9 on catastrophe derivatives). The leading concern is about the capital that will be available when there is an urgent need for it, the likelihood of a panic or run on the financial system, and the ability to absorb the cultural shock that debit derivatives markets entail.

- With vanilla-ice-cream banking, institutions lend a line of credit assuming that they will carry the loan at its full value until the borrower repays.
- The new strategy is to get around the loan's illiquidity, which binds the bank to the counterparty by means of novel instruments that unbundle credit risk from market risk.

Still some characteristics of the old culture remain. If the counterparty in a loan runs into trouble, it is a foregone conclusion that—up to a point—it will expect help from the bank. With credit derivatives the party that may expect the bank to perform is the investor that bought the packaged product.

If banks begin to value loans like securities, they will trade their loans just as readily. Contrary to mortgage-backed financing, for about two decades there has been no market for most corporate loans held by banks.

- Such a market, however, can nicely develop as already happened with credit cards and auto loans.
- Once the links between borrower and banker are altered, banks can buy and sell loans to commercial and industrial companies, mutual funds, pension funds, insurance companies, and other investors.

Technology has a vital role to play with credit derivatives. Securities markets need data and models to price and trade their loans whose securitization might make the classical argument of core deposits nearly irrelevant. Hence the interest in advancing solutions that would subject all financial assets and liabilities, not just traditional bonds and equity securities, to market value accounting.

For securities, the fair value is the market price or something close to it. For loans, it is the banks' best guess, but it has to be reasonable, factual, and documented. Eventually, the Financial Accounting Standards Board may require financial institutions to mark-to-market the bulk of their balance sheets. That would revolutionize the way financial institutions work.

The whole concept behind an active market in credit derivatives can be encapsulated in one phrase: "Capitalizing on the revolution in the marketplace for credit." Because of credit derivatives, banks are both able to buy credit risk and sell it short. Many credit institutions now want to be at the forefront of that business.

In April 1999, as this text was finalized, there has been good news and bad news in connection with credit derivatives. Regarding marketing, the good news of the first quarter of 1999 is that there is no big difference in the acceptance between the United States and Europe. The credit derivatives market is global, like the derivatives market at large.

Another piece of good news is that in the Group of Ten countries the credit derivatives market is now growing at a rate of between 40 percent and 80 percent per year, depending on the country. For some institutions, the growth rate of their trades is faster at 20 percent to 25 percent level in a quarter.

The bad news is that bank mergers, particularly mega-mergers, reduced the number of counterparty names. this has led to concentration, which increases by so much the amount of counterparty risk. Big institutions are no less default-prone than small institutions, and they are just as exposed to the law of unintended consequences.

CHAPTER 2

Assets, Liabilities, the Trading Book, and the Banking Book

1. INTRODUCTION

Globalization, deregulation, and liberalization of market access increase the pressure to be more competitive, cut costs, and rationalize as well as to use our assets in a more effective way. This enhances overall efficiency but also changes the market structure the players have known for the past few years.

This change is welcome. A new, more rigorous look at assets and liabilities is necessary for survival reasons. Obstacles to new financial companies entering the market are being dismantled. Nonbank banks particularly profit from deregulation of prices and conditions, enhancing their ability to penetrate local and foreign markets.

A shrinking world represents enormous opportunities for an institution that can think beyond its own borders, physically, financially, and psychologically. Globalization is both a product design and a marketing concept, which is further promoted through high technology. The business opportunities presented by the synergy of globalization, innovation, and technology, however, can be successfully exploited only when we are able to instantly communicate with our business partners—and to maintain high product quality at all times.

Globalization and innovation have had an interesting aftermath affecting financing. The line dividing the trading book and the banking book has been blurred, and derivatives are responsible for this. At the same time, the flow of capital to finance new projects is increasing.

- As many companies become multinational, the global competition grows and so do the information requirements.

- Companies that require access to the capital market find it necessary to enlarge their perspective and think of the entire world.

Credit derivatives help in this transformation toward a broad geographic setting, but also fundamentally affect market behavior. The strategy of maximizing turnover in the classical, linear manner is no longer a recipe for success. Banks and nonbanks must now compete over new products, prices and conditions, innovative sales methods, credit criteria, and financial standing.

This ongoing change in market behavior culminates in results with great market impact, including the freedom to set prices, the emergence of alternative sales methods, and stiffer competition from new suppliers of the same or similar services. The likely outcome is dwindling premium margins, accompanied by more volatile market behavior, with profits going to those companies that manage their liabilities and assets in ingenious ways.

2. THE MARKET'S SWITCH FROM ASSETS TO LIABILITIES

Traditionally, bankers have been preoccupied with the *asset* side of business, which is the basis for the whole process of giving loans. But in the 1980s, the *liability* side took on equal importance. Buying money cheaply in the marketplace, rather than collecting deposits, is one example of the emphasis placed on liabilities. Derivatives at large and credit derivatives in particular are another.

Invented by money center banks, the new world of wholesale money markets worked to the benefit of the institution's clients, particularly the more sophisticated ones. Just as a global bank could sell certificates of deposit (CDs) around the world, a big multinational corporation could circumvent the bank and sell promissory notes, or commercial paper, at interest rates lower than those a bank demands for a loan.

Innovation in banking saw to it that both assets and liabilities became products that could be designed to suit a client's needs. They could be parochial or world class, sold only when a client asks for them, or marketed aggressively by a sales force. A financial instrument is any contract that gives rise to

- A financial asset of one entity and
- A financial liability of the counterparty.

A *financial asset* may be cash, a contractual right to receive cash, the right to receive another financial asset from a counterparty, or the right to receive an equity instrument of another entity. A *financial liability* is a contractual obligation to deliver cash or another financial asset to a counterparty, or to exchange financial instruments with another entity under potentially unfavorable conditions.

Depending on the economy and the business environment, financial liabilities may increase faster than financial events. With 1998 and 1999 profits sluggish, companies have been taking on a mountain of debt to finance capital spending. Many analysts believe that when the boom ends, some companies may have a tougher time weathering a slowdown.

According to Securities Data Co., about $650 billion in investment-grade corporate debt was issued in 1998, up 39 percent from the previous year. Junk bond level debt was also up about 29 percent. By contrast, new equity issuance has been about flat, at just under $210 billion per year.[1]

In spite of what these numbers might suggest, bankers, investors, and analysts who favor credit derivatives believe that

---

[1] *Business Week,* February 22, 1999.

innovation will do its magic. They also point out that, drawn by the possibility of gains, investors are willing to fund a wide variety of new instruments, just like they do with new companies in the stock market—with the result to move the economy forward at a faster pace.

Back to the fundamentals. Financial instruments include both *primary products* (such as receivables, payables, and equities) and *derivatives*. When a financial transaction concerns an item that meets the established definition of an asset or liability, such item must be recognized on the balance sheet. There are, however, conditions to be observed in this process. For instance,

- There must be sufficient evidence of the existence of the item, including evidence that a future cash flow will occur, where appropriate, and
- The transaction taking place can be measured with sufficient dependability in terms of its worth, which is increasingly taken as equal to its market value.

Assets and liabilities subject to this recognition in the balance sheet are also subject to reporting. The same is true about exposure to the risks inherent in the benefits expected to result from the transaction. Therefore, rules and regulations are in place establishing how and under which conditions the asset or liability will be recognized or, alternatively, derecognized.

- The definition of asset requires that access to future economic benefits is controlled by the reporting company.
- Access to economic benefits normally rests on *legal rights,* even if legally enforceable rights are not essential to secure access.

Future financial benefits inherent in an asset are never completely certain in amount or timing. There is always the possibility that actual benefits will be less or greater than those expected. Such uncertainty regarding eventual benefits and their timing is the very sense of risk. *Risk* represents uncertainty about the outcome and it includes both

- An upside element of potential gain and
- A downside possibility such as exposure to loss.

The definition of *liability* includes the obligation to transfer economic benefits. With liabilities as with assets, while most obligations are legally enforceable, a legal obligation is not a necessary condition. Both in regard to liabilities and to assets, a company may be commercially obliged to adopt a certain course of action that is in its long-term best interests even if no counterparty can legally enforce such a course.

The notion of *obligation* implies that the entity is not free to avoid an outflow of resources. For instance, there can be circumstances in which the company is unable to stop an outflow of money, whether the constraint has its origin in legal or commercial reasons. In such a case, its obligation is a liability.

One of the important rules in regulatory reporting, according to classical accounting, is that assets and liabilities should not be offset.

The practice, however, has been bent through creative accounting as well as by means of netting, which under certain conditions is allowed by the supervisory authorities. *Netting* is the practice of balancing payments in one direction with those in the opposite way. This sets off assets and liabilities against one another. The difference between gross replacement value (GRV) and net replacement value (NRV) of assets in *our* portfolio is the amount of assets and liabilities we can net in full observance of prevailing rules and regulations.

Master netting agreements make it possible to net out exposure to a given counterparty, rather than having the exposure from each individual transaction count on its own. Both payments and balances can be included in netting. The problem is that the assumptions made that certain accounts will net out often prove incorrect, leaving the institution with significant financial waste in its books. What about having netted transactions with LTCM, then seeing this highly geared hedge fund go bust?

3. EXTREME EVENTS IN CREDIT RISK: THE CASE OF LONG-TERM CAPITAL MANAGEMENT

In its fundamentals netting has many weaknesses even if central banks consider it to be a rather acceptable practice. One of the major weaknesses is that it does not account for extreme events. (A similar criticism is true of value-at-risk and many other models.) There is no better example of an extreme event that nearly tore apart the world's financial fabric than the near-bankruptcy of Long-Term Capital Management (LTCM).

Salvaged on the twelfth hour, on September 28, 1998, through a deal brokered by the New York Fed, LTCM had what it takes to demonstrate how undocumented netting practices are. Also, how lighthearted can its partner financial institutions be when hedged for market risk but not for credit risk, as if LTCM was the Rock of Gibraltar. Overleveraging was another major LTCM weakness, and this critique is not only valid for the hedge fund. Recently released statistics by BIS indicate that:

- The commercial banks' risks in derivatives vis-à-vis other credit institutions have tremendously increased.

In notional principal, more than 85 percent of currency-exchange related-exposures of German, Italian, and Luxembourg banks arose from interbank transactions. In other countries, the interbank portion in Forex averages 60 percent—which is still too high.

- With interest rate related derivatives, this bank-to-bank exposure reaches 70 percent or more—an irresponsible figure.

These statistics are way up from 1994 findings, when 50 percent of derivatives exposure was bank-to-bank. Even then, in a meeting in Frankfurt, a senior German banker suggested during our discussion: "It is as if Daimler-Benz sold 50 percent of its production to Volkswagen."

Such concentration of derivatives trades among financial institutions is dangerous because there are plenty of events during the year that contribute to market nervousness, including the collapse of a big company and of a country or two. Table 2.1 highlights the currency, stocks, and loans turmoil from June 1998 to February 1999. In just nine months there have been 11 events of significance to the financial markets. The risk hidden behind these references is the high leverage of some institutions that seem to be living in the virtual world of sustained unthinkable profits.

Cognizant analysts say that most worrisome in the LTCM crash was the unprecedented amount of borrowed money used for speculation:

- Borrowed money allowed the 50:1 supergearing, and
- When LTCM tumbled, the markets feared a snowball effect.

The next most unsettling fact is that this was done through such complex credit arrangements that lenders, trading partners, and reg-

Table 2.1 Currency, Stocks, and Loans Turmoil, June 1998 to February 1999

June 15, 1998	Japanese yen plummets to 146 to the dollar.
August 17, 1998	Russia defaults on its foreign debts.
August 31, 1998	Dow Jones drops 512 points.
September 28, 1998	Bailout of LTCM led by New York Fed.
October 5, 1998	Thirty-year treasury hits 4.76 percent, an all-time low.
November 13, 1998	IMF announces a $41.5 billion Brazilian bailout.
January 4, 1999	With Euro euphoria, stock markets surge in Europe and United States.
January 11, 1999	Yen hits 28-month high of 108.6 to the dollar.
January 13, 1999	Brazil devalues the real and stock markets tumble.
January 29, 1999	Within a fortnight the 8.5 percent devaluation of the real becomes 42.5 percent.
February 19, 1999	Within a month and a half, the Euro drops from 1.18 to below 1.10 to the dollar.

ulators could not find an easy way out. The bottom line is that today's global financial markets:

- Feature a whole series of structural changes and these have many unknowns,
- Therefore, when we come to the edge of chaos we find the old formulas no longer work.

"That is what this LTCM crisis is about," said Dr. Henry Kaufman. Even institutions that should know better than gambling their assets find it difficult to exercise self-control. Their hedging, too, is imperfect. For instance, UBS bought over $1 billion in LTCM stock to cover itself for the $800 million it sold in options, plus the proprietary trading it did with the $266 million fee for writing these options.

- But though the bank hedged itself for market risk,
- It did not bother to hedge for credit risk, in case its counterparty went bust.

This is a dramatic example on how senior bankers can blunder several times on the same deal. Also, on how error-prone and unsafe are the hedging strategies. As the LTCM-UBS case has demonstrated, banks are not that careful with credit risk. Credit risk is the oldest form of exposure in financial markets. But good credit is a valuable and scarce commodity. Therefore, rare to come by.

Many institutions bend their own principles and conditions in lending and in trading. This way they are exposed to the probability of default by the obligor. Management, however, should know better. Unsafe credits can explode at the cost of billions, particularly if there is leverage because the bank goes *short on credit*.

The composition of the risk council at UBS and the conflicting duties of its members are another example of organizational carelessness. In late 1996, the bank instituted a risk council with four members: The director of treasury and trading (later president and chairman of the bank), the chief credit officer, the assistant director of trading, and the chief risk manager, reporting to the director of trading. This violated two cardinal rules at the same time:

1. That traders and loan officers should never be entrusted with risk control, and
2. The functions of the front desk and the back office should be separated by a thick wall.

Financial analysts also said that the creation of another risk control function, under trading, diluted rather than strengthened the bank's risk management structure, which prior to these changes was in good shape. When this happens, the sky can break loose, as the Peregrine case demonstrates.

Leveraging can easily go beyond conventional bounds. The now-bankrupt Peregrine Fixed Income Ltd., of Hong Kong, had for every $1 it lent $10 in foreign exchange contracts or other derivatives with overexposure in Indonesia. "The total size of Indonesian companies' derivative contracts is almost impossible to calculate," some analysts suggested after the East-Asia meltdown, "because of the wild swings in the value of the rupiah and the hidden nature of many of those transactions, which the Indonesian government keeps in the shadow."

Secrets, however, do not last long and derivatives failures travel electronically from bank to bank and country to country, as they are connected across markets and across continents. An Asian derivatives disaster that happens in the morning turns into a European disaster by lunchtime, and an American one well before dinner. Secrets are no longer kept as close to the chest as they used to be. A good example of a secret that broke loose is the business opportunity suggested by Dr. Myron Scholes to UBS. That:

- UBS write options on the hedge fund's stock to the tune of $800 million,
- While the LTCM partners pay $266 million for the options.

These options would have permitted them to acquire from the bank the original $800 million of stock at a fixed price. If the shares rose to, say, $4 billion, then the LTCM partners and managers could sell the options and profit from the difference.

- The $3.2 billion windfall would have been taxed at 20 percent.

- This would have left $2.56 billion as net profit to the LTCM partners.

Consider for a moment the two alternatives: old-fashioned investing and gearing. If the partners had borrowed $800 million and invested in LTCM, this would have meant:

- Increasing the spot price of the stock,
- Paying a high interest cost,
- Paying 39.6 percent in taxes, and
- Possibly losing all of the $800 million, in a downside.

As it were, UBS lost all of the $800 million. UBS also lost the $266 million in option fees it had got from the partners. In short, from the $1.066 billion in total investment, the bank lost $960 million. It also had to pour another $300 million into LTCM, under pressure by the New York Fed. LTCM, incidentally, did not fare much better: Both its partners and its investors lost 90 percent of their equity. Remember that next time you think of gearing.

4. DEFAULTS THAT FOLLOWED THE GLOBALIZATION OF TRADES IN LIABILITIES

Derivatives based on credit are no invention of the 1990s. As briefly stated in Chapter 1, three-quarters of a century ago, in the 1920s (when people gambled on stocks and bonds), banks would take unsecured real estate loans, repackage them as bonds, and sell them to investors.

This was followed by a repackaging of bad loans, which hurt investors. National City, for instance, securitized its Latin American loans whose creditworthiness was in doubt. Banks would even lend people and companies money to buy these liabilities. Because commercial banking and brokerage were not yet segregated, the Federal Reserve had to stand behind both speculators and depositors.

This case of repackaging and selling other peoples' loans is an important lesson to be remembered when discussing credit derivatives. During the 1920s, while intermittently assuring everybody who wanted to listen that investors were not directly at risk, banks negotiated restructuring terms with Latin American debtors. They did so on their own account, but also acted as moral trustees for small bondholders devastated by Latin American defaults.

In the early decades of this century, American investors alone had poured south of the border $1 billion in that time's money—or more than $25 billion in today's money. Over and above that was the money of British and other investors. In the case of Mexico, the trap has been that this resource-rich country theoretically could also enrich those investing in its future. But these seductive promises of prosperity were never really fulfilled.

This case matters for two reasons. First, it exemplifies how risk and return promises can turn belly up. Second, this is an early example of global market structure and behavior, with the added flavor that today large money flows and minimal government supervision make it more necessary than ever to place emphasis on *future risks* with the past providing a frame of reference.

While many people appreciate that new market freedoms make it possible to use prices and products to wrest market share from other suppliers, few pay due attention to what can go wrong. Yet, the surge in competition is accompanied by significant volatility leading to both higher expectations and greater risk of downturn.

Today the securitization and sale of liabilities are promoted by increasingly demanding, globally linked financial markets. Many of these markets are little known to investors. While the growing importance of rating agencies is welcome (see Chapter 10), it is also wise not to forget the fundamentals of good credit standing as bankers perceive it.

"I have come to the conclusion that neither my firm nor myself will have anything to do, directly or indirectly, with the negotiation of securities of any undertaking not entirely completed. Or, one whose status by experience would not prove it entitled to a credit in every respect unassailable," Dr. J.P. Morgan said at the beginning of this century.[2]

---

[2] Ron Chernow, *The House of Morgan,* Touchstone/Simon & Schuster, New York, 1990.

Morgan's policy is still valid even if over nine decades the banker's job has significantly changed. I have already spoken of the fact that big companies issue commercial paper rather than taking loans. But the defection of clients is only one factor. There are other reasons why during the last 20 years there has been a shift in the business of commercial banks away from classical lending and toward other theoretically more lucrative products.

The first among the events of the 1980s that followed the oil shocks and harmed the credit function was the failures associated with Latin American sovereign loans, in a repetition of the events of the 1920s. Loans by money-center banks were interpreted by politicians in Mexico, Brazil, Argentina, Venezuela, and Peru—among other countries—as a sort of U.S. government handout in disguise.

This was followed by the junk bond market's collapse, as shown in Figure 2.1, and by the meltdown of the savings and loans. The latter was largely due to the mismatch in interest rates between deposits and mortgage loans in their books, which is a good example of position risk with other people's liabilities. (See also the discussion on credit derivatives and junk bonds in Chapter 5.)

The failures in the thrift industry were followed by a credit crunch in which the supply of credit was constrained by bank managers' reluctance to lend. This U.S. event of the late 1980s and early

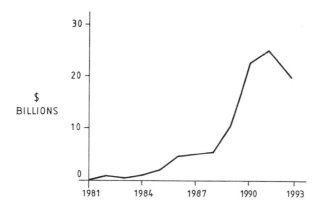

FIGURE 2.1 DEFAULTS OF JUNK BONDS OVER A 12-YEAR PERIOD

1990s has been repeated on a global scale with the Asian meltdown of 1997 and the Asian credit crunch of 1998 largely due to the reluctance of Japanese, South Korean, Indonesian, and other banks to lend.

The careful reader will not miss the parallels that exist with securitized liabilities. Part and parcel of the equation are the unknowns. Many financial analysts believe that in the United States today, securitized credit card operations have the potential for large exposure—even more than plain vanilla derivatives.

Just the same, because credit risk is on the increase (see Chapter 8), securitized corporates have a significant but not precisely known amount of exposure embedded in them. There are financial analysts who point to the deteriorating creditworthiness of some borrowers as a warning to investors that they must do their homework before committing capital to securitized loans.

Scams can happen with any product, including rather popular securitizations like that of credit cards. Take Commercial Financial Services (CFS) as an example. It has been a company that pioneered the business of buying up bad credit-card debts and securitizing them. This started in May 1995. But in October 1998, Moody's, Standard & Poor's, Fitch IBCA, and Duff & Phelps Credit Rating have all suspended or cut ratings on CFS deals after receiving information alleging improprieties at senior management level.

On the surface, CFS was a success story. Since it began securitizing consumer loans in 1995, it leaped onto the Forbes 400 list, got itself on the cover of *Inc.* magazine, and its chief executive was among *Business Week's* 1997 Entrepreneurs of the Year. For more than three years, CFS expanded its business. In November 1997 it had formed an international affiliate, and in August 1998 it bought an Arkansas savings and loan.

The rating agencies got alarmed when, in October 1998, they received a letter from an anonymous source, alleging improper sales of receivables by CFS and falsification of data. Until then, the company has not missed any payments on its $1.6 billion of deals outstanding. But the rating agencies expected CFS to default on some notes.

"Is this company potentially self-supporting or a Ponzi scheme?" said Stephen C. Macy, a vice-president at Moody's

Investors Service.[3] Other credit card securitization companies questioned how CFS:

- Could pay top dollar for charge-offs of about 10 cents on the dollar, and
- Collect the 30 cents or more it claimed it can get in market deals.

Competitors noted that banks typically collect 15 cents to 23 cents on the dollar over three to five years on bad credit-card debt. It was therefore difficult to conceive how one could claim to steadily outperform the rest of the industry short of smoke and mirrors, which were bound to get unstuck. Buyers of credit derivatives beware. Without depriving yourself of market opportunity, challenge the obvious. That's the only way to find out if nuclear waste has been repackaged as triple A.

5. CREDIT DERIVATIVES, BANKING BOOK, AND TRADING BOOK

The *banking book* consists of three main parts: loans, deposits, and the investment portfolio of the institution. The investment portfolio comprises all debt securities (including fixed income) as well as shares and other variable-yield instruments. Typically, these are held as fixed assets for investment purposes.

Traditionally, the *trading book* has assets bought and held principally for selling them in the near term. Usually, this means less than six months, though in some countries (for instance, France), it is taken to be up to one year. The aim of holding assets in the short term is to capitalize on price differences.

The exception to the short-term rule of the trading book is *derivatives*. Swaps and other less liquid assets are held over long periods.

---

[3] *Business Week,* November 9, 1998.

Generally, derivative instruments are not part of active buying and selling, but they are part of the trading book.

This distinction between banking book and trading book is not done with the same clarity in all countries. For instance, in the Federal Republic of Germany, Statement 95 made no separation between trading book and banking book in terms of calculating and reporting exposure. What Statement 95 essentially said is that a bank has a *third risk,* and it has to establish internal controls and risk management procedures to face it.

Subsequently, in compliance with the 1996 Market Risk Amendment by the Basle Committee, German supervisors require that assets and liabilities held for the short term as well as derivatives are marked to market or to model. There is no similar rule for marking to market parts of the banking book. "The idea of marking the banking book was discussed some years ago, but it was shot down," said a senior executive of the German Federal Banking Supervisory Office. "Most likely it will come up again."

In the United States, Financial Accounting Standards (FAS) Statement No. 115, Accounting for Certain Investments in Debt and Equity Securities, defines *trading securities* as "securities that are bought and held principally for the purpose of selling them in the near term" and therefore held for only a short period of time. The problem with this definition in connection to derivative financial instruments is that the term *short period of time* does not readily apply because some traders of swaps and other less liquid customized derivatives commonly maintain their positions for longer periods, but report them as part of their trading portfolios.

The recent FAS Statement No. 133 has provided a clear framework for financial reporting. Particularly important are the rules distinguishing between active, frequent buying and selling, with the objective of generating profits on short-term price differences, and long-term holding of assets and liabilities.

- If the goal is short-term, then the financial instruments must be marked to market, or to model if they have no active market.

- If the objective is long-term (for instance, to maturity), then they can be reflected in the bank's financial statement at their acquisition price.

This otherwise clear distinction brings with it the notion of *management intent,* which is known in America from earlier financial accounting standards by FASB, but it is alien to regulators and companies in Continental Europe and even more so in Asia and Latin America.

According to the new U.S. regulations, financial instruments on the trading book can be offset against each other and therefore receive regulatory relief. This is not true with the contents of the banking book. The current capital adequacy rules do not recognize offers for credit derivatives unless the position is perfectly hedged.

Neither do the present rules recognize the potential benefits of shorting credit risk (for instance, by selling a credit derivative) to hedge a long position in a bond or loan. Across other asset classes, a partial offsetting of positions is recognized by the European Union's Capital Adequacy Directive (CAD). Relief is accorded on a sliding scale, but it depends on how closely the hedge matches the underlying position.

Some experts think that the incorporation of default products into the trading book should lead to a general reform of rules and regulations by the Basle Committee on Banking Supervision. Major players in the banking industry are also lobbying the Bank for International Settlements (BIS) to recognize credit risk models in capital requirements.

6. FIXED-RATE/FLOATING-RATE SWAPS BETWEEN BANKING BOOK AND TRADING BOOK

Credit risk, which has traditionally been a banking book issue, enters the trading book because of credit derivatives. This, however, is not the first major change. Interest rate risk which is part of fixed interest rate loans has been already switched out of the banking book and into the trading book through internal interest rate swaps.

This rests on a fairly simple concept. An institution can issue a fixed-rate loan and enter into a floating-rate swap with itself (it could also be a counterparty—for instance, another bank—but in this case it is not an internal swap). If the swap is internal, the institution continues carrying the mismatch risk in its trading book.

- The trading book receives fixed rate and pays floating rate.
- The banking book, however, does away with the interest rate risk.

If the interest rate swap is done with a third party, the result is that it redistributes interest rate risk among banks, without changing the level of interest rate risk in the banking industry. The result is that some risk-prone banks end up holding unhedged swap positions.

- This would leave overall risk in the banking system concentrated in those banks that think that they know best which way interest rates will go.
- The very fact of entering into a fixed-rate/floating-rate trade with a counterparty introduces credit risk—which is not the case with the internal swap.

The benefit the bank gets is that once the mismatch risk is in the trading book, it can be managed there rather than in the banking book. The derivatives dealers of the bank provide hedging instruments for the banking book that exactly fill the interest rate gaps.

Not all the regulators accept internal interest rate swaps for financial reporting reasons. In the UK, the Bank of England's position is that institutions are welcome, indeed advised, to do internal interest rate swaps for management accounting purposes—but not for reporting to the supervisory authorities.

Whether or not the regulators permit it, there are difficulties in hedging the overall interest rate exposure of a banking book. These come from the fact that its contents are typically valued at cost. At least today banking books are not marked to market. Also, with the exception of tier-1 banks, the banking industry uses relatively low technology that does not permit it to have current market value day to day, much less intraday.

The prevalence of historical costs biases the contents of the balance sheet because they give an outdated picture of assets and liabilities. To improve upon this situation and therefore contain the interest rate risk in their loans portfolio, some banks match the interest term of each loan with that of funds used to finance it. This process is known as *match funding.*

In what concerns the introduction of credit risk in connection to interest rate swaps made with a counterparty, tier-1 banks are working on more sophisticated methods for measuring it. The goal is a better understanding of likely losses connected to the credit risk of swaps over their lives. Models permit integration of interest rate risk and credit risk taken in such transactions—a matter made more complex if currency exchange risk is also introduced.

Clearly, the rule book for the calculation of all risks taken with derivatives is still being written. Credit derivatives are no exception to this statement. Even the rule book of the regulatory framework is evolving, but some jurisdictions are more settled than others. The Federal Reserve's new guidelines clarify the capital treatment of credit derivatives held on banks' trading books, stating that

- Capital requirements for credit derivatives will be the same as for other derivatives in the trading book, and
- Banks are allowed to use internal models but with an extra add-on to account for counterparty risk.

One of the policies followed by regulators of the Group of Ten (G-10)[4] countries is to look at credit derivatives transaction by transaction, which is feasible because the market is still relatively small, but would become impractical as the market grows. Clear-eyed regulators are now looking for models that mirror the fact that credit derivatives

- Make it possible for banks to take on assets and convert them to debt, and
- Do so without going through the usual reserve requirements associated with classical loans.

---

[4] United States, United Kingdom, Germany, France, Italy, Canada, and Japan, which make the Group of Seven (G-7); plus Switzerland, Sweden, Holland, Belgium, and Luxembourg as an observer, actually numbering 11½.

An example is a December 1995 judgment by the U.S. Office of the Comptroller of the Currency (OCC) concerning credit derivatives transactions. This set a precedent and started to crystallize some regulatory thinking.[5]

In the background was the fact that an American bank made a substantial loan to an industrial company. Subsequently, the bank entered into a total return swap that was fully collateralized.

- The rules in effect at that time considered each transaction discretely.
- An interpretation close to the book would have required the OCC to charge regulatory capital on the derivative.

To the contrary, the OCC ruled that in economic terms the credit derivative fully hedged the loan. Therefore, the bank was required to hold no capital against that loan. In retrospect, analysts say, any other ruling would have removed the incentives to hedge using credit derivatives.

7. THE EVOLUTION TOWARD MORE SOPHISTICATED BOOKKEEPING METHODS

The usefulness of some form of bookkeeping has never been seriously questioned in the history of banking and finance. Different methods have evolved over the centuries, but also in several cases there have been reverses. The current method of the general ledger and double-entry accounting was formalized in 1495 by Luca Paciolo, an Italian monk and mathematician, who wrote a treatise on the mathematical aspects of accounting.[6]

Both before and after Paciolo, other approaches have also been used. In the ancient world, merchants and bookkeepers would tally accounts on clay. Tablets found in Babylon and other Mesopotamian cities demonstrate that their accounting was a very orderly enterprise and quite likely enforceable before a court of law.

---

[5] *Risk,* July 1997.
[6] See D.N. Chorafas, *Financial Models and Simulation: Concepts, Processes and Technology*, Macmillan, London, 1995.

A relic from medieval times has been the use of tallies to keep a count, the tallies being notches on sticks. If the counterparties disagreed, the judge would see if wood and tallies matched and then render a decision.

In the Middle Ages, for example, notches in a tally that stood for quantities of goods delivered or money owed were considered to be adequate. In fact, they were officially in use until the early 19th century because the bureaucracy could not give up the old-fashioned bookkeeping methods.

England abolished the tallies in 1826, but not without a major catastrophe. In 1834 the accumulation of tallies was so large that there arose a question of what to do with them. It was decided to burn them in the House of Lords, but the fire escaped and burned down the House of Lords. From there, the fire spread and burned the Parliament—as if the downgraded talliers wanted to take their revenge.

The lesson to remember from history is that some type of catastrophe can also happen with models (see Part Three). Marking to model is tallying, but not through notches on sticks. It blends together measurement with the method sophisticated merchants used in the Middle Ages that led to the work by Luca Paciolo.

There have also been problems with the early accounting methods of double-entry bookkeeping and general ledgers. A major one has been the numbering system—as anyone who tried to add, subtract, or multiply with ancient Greek and Roman numerals would appreciate.

Arabic numerals, the decimal system we use today, solved the computational problem in an elegant manner but their introduction faced stiff resistance. In Amsterdam merchants who used Arabic rather than the time-honored Roman numerals were prosecuted by the city fathers for having turned the tables to the detriment of other merchants and consumers.

Eventually, the decimal system established itself in accounting, and the industrial society developed cost accounting methods. Slowly merchants and bankers began keeping track of cash flows, profits, and losses as a better way to manage a business. And in the age of financial derivatives, particularly for over-the-counter trades, marking to model has become essential.

But failures can always happen in accounting, as a brief news item documents.[7] Gloom reigned at Informix, the California database software firm that once was a hot technology stock. As Informix management revealed, accounting errors meant that 1996 sales originally thought to be $939 million were really $200 million less. As a result, despite a reported profit of $97.9 million, actually there was a loss.

I am not privy to how and why this error occurred. The reason I bring this example to your attention is to underscore the fact that accurate accounting is crucial when we deal with sophisticated instruments like credit derivatives. Our methodology must account for the transaction in the most dependable way that is transparent and auditable, but it must also reflect future risk which, in the bottom line, adds significantly to the costs.

This risk-oriented transaction costing must take into account the effects of collateralization and securitization—and this is true all the way from mortgage-backed financing to credit derivatives. It must also map future risks into the incentive program and bonuses for traders and salespeople, because otherwise they end up distorting the bank's compensation system, inciting traders into taking inordinate risks.

A growing number of senior bankers now think that many of the current lavish reward schemes for star salespeople in the banking industry promote the wrong behavior—and this leads to pretty large losses like those suffered by Kidder Peabody, NatWest Markets, and others that ended with the disappearance of these brokers from the business scene.

While traders work hard and are entitled to a good compensation, the bank should take care not to be left with toxic waste in its trading book. This matches what was said in Chapter 1: Financial institutions should appreciate that one of the factors connected to the securitization of assets is that

- The high leverage of corporates hides the low quality of remaining assets.

---

[7] *The Economist,* September 7, 1997.

- Accounting systems must therefore be devised that do not underestimate the quality of assets.

   While the bookkeeping method of Luca Paciolo with its clear distinction of assets and liabilities is still valid, this cannot be said of the classical subdivisions into short-, medium-, and long-term assets and liabilities. A better classification would be by *risk factor,* which integrates maturity as well as market risk and credit risk.

   It is also wise to have a methodology that accounts for the fact that with leveraged instruments assets can rapidly turn into liabilities, and liabilities into assets. Nowhere is this better exemplified than in the annual reports of Swiss banks, which since 1996 have to include recognized but not realized gains in derivatives as "Other Assets" and must include recognized but not realized losses in derivatives as "Other Liabilities."

CHAPTER 3

Information Requirements for Issuers and Users of Credit Derivatives

1. INTRODUCTION

Issuers give two reasons for the desirability of securitizing corporate loans. In America and in foreign branches of U.S. credit institutions operating under U.S. law, banks are attracted by the ability to execute decoupled structures without borrower notification. Then, there is the benefit of asset derecognition under the Generally Accepted Accounting Principles (GAAP) and rules connected to regulatory accounting.

Asset deregulation provides the opportunity of improving capital efficiency. While many banks have securitized mortgages, credit cards, and auto and other small-ticket receivables, until recently, commercial loans were considered too difficult to securitize because of less standardized loan terms and larger credit risk concentrations.

Some financial analysts believe that this attitude began to change in late 1996 with NatWest's securitization of corporates. Others think that the time for loan securitization had come anyway. The fact is that since the mid-1990s a number of larger U.S., European, and Asian banks have begun to securitize commercial loans, with varying degrees of decoupling from the underlying seller.

An important development occurred in 1997, when for the first time an issuer was able to achieve a sale of loan participation without borrower notification. This opened the door for branches of foreign banks operating in America to execute fully decoupled securitizations.

This is an interesting procedure because it results in tighter offering spreads for asset-backed securities due to the lack of influence from the seller's rating. Another advantage to the issuer is the relative flexibility of the structure; but decoupling means disintermediation.

By using input from rating agencies and focusing on historical pool and servicer performance, restrictive collateral maintenance tests can be reduced. At the same time, from the perspective of an investor, financial products based on the securitization of corporate loans offer diversification in the asset-backed securities market and other fixed-income investments—albeit at the price of assumed credit risk.

The reader's attention should also be brought to another issue. Capital markets tend to be more efficient than the banks. One of the reasons why commercial paper and different forms of asset-backed financing have, to a significant extent, replaced classical bank loans is because of the inefficiency of the banking system. The total cost of intermediating a security over the life of an asset: under 50 basis points in capital market operations, and over 200 basis points in banking intermediation.[1]

2. CONCENTRATION AND LEVERAGE WITH CREDIT DERIVATIVES

As has been said, a prime motivation for credit derivatives among commercial banks is the avoidance of prudential capital requirements. Naturally, this is of particular concern to supervisors. There is also a more general concern that credit derivatives may have the

---

[1] J.B. Caouette, E.I. Altman, P. Narayanan, *Managing Credit Risk,* John Wiley, New York, 1998.

effect of concentrating risks within the financial system, while such risks were previously more widely dispersed (see Chapter 1; there are two different opinions on this argument).

Fundamentally, the individual types of risk associated with credit derivatives should, in principle, be no different from those associated with the loans held in the bank's portfolio. But financial analysts point out that this is not 100 percent true because of concentration and leverage.

A similar argument can be made about all risks with off-balance-sheet business which, as shown in Chapter 2 in connection with internal interest rate swaps, connect to items in the balance sheet. Therefore, regulators increasingly suggest that balance sheet risks cannot and should not be analyzed separately from the risks arising from on-balance-sheet activities, but should be regarded as an integral part of the banks' overall risk profiles.

This method of approaching credit derivatives exposure has the additional merit of accounting for the associated risks while recognizing their value when they serve in bettering the bank's cash flow. But how large is the potential of this market and how fast may it be growing?

According to some estimates, there are about $750 billion of corporate loans on the balance sheets of U.S. banks, accounting for roughly one-third of the assets of all insured banks. Based on these estimates, and given that in 1997 commercial loan securitization hardly reached $14 billion while the sum of all securitized corporates in the 1991–97 time frame is below $30 billion—this market has not yet reached 5 percent of its potential. It is just taking off, as shown in Figure 3.1.

The way to bet is that this market will develop, but will credit derivatives change some of the culture associated with designing and selling financial products? Will they lead to great responsibility in salesmanship? John Caouette thinks that this will happen. "A broker," he said, "has today a fiduciary responsibility of what his client is doing and how much is too much in exposure." Because of this,

- The salesman needs to know the client better, and
- He should be sure that what is done is appropriate for him.

This sort of concern by the salesperson, if it materializes, fits well with the preoccupations expressed by regulators who are worried by the fact that lots of derivatives products are new, and lots of people and organizations who buy them don't understand them. As a result, they are not able to manage their exposure, as the December 1994 Orange County case and so many others document.

- The right salesmanship should be embedded into the instrument when it is still at the drafting board.
- This can be effectively done through real-time simulation of product sales and through fulfillment of minimum standards.

The ability to manage exposure with leveraged products is not only a problem for investors but also one concerning the management of institutions that address the market with innovative instruments. Litigation is very expensive and out-of-court settlements may eat up a big chunk of the institution's profits, as the case of Bankers Trust and Procter & Gamble as well as those of Merrill Lynch and Orange County document.

Few issuers and users of credit derivatives appreciate how much they compound the problem of product understanding and

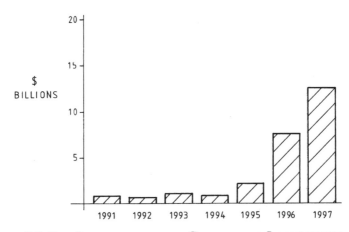

FIGURE 3.1 THE SECURITIZATION OF COMMERCIAL LOANS IN THE UNITED STATES, 1991–1997

therefore sales management. "You really have to have a strong internal control structure," said Edward A. Ryan, Jr., of the Securities and Exchange Commission's Boston office, "but many people say, 'Barings can never happen to me.'"

Part of the problem, cognizant executives said during my research in the United States and Europe, is that management does not fully understand that the ability to control risk diminishes as the sophistication of financial products increases and the market's desire for innovation grows. To face the challenge, the managements of both issuers and users need to establish preventive controls and detective controls.

Preventive controls help the company work in a proactive mode, which is important because traders get very creative and the market's behavior is complex—a fact reflected in greater volatility. At the same time, legal and regulatory requirements change, and this alters the risk profile of the trades being concluded.

Detective control can be developed and applied by the institution itself, or it may be implemented in compliance to regulatory rules. There are lots of conditions to be fulfilled for credit derivatives, according to the German Federal Banking Supervision Bureau. The first directives were issued in 1997. Then new rules came along:

- Including the fine print of the original detective controls regulation, and
- Explaining how banks should recognize credit derivatives in their financial statements.

The Federal Banking Supervision Bureau underlined that this is the right time for credit derivatives regulation because, until late 1998, German banks had not been big players in this market. They are only getting started, and there is some uncertainty on how the market develops in liquidity terms.

The answer many bankers give to the problem of preventive and detective controls centers around the need to develop new, more powerful metrics and solutions for reporting risk. "Classically the banker managed risk without instruments," said a senior German banker. "Therefore complexity was hidden. Now we appreciate that we need both instruments and transparency."

Another problem that impacts on both preventive and detective controls is cultural. "We are a user of credit derivatives," said Hans Voit of Deutsche Bank. "We trade in credit derivatives, but like any other bank, we are still in a learning curve." Generally, European banks are not so sure they wish to enter this market because it will reduce the amount of handholding with their clients—and this might develop into a competitive disadvantage.

"Credit derivatives will bring market risk and credit risk closer together," said Peter Bürger of Commerzbank. In terms of responsibilities, the credit derivatives team at Commerzbank is part of Global Bond operations. Its instruments are evaluated and controlled by the institution's New Product Committee, which meets weekly and brings every single product through the treadmill of internal control (see section 6)—with legal issues, marketing, accounting, and information technology also being part of the evaluation procedure.

The Ministry of Justice, which has the responsibility for accounting standards in the German Federal Republic, seems concerned about the risk involved with credit derivatives, and the nature of controls that will be the most appropriate. Therefore, it is doing its own research to establish advantages, problem pitfalls, and the accounting procedures better positioned to reflect credit risk.

Another of the senior executives who participated in my research added this afterthought: The banker grew powerful when capital markets were limited and there were few financial intermediaries to tap them. When capital markets became plentiful, the banker developed into a salesman pushing the bountiful stuff and its derivatives on wealthy customers. But this means new responsibilities that go beyond those of classical banking.

3. INVESTORS, LENDERS, AND THE RESPONSIBILITIES OF SENIOR MANAGEMENT

As new financial products are introduced in the market, investors have to learn their characteristics, risks, and rewards. By doing so they become more sophisticated and able to search for better yield while limiting risk. Over time, many investors have progressed from handling commodity-type bonds to becoming specialists in emerging asset instruments which, in their judgment, can offer a much better pattern of return.

Lenders, too, have acquired not only new skills in designing new financial products but also new ways and means to market them. Today, lenders have several alternatives in choosing where to issue securitized paper, including

- The public market,
- The private market,
- The private 144A qualified market, and
- The asset-backed commercial paper market.

Each of these has unique advantages but also disadvantages. Therefore a bank must evaluate the conduit it chooses in relation to its marketing muscle. Part of its concerns are factors beyond these more classical issues, such as the composition of its portfolio, cash flow, and profits. Its long-term strategic goals are also part of the picture.

The greater the diversity of instruments offered in the market, the more one has to be a virtuoso in the design as well as in the choice of financial products, and on what makes the market tick. Since October 1998, for instance, bank credit has played a large role in U.S. capital market rallies. At one point in the fourth quarter of 1998, bank lending for securities purchases and bank purchases of non-Treasury securities was rising at an annual rate of more than 100 percent.

Then the pattern changed. In the first quarter of 1999, the growth in bank credit had been running only at 15 percent. But then the growth in other securities, such as mortgages and corporate issues, sped up at a rate of 110 percent. Subsequently, that market slowed down to a 30 percent rate, suggesting that banks are moving back to Treasuries. This explains part of the renewed widening in corporate quality spreads.

"Trends" are not lasting, but in the late 1990s in the United States they were changing at a weekly or monthly pace, while in emerging countries conditions may do so daily. As a result, investors active in the Brazilian market need to monitor a wide variety of factors on what is virtually day-to-day. Among the reasons for that pace are developments associated with:

- The change in political winds,
- Tightening of the country's fiscal policy,
- Movements in spreads on external debt,
- Foreign-exchange and inflation trends, and
- IMF and U.S. response to the local crises.

Designing a new financial instrument, experimenting with its characteristics, and building into it attractive features for better marketing are interrelated tasks calling for skills from many professionals whose knowledge is essential to completing a transaction. In fact,

- The need for credit derivatives know-how begins at the board and senior management levels.
- These levels should be setting the strategic goals and orientation of the transactions to be done.

In terms of legwork, an internal credit derivatives transaction team will typically include personnel from the treasury, commercial, accounting, legal, credit risk, market risk, and operations departments. Another important partner is information technology.

Any modern financial product that does not benefit from high technology is doomed. It will be void of innovation, its sophistication will be low, its risks will be high, and its costs will make it unprofitable even if it rests on a good idea.

- Low technology sees to it that the institution takes huge risks and the transaction is badly executed.
- Both issuers and users of credit derivatives need sophisticated technology for rigorous analysis, for pricing, and to control exposure.

In executing the strategic plans established by the board, a team of financial wizards supported by rocket scientists (see

Chapter 16) and state-of-the-art technology should work to develop ways to meet objectives. In driving for targeted achievements, this team should always keep the clients' needs in perspective.

Experts in this field suggest that an external team's contribution is just as valuable as the internal team's input from clients. The external team includes investment bankers, rating agencies, law firms, accounting firms, trustees, credit enhancers, custodians, and back-up services. These outside experts can help to ensure that a credit derivatives transaction is properly structured and marketed in an able manner.

Each lender who engages in credit derivatives or considers doing so is unique in its strategic objectives as well as in its reasoning why he wants to employ securitization. But there are also common issues that drive this kind of decision. For instance,

1. The desire to receive off-balance-sheet treatment, also known as Sale of GAAP.

For this purpose, the transaction must be structured in accordance with Statement of Financial Accounting Standards (SFAS) No. 125, "Accounting for Transfers and Servicing of Financial Assets and Extinguishments of Liabilities."

2. The intent to realize a gain on the sale of liabilities or assets.

Booking a gain on such sale would need to comply with SFAS 125. Notice, however, that unguaranteed residuals are not considered financial assets and therefore would not qualify.

3. A plan for diversification of the funding base.

This helps to ensure a consistent access to capital, while the bank designs and manages the instrument in a way permitting it to maintain its relationship with (most of) its clients.

4. A favorable accounting treatment for tax purposes.

Here, the goal is to have the credit derivatives transaction treated as debt, so that the interest is tax deductible, thereby optimizing what the institution declares to the authorities as taxable income. Both lenders and buyers aim to control the timing of earnings recognition.

4. INFORMATION REQUIREMENTS WITH CREDIT DERIVATIVES

Section 2 has brought the reader's attention to the fact that marketing new financial instruments is a preoccupation that should start at the drafting board, not postmortem. Whether in banking or in manufacturing, the most successful product is one the user cannot imagine life without—and this should be embedded into product design.

A 19th-century merchant from Frankfurt is credited with saying that to buy a gem from a man who wants to sell it and then to resell it to one who wants to buy it is very easy. But to buy a diamond from one who does not want to sell it and then to sell to one who does not care to buy it, that is business. This is also, in a nutshell, the function of marketing securitized corporate loans. The difference is that securitized corporates can have toxic waste, hence the need for information to manage them.

Information requirements for credit derivatives are significant for three reasons: the need to optimize the design of the instrument; subsequent marketing purposes; and the control of exposure. The information needed for the securitization of loans is both qualitative and quantitative. The qualitative side includes well-documented and updated credit and collection policies and associated procedures.

The users of corporates are entitled to know about the issuer; sophisticated clients of credit derivatives would also like to have information about the companies whose loans are in the pool (which contrasts with some of the notions presented in Chapter 2). They would also like to know about the history of the bank audits, management experience, marketing channels being used, current competition, and future growth areas.

Among the information requirements are skills the bank currently possesses and those the users need as well as down-to-earth issues like how the business is managed on a daily and long-term basis.

In regard to quantitative information, cognizant users of credit derivatives require at least five years of historic portfolio performance by quarter at a minimum. This must be in a form that can be audited both by the bank and by the parties in the transaction.

Sometimes banks try to put on the rails a securitization of corporates with fewer years of financial data by extrapolating loss curves from industry information. Investors, rating agencies, and other parties are not comfortable with this approach because it reduces visibility in analyzing the information made available. Knowledgeable people in the industry advise that the file of historical data should also include data on delinquencies such as

- Delinquency references,
- Gross and net defaults (if any), and
- Detailed reference to such defaults.

The latter would show the events that occurred month by month after origination for all transactions that took place in a specific time period defined by the buyer. This figure is usually divided by the total origination for that same time period to give a control ratio.

This is the general trend that I found, but there was also evidence that not everybody is happy with such statistics. While this information could give a good picture of how a bank's portfolio performs and of how it might perform over the amortization of a transaction, some financial analysts maintain that greater detail may at times be revealing.

Issuers often argue that it is possible to complete a securitization with only general financial accounting default data—for instance, all defaults that occurred in a given period divided by the average receivables outstanding in that same period. Analysts with a sharp mind answer that

- This is a summary approach based on averages, making prognostication on a specific issue difficult, and
- In the majority of cases simple summaries impact negatively on how other parties look at a portfolio and its risks.

Other information on the loans entering into the portfolio is important too—for instance, audited annual and quarterly financial statements, average ticket size, weighted average of original term, weighted average of remaining term, weighted average of implicit yield, and weighted average seasoning. Audited quarterly and annual statements of the issuing bank are also required by some investors.

The information requirements for effective marketing of securitized loans don't end with the aforementioned topics. Each user of credit derivatives may have his own information needs. Nor do the information requirements end with the sale of a credit derivatives issue.

- After securitizing assets, the bank has a new group of parties interested in obtaining information.
- These parties need timely and accurate data in a format that they can easily understand and exploit.

To answer these requests in an able manner, the issuer often must adjust its information technology, adding new tools that permit simulation, optimization, and verification within the contractual time frames. This is a major reason why I press the point that banks and investors with low technology had better avoid credit derivatives.

Keeping the investors, rating agencies, credit enhancers, and supervisors satisfied with a securitization transaction after closing will prove to be helpful the next time the bank makes a new issue. The problem is that in many cases the lender's organization and technology are not able to cope with clients' sophisticated requests for information. Other things equal, the issuers with better organizational solutions win.

5. WHAT CAN WE LEARN FROM SINGLE-TRANSACTION MANAGEMENT?

The concept of single-transaction management is an important supplement to the discussion of information requirements because it deals with credit decisions and execution activities for a specific borrower. It also addresses particular credit facilities extended to that borrower, in an aggregate of decisions and activities including

- Deal structuring,
- Product pricing,
- Limit setting,
- Account management, and
- Risk assessment.

In its fundamentals, single-transaction management is designed to price and control possible future credit losses for each individual borrower. The basic relationship is given by the algorithm

$$\text{Expected net loss} = (\text{Default probability}) \times (\text{Expected exposure at time of default}) \times (1 - \text{Expected recovery rate}).$$

For each borrower, default probability should be assessed by the loans office with the help of a scoring system and of database mining. This concept can be extended to cover a pool of borrowers whose loans are securitized. The use of operating characteristics curves can significantly help in this effort.[2]

The information requirement of investors looks tough because they have learned from banks how to proceed. When they evaluate creditworthiness for their loans, banks use financial ratios from the borrower's balance sheet. They also project cash flows under different assumptions for sales volume, unit prices, unit costs, and the like. Such exercises help to judge the borrower's

- Adequacy of capital,
- Capacity to pay the interest, and
- Ability to repay the capital.

Notice the similarity between these elements and the information requirements in section 4. Financial analysts add that other cru-

---

[2] See D.N. Chorafas, *Statistical Processes and Reliability Engineering*, D. Van Nostrand Co., Princeton, NJ, 1960.

cial decision elements are the borrower's management competence, willingness to repay, and character. A vital component of judgmental assessment is the identification and study of key risk factors that can affect ability to repay. These factors include

- Product appeal,
- Competition,
- Financial risks, and
- Operational risks.

One of the quantitative approaches followed for default assessment is Contingent Claims Analysis (CCA). Also known as option modeling, it assumes that the borrower has an option to default that he might exercise. This can be modeled as a put option.

- The underlying for this option represents the borrower's assets.
- Default parameters are the present asset value and its volatility due to earnings volatility.

The strike price of the borrower's default option is represented by the present value of the borrower's liabilities. Models of this type assume that the put will be exercised—hence, the borrower will opt to default—when the present value of his assets falls below the present value of his liabilities.

The process of estimating expected exposure at the time of default per single transaction must address the likelihood of both expected and unexpected losses at the borrower's side (see Chapter 11). In the case of loans, what we are interested in is loan value plus accrued interest outstanding at time of default. Basic elements in estimating the term structure of default probabilities are

- The transaction structure and
- The setting of borrower limits.

Pricing should account for these elements. The same is true of supervisory norms. In terms of limits, regulators specify a bank's legal lending limit to any borrower or group of related borrowers, as a percentage of the bank's capital. The exact percent level depends upon the jurisdiction.

Limits connected to counterparty risk and borrowing ability in regard to the bank's capital help to ensure against the possibility that one catastrophic default can wipe out the institution. Theoretically, credit derivatives spread out this sort of risk. Practically, it is always wise to watch out for these factors.

In most banks the board sets an overall borrower limit that is well below the legal lending limit. This is based upon assessment of borrower risk and the long-term profitability of the relationship.

Banks also set product sublimits to diversify product exposure, to meet market objectives, and for other reasons. Prudential limits help in establishing the total amount of credit that the bank is willing to make available to a particular counterparty. This information is critical to financial analysts in their examination of a pool of securitized corporates—and it should be added to the information elements outlined in section 4.

6. INTERNAL CONTROLS AND CREDIT DERIVATIVES

"The products to which the International Swaps and Derivatives Association addresses itself are over the counter; hence, they are not regulated per se," said Susan Hinko, the International Swaps and Derivatives Association (ISDA) technical director. "But the institutions are regulated." In ISDA's opinion, the fact that derivative financial instruments are deregulated and flexible (1) is conductive to innovation and dynamism in the market and (2) allows many new instruments like credit derivatives to develop.

But the institutions handling them must see this opportunity as an incentive to implement a first-class internal control system. Susan Hinko has suggested that credit derivatives is a demanding business, requiring the appropriate management culture, including the observance of internal controls that should cover the many aspects of exposure.

This thesis closely parallels the position taken by the Federal Deposit Insurance Corporation (FDIC), which pointed to the need for bankers and examiners to carefully evaluate the assumptions used in valuing economic interests in assets transferred or sold. Under gain-on-sale accounting rules, effective in 1997,

- Some lenders reported substantial income based on assumptions about future performance of subprime loans sold in securitizations.
- But substantial write-downs showed up in a number of cases when the assumptions proved incorrect.

FDIC analysts cited financial reports by several major credit rating agencies that have drawn attention to pctential inflation of companies' reported earnings and capital that can result from gain-on-sale and other creative accounting practices. Because credit derivatives are part of the picture painted by such reports, senior management must be very careful in the pricing and valuation of assets. The same is true for risk managers.

Valuable lessons can be learned from the insurance industry, which presents a certain similitude to risk issues encountered with credit derivatives. One of these lessons is the wisdom of spreading the risk through diversification of the exposure being taken. This principle is violated when a bank looks at credit derivatives as a way to free up internal credit lines to serve the same borrower.

For instance, a commercial bank has reached its internal lending limit with respect to a certain counterparty, but might feel obliged to continue to provide the upcoming funding needs or derivative transactions of that client. Theoretically, the institution could address this dual challenge by entering into a total return swap tied to an underlying loan (see Chapter 6). Under the swap, the bank pays the total return on the existing loan positions in consideration for a payment based on the London Interbank Offered Rate (LIBOR).

Alternatively, the bank looks for default protection on a specific derivative transaction while the reference assets stay on the books. This way, the bank effectively swaps the borrower's (or the derivative counterparty's) credit risk for its own. Through this process management thinks that it is freeing up corresponding credit lines. But is it really?

The query is made in full understanding that credit derivatives might be used for hedging default risk in respect to a single, credit-sensitive asset. But the market may not be behaving in a way that confirms management's or the trader's hypothesis.

In essence, the bank exchanges the credit risk of the borrower for that of the swap counterparty. The periodic payment amount will depend primarily on the credit of the underlying reference asset. But because of an amount to be paid in the event of default or some other significant credit event, the bank in essence has assumed another layer of credit risk.

CHAPTER 4

Credit Derivatives, Transparency, and Collateralization

1. INTRODUCTION

The concept of credit derivatives has been described as being based on (1) the bank's desire to liquify its corporate loans and (2) the belief that the credit universe is evolving into a liquid, transparent market of the type characterizing other global markets like foreign exchange. Historically, however, the hypothesis regarding this second motor behind the credit derivatives drive is not foolproof.

- The measurement of credit risk from lending has been often expressed by imposing arbitrary limits on the total outstanding exposure, which is not appealing to investors.
- While mortgage-backed financing (MBF) prospered, the securitization of corporate loans lagged behind because they are not easily liquified.

Only rarely have there been attempts to rid the balance sheet of unwanted loans risks, a key reason being that classically corporate loans are not transparent. The bank holding them keeps many secrets close to its chest. The equity market would never have

71

reached its current level of liquidity and efficiency were it not for well-regulated financial disclosure and *transparency.*

Transparency is a precondition for an efficient market—a fact emerging countries and, sometimes, emerging products do not fully appreciate. Short of a regulated disclosure system, investors feel constrained and have to account for loan market inefficiency. Alternatively they might accept assurance provided through a guarantor.

The role of the *guarantor* in the broker capital market is relatively new, and for the time being it primarily focuses on municipals. Because the notion of a guarantor holds promise for the future, Figure 4.1 presents in a nutshell his position in the securitization circuit. His action is intended to make up for the difference between the values assigned to a loan or pool of loans by (1) the free market and (2) the lender who is not making public the dependability of the pool.

To close the gap between these two values, Chapter 3 has listed the information requirements for the securitization of corpo-

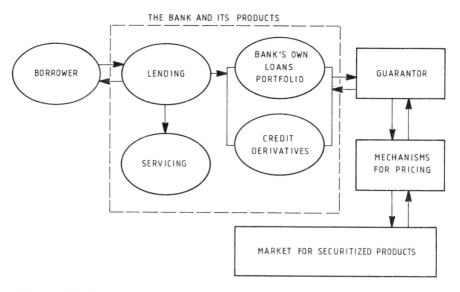

FIGURE 4.1 HANDLING CREDIT RISK THROUGH A REINSURANCE PROVIDED BY A GUARANTOR

rates. The service the guarantor can assure is not only as an insurer but also as an interpreter of information requirements that permit the assigning of a net present value (NPV) to the securities.

2. THE DIFFICULTY OF OBTAINING FAIR VALUE ESTIMATES

Ideally, what an institutional investor or a guarantor tries to do is to qualify and quantify a given pool of loans in terms of expected net present value. By comparing loan values derived from internally calibrated risk premiums with those obtained from market risk premiums, it is possible to come up with pricing disparities.

This business is not simple and transparency can go a long way in making feasible informed judgments about how to reconcile pricing dictated by the marketplace with the bank's internal pricing of credit risk, including its loan servicing costs. A "must" is the existence of risk management models that, based on available information, help to identify and quantify credit risk (see Part Three).

The work the guarantor's analysts need to do is not that different from that classically done by banking analysts. This includes their estimates. Practically all commercial banks have problems in managing their loan portfolios because these portfolios tend to be illiquid and not diversified.

Bankers who work on the securitization of loans appreciate that the analytical aspects of this work are different from those characterizing the mission of fund managers (see Chapter 5), who design and build their portfolios practically from scratch. While in both cases the precondition is understanding the risk/reward profile, the information hidden in the loans portfolio the bank owns is much more complex than that found in assets management.

Bankers who securitize or aim to securitize their corporates must also cope with the rather general feeling that this market is not yet mature. Therefore, it might become illiquid, with illiquidity introducing some major variances in fair value estimates that may be harmful to investors.

The Group of Thirty has made reference to a study conducted by KPMG which has shown existing variances in fair value estimates.[1] As it is to be expected, the variance is relatively small for good assets, but becomes big for assets that have turned sour. For example,

- For residential mortgages with an active secondary market, test values varied between 2 and 5 percent.
- For many traditional loans with good standing, the expected value of the deviation was about 3.5 percent.
- But for poor-quality loans, the deviation grew significantly to 30 percent.

This is telling in terms of risks both guarantors and investors take with new financial instruments. There is, evidently, a competition for "good" risks matched by the development of alternative sales methods. There is as well a pressure on prices resulting from increased competition which is likely to have the greater effect on markets where

- Regulation used to be strict,
- There are thick equity cushions available to fight price wars, and
- The number of new suppliers exceeds the number of those dropping out of the market because they are no longer competitive.

We have been talking about guarantors, but as shown in Figure 4.2 we should not forget the role played by rating agencies and nascent global regulation. The 1988 Capital Accord and the 1996 Market Risk Amendment are examples.

As discussed in Chapter 10, over the last few years independent rating agencies have become more important not only due to the relative reduction in government supervision but also because globalization has worked like a thin wedge between supervisors.

---

[1] "Defining the Roles of Accountants, Bankers, and Regulators in the United States," Group of Thirty, Washington, DC, 1994.

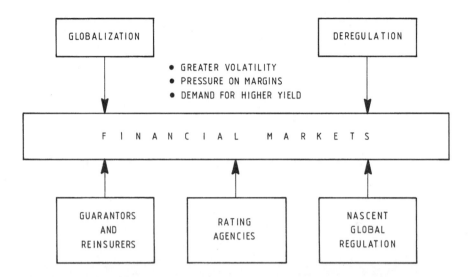

FIGURE 4.2 NEW CONDITIONS IN THE FINANCIAL MARKET LEAD TO
GREATER EXPECTATION OF CAPITAL MANAGEMENT.

This division is now closing thanks to the seminal work by the Basle
Committee on Banking Supervision, which leads to a higher level of
regulatory activities.

Taken together these conditions produce a need for adjust-
ments, and it is proper to assume that, during this phase, price rises
for "bad" risks will only partially be compensated for by price reduc-
tions for more favorable risks. This is one way to interpret the
KPMG findings.

It is not difficult to detect the way the mind of management
would work within this frame of reference. At first, institutions will
probably concentrate on their positioning in the new competitive
environment and, above all, on securing or even gaining new market
share. This will most likely lead to shrinking premium income and
margins. But at the same time, market-induced price changes will
result in more volatile technical results.

One also has to factor in the results of consolidation. As the
number of banks shrinks because of mergers and acquisitions, and
as these banks get larger as well as loaded with the exposures of the

merged parties, the magnitude of the credit risk that they securitize increases.

3. SECURITIZED BALANCE SHEETS, EVENT RISK, AND STRUCTURAL SHOCK

Many analysts look at credit derivatives as being essentially a securitization of conventional balance sheets of the firms whose liabilities enter the pool of corporate loans. But there is also legal risk, because under the laws of some countries an underwriter may be liable for failing to adequately ascertain and disclose to investors material information pertaining to the securities he issues.

If there is any default by a company in the pool or decline in the market price of the securities as a result of adverse financial results within a short time after the underwriting, investors are likely to seek to hold the underwriter liable. Alternatively, they may hold liable the guarantor.

There is as well the fact that in many countries institutions are subject to guidelines or limits on large exposures, and they are also expected to diversify risk in a prudent manner.

For these reasons, the board should ask senior management to offer evidence of whether the present scale of corporate loans in the bank's portfolio (1) provides a sound basis for loans securitization or (2) can leave the institution excessively exposed to a few counterparties.

This is not alien to the preoccupation of many supervisors. Board members should also appreciate that a lopsided exposure in the bank's loans portfolio can happen without even realizing it. The board should therefore explicitly ask senior management to ensure that

- Credit derivatives and other off-balance-sheet items are included in a systematic manner in the internal counterparty limits, and
- They are subject to prudent measurements and timely, accurate reports to board members.

These demands by the board essentially amount to a frequent evaluation of the loans book. There should be internal control rules that permit one to judge the health of the lending commitments, at any time, with any counterparty, anywhere in the world. A rigorous sensitivity analysis and online visualization of result can be most helpful.

The previous paragraphs' implication is valid both for the companies whose loans are in the bank's portfolio and for the balance sheet of the bank itself. The securitization of balance sheets and collateralized debt obligations are obligations that go beyond the classical criteria for diversification in loans and investments focusing on

- Counterparty,
- Industry,
- Interest rate,
- Maturity,
- Currency, and
- Country.

The balance sheet, for instance, might have been wounded even with loans in the same currency and in the same country where the bank resides. As an example, on September 20, 1996, Michel Pebereau, chairman of Banque National de Paris, told investment analysts in Paris that his bank is happy with the proposed agreement regarding the Eurotunnel debt and is ready to sign it.

The financial analysts were not convinced. They thereafter commented that Pebereau's statement should be seen in the light of the particular difficulties French banks face as a result of their involvement in the Eurotunnel. Part of the equation was also the fact that the French banking sector has been struggling with low profitability and a rash of bad property loans.

A year prior to this event, in 1995, the French banking regulator had instructed all French banks to make provisions equivalent to 30 percent of their exposure to Eurotunnel. Any agreement was therefore expected to lead to further provisions and write-downs. Banking analysts have been concerned about the impact of any Eurotunnel restructuring on the banks' balance sheets.

Losses can be significantly more severe when loans are given to companies and sovereigns in countries where the uncertainty quotient is especially high. On September 1, 1998, Barclays Bank

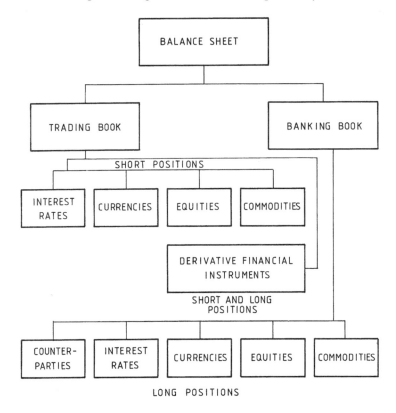

FIGURE 4.3 ORIGINS OF PROBLEMS FOUND IN A BANK'S BALANCE SHEET

announced that it set aside reserves of £250 million ($420 million) to cover losses because of the Russian meltdown. NatWest then declared that it felt comfortable with £100 million ($166 million) in provisions for the same disaster. Here we have two wounded balance sheets, the difference being one of degree.

The lesson taught by all these examples is that investors interested in securitized balance sheets must pay particular attention to *specific risk,* which is a function of the quality of the issuer and reflects that quality in numbers. As Figure 4.3 shows, problems in a bank's balance sheet may originate from the following:

- Long-term positions (the Eurotunnel's case),

- Medium-term positions (the case of Russia's loans),
- Short-term positions in the trading book, and
- Derivative financial instruments.

But there may also be *event risk*. Event risk is a situation in which a change in creditworthiness is likely to be transitory, as with the credit rating of Reynolds Nabisco after the leveraged buyout (LBO) by Kohlberg, Kravis, Roberts.

Event risk contrasts to the cases of the Eurotunnel and Russia, which have been *structural shocks*. This means a rather long-lasting change in creditworthiness. Another example of structural shock that has wounded many banks' balance sheets was the East-Asia meltdown.

While there are some approaches today that seem to be accounting for event risk, no model as yet has been able to handle structural shock. This is largely because most banks keep that information secret with outsiders suspecting rather than knowing the size of the damage. Yet structural changes have a significant value to investors apart from creating arbitrage opportunities.

4. DERIVATIVES TRADES AND THE USE OF COLLATERAL

In the derivatives industry, collateralization is a technique frequently used for risk reduction. Basic issues are the decision to allocate collateral for a single transaction or an entire portfolio; determining the nature and pricing of the underlying collateral; its posting on an upfront or periodic basis; and the structuring of collateral agreements.

Few banks are able to proceed with a real-time evaluation of what is involved in a collateral requirement. For this reason, as well as because of conservative management, many banks have a policy of accepting as collateral cash or high-rated government bonds. By contrast, high tech institutions have broadened the list of acceptable collateral to include mortgage-backed securities, corporate bonds, junk bonds, and equities.

Credit derivatives may be next in line. When handling collateral, banks apply standard discounts, or haircuts, to the upfront market value. Haircuts help to protect against volatility in the collateral's value by providing an extra margin, but the use of old technology causes haircuts to be fixed. By contrast, the use of fuzzy engineering increases both flexibility and accuracy in the evaluation of the collateral's value.[2]

Any collateral is subject to constraints such as liquidity and creditworthiness. Therefore, counterparties accepting collateral should improve their ability to price and monitor it on a real-time basis. They should also account for the fact that while lower volatility, higher liquidity, and better credit rating influence the calculations, the market can turn around at any time.

The concept of *upfront collateral* is that of posting a guarantee at the inception of a transaction, and doing so in an amount sufficient to cover future market movements. By contrast, *periodic collateral* is taken at selected milestones during the life of the transaction. It is computed on the basis of current marking to market of the inventoried transaction, plus a buffer.

Generally, a bank requires a counterparty to post upfront collateral as a guarantee with the discount (or haircut) helping to cover the margin. Banks with low technology don't even have the operational capability to do accurate calculations of haircuts in volatile markets. Typically,

- The upfront collateral reflects the final maturity date of the transaction,
- While the haircut takes care of the possibility the counterparty will not be able to post additional collateral down the line.

Upfront collateral sometimes acts as a break to derivatives deals because it represents a significant sum that the counterparty may have difficulty putting together. This is particularly true when dealing with high-risk complex derivatives.

This discussion is relevant to credit derivatives. If the bank continues holding the loans in the pool for relationship banking or

---

[2] For a practical example, see D.N. Chorafas, *Chaos Theory in the Financial Markets,* Probus, Chicago, 1994.

other reasons, then these loans are the collateral of the bonds being issued. And because these bonds are derivatives they are also the underlying.

- This dual status requires a more complex procedure than the simple haircut classically applied to collateral.
- Users of credit derivatives will be well advised to ask for special guarantees, because at the end of the day they will be carrying the underlying's risk.

A critical decision in collateralization, pertinent with credit derivatives, is that of a transaction-specific versus a pooled portfolio. Transaction-specific collateral is taken against a precise deal. By contrast, pooled collateral addresses a portfolio of derivatives or a securitization.

The transaction-specific basis is preferred when a counterparty is not a frequent partner of the bank in derivatives and other deals. In a transaction-specific case, termination or unwind of the deal for which the collateral was put up results in its release.

Combining collateral into a single pool and using the pool in securing the entire derivatives portfolio has advantages. But the pooled collateral agreement must be appropriately documented from both security and legal standpoints. It is a good policy to ensure that enough money is available to face adversity.

5. LESSONS TO BE LEARNED FROM COLLATERALIZATIONS OF THE 1920S

The structuring of a collateral agreement can be a challenging proposition. The contrast is between one-way and two-way collateral. The former arrangement calls for only one of the two parties to a derivative transaction to post collateral; the latter requires that collateral is posted by both counterparties.

- One-way collateral agreements are a more common form of the securitized derivatives business.
- Two-way agreements are more prevalent between institutions of an equal credit quality.

A one-way collateral agreement is the rule when the other party's credit quality is not high. This has led to an escape strategy through AAA-rated Derivative Products Companies (DPC). The basic element of a DPC's enhanced rating comes from the endowment it has received from its mother firm (see also Chapter 7).

The concept of specifically designed DPCs, or some form similar to them, has not yet been used with credit derivatives—at least to my knowledge. But if the pool of loans is kept as underlying and the issuer guarantees the bonds it underwrites, then special companies endowed with financial staying power may come into being. This will be particularly true when the buyers of credit derivatives find out that collateralization may not provide the guarantees it is supposed to offer.

Let me take a lesson from financial history to explain my point. In the 1920s, in the United States most domestic bank loans went directly to finance securities purchases, largely stocks. This trend had developed after World War I as

- A growing number of large U.S. corporations had turned to the New York Stock Exchange to raise capital, and
- They financed their expanded investments through new issues of shares sold to the capital market.

For instance, the American automobile industry was expanding at high speed with most of the expansion of plant and equipment financed by new stock issues. But at the same time banks were awash with liquidity. As a result, commercial banks extended credit for the purchase of stocks on an unprecedented scale, with shares and other securities taken by banks as collateral for new lending.

- People were encouraged to borrow money to buy stocks on margin, further fueling the market's rise.
- Stock prices ballooned 69 percent from the end of 1927 to the peak in September 1929—albeit less than in the 1995–98 period.

This risky practice of a synergy between loans and shares pushed the stock prices higher and higher, drawing ever more people into the market at ever riskier levels. In 1925 alone, bank loans to stockbrokers to finance stock purchases more than doubled to a record $2.8 billion. With this, the New York Stock Exchange index rose by 40 percent.

By early 1929, fully two-thirds of all U.S. bank credit was collateralized by various securities, usually shares. This tremendously increased the possibility of a stock market collapse and such a collapse's ability to bring down the entire banking system. As the stock market itself continued to rise on the back of new demand, mostly on borrowed money, the public's interest in stock ownership grew even more. But when the stock market prices caved in, the collateral held by the banks for their loans also collapsed.

There is a proverb that who forgets the lessons of the past condemns himself to repeat them. Gearing is always a cause of concern. On May 31, 1998, the outstanding *margin credit* had expanded from $127 billion at the end of 1997 to $143 billion, according to Federal Reserve figures. These were loans to financial investments, mainly margins in shares.

Loans for financial investments become very risky when the mood of the market changes. In bear markets leveraged shares are highly unreliable as collateral. As the professionals know, lower share prices force margin investors either to deposit more cash with their brokers or, if they don't have the cash, to liquidate some or all of their holdings.

The high gearing with securitized loans some bankers project for the first years of the 21st century—some $750 billion of them—has a sinister resemblance to the high gearing with shares in the late 1920s and late 1990s.

- In the 1920s, bought shares constituted the collateral of the loans banks were giving.
- Around year 2000, securitized loans will likely be the collateral of other loans.

But loans collapse when creditworthiness does, and that takes care of the collateral. It is important to keep in mind the lesson from the 1920s: Collateralization was not invented with credit derivatives. Using an existing infrastructure with a new leveraged instrument makes me nervous.

Bank supervisory authorities feel the same way, as I found in my research. A major issue confronting regulators in connection to their supervisory duties, particularly because of the risks taken by institutional investors (see Chapter 5), is that individual transactions are increasingly collateralized. This means that

- As a result of collateralization, many of a bank's good assets go out of its reach.
- Therefore, the other asset holders will find themselves secured against little or nothing.

Regulators are sanguine about the effects of an extensive collateralization. Because of cherry picking by lenders and counterparties, the best assets may be gone as credit derivatives and other leveraged instruments pick up momentum. Eventually this will become a bubble that will burst and the financial institution might be worth 10 cents to the dollar—much less than an emerging country's credit.[3]

6. CREDIT DERIVATIVES, RISK PREMIUMS, AND LONG-TERM LOANS

Commercial and investment bankers with whom I spoke of these concerns assured me that they can be taken care of through risk premiums. In all fairness, I don't believe that risk premiums can go a long way because, after all, we work in a highly competitive market. However, to inform the reader of all viewpoints it is proper to briefly examine what lies behind this suggestion.

Banks tend to extend the notion of risk premiums to long-term loans by using the concept of an expected net present value: NPV_E. Specifically, they exploit the difference between the amount the lender realizes by holding the loan for its cash flows, L_{CF}, and the amount the lender realizes if he sells the loan at fair value, L_{FV} :

---

[3] See D.N. Chorafas, *Managing Derivatives Risk,* Irwin/Probus, Chicago, 1996.

$$L_{CF} - L_{FV} \quad (1)$$

A clear definition of *fair value* has been given by the Financial Accounting Standards Board (FASB). It is the price a willing buyer will pay a willing seller under conditions other than fire sale. Fair value and market value are not quite the same because market value may include fire sale prices and special discounts. Also present value, which is practically market value, is not as clearly defined by regulators as fair value.

Many bankers believe that fair value can be interpreted as market value if the expected net present value is calculated with regard to the open market credit spreads. Otherwise, fair value relates to the lender's internal credit spreads—which is not exactly FASB's definition, but it is used frequently in finance.

One way a lender can sell the credit risk of the loan is to himself, through an internal credit. The effect of this internal transaction is that of transferring credit risk directly to the lender's shareholders. Alternatively, the lender can sell part or all of his portfolio to the market through credit derivatives. In this case he eliminates credit risk provided he dissociates himself from the pool used as underlying.

To appreciate the flows of cash and risk, we can think of lenders as maintaining separate entrepreneurial capital and economic capital accounts. The exchange of cash flows is managed through the entrepreneurial capital account, but default losses are underwritten by the economic capital account.

- The transfer of credit risk from the entrepreneurial account to the economic account is effected through an internal return swap.
- If arbitrage pricing is used, this swap has a fair price which most banks believe to be the market price, L_{FV}.

The net cash flow into the entrepreneurial capital account under the swap is this fair price. The expected cash flow into the economic capital account that results from acquiring and holding the swap was shown in equation (1): $L_{CF} - L_{FV}$

This difference, the pros say, can be seen as being equal to the *risk premium*. In other words, in the expected present value notion the risk premium derived from a loan represents the net flow of cash into the lender's capital account in return for the credit risk which is that account.

This looks like a neat algorithm, but I am not convinced that it will pass the market test in the long run. Another issue to which I do not subscribe, though it should be brought to the reader's attention, is the use of netting in connection to the exposures just being mentioned or any other exposure, for that matter.

There is a breed of bankers who believe that netting by fair value does away with part of the capital requirements, particularly those connected to the transactions and positions being netted. This argument is wrong for two reasons. First, there should always be prudential capital. Second, something that might look nice on paper could turn into a disaster in real life.

To gain a good foothold in the American oil market, the U.S. subsidiary of the German Metallgesellschaft entered into five-year contracts. For hedging reasons it bought futures. But when the price of oil skyrocketed because of the Iraqi invasion of Kuwait, the huge losses in the cash oil market were very unevenly covered by gains in oil futures, and Metallgesellschaft nearly went bankrupt. There is a fundamental issue with capital requirements no derivatives contracts can cover:

- The amount of capital the bank needs is related to the financial riskiness of the business it is conducting.
- This amount is best measured by the volatility of its income and its cash flow plus the exposures it has taken.

A valid way to address the income issue is to take operating income and the gain or loss in the value of assets and liabilities—including the bank's portfolio of derivatives. This means marking to market or marking to model, and passing gains or losses into the income stream.

Cash flow is typically generated through business transactions. But *cash flow* is a term that does not have only one definition and method of computation.[4] Banks need to improve significantly the accuracy with which cash flows are estimated and recorded, borrowing concepts and tools from actuarial science:

- Any asset or liability that has an expected future cash flow can be marked to market or to model by discounting that cash flow.
- Traditional loans meet this criterion. So do many derivative financial instruments if properly studied.

"Prudential supervision requires capital charge," one regulator commented. Since 1993 the Deutsche Bundesbank has seen to it that the basis for supervisory controls is the sum of cash flows. The principle is that the solution to be chosen should be valid for each individual bank, in its risk management effort, and should provide transparency for the regulators.

The solution to be retained should link cash flow to *liquidity* and hence to the ability to pay off quickly by either having available cash, raising money, selling short-term investments, or liquifying long-term commitments without undue losses. Together with capital, cash flow and a liquid market amount to *financial staying power*.

---

[4] See D.N. Chorafas, *Financial Models and Simulation,* Macmillan, London, 1995.

CHAPTER 5

Fund Managers and Credit Derivatives Markets

1. INTRODUCTION

Several of the executives I met in the course of my research described credit derivatives as a by-product of perfect capital mobility on a global scale. A reference to perfect capital mobility implies the existence of a global capital market, and vice versa. This contrasts to the point of view of a single country, where perfect capital mobility requires that

- National savings are being channeled not only to retail banks but also to a capital market, and
- Capital is obtained for investment purposes from a golden horde of instruments, new and old.

In any country, perfect capital mobility would see to it that the relation that has classically existed between savings and investments tends to disappear as a formerly closed economy opens up. But there is no reason to believe that this model is valid with current globalization, because there are still so many barriers in the way.

- Empirical analyses point to the fact that though globalization is ongoing, there is still no high degree of international capital mobility.
- Investors are still concerned about credit risk, currency risk, and country risk in the so-called emerging markets.

There are other reasons as well why capital mobility is imperfect in a global sense. An example is the avoidance of dispersion of securities portfolios. Comparative studies generally support the hypothesis of clear preference for domestic stocks, bonds, and notes—though this might be changing in the years to come.

These references are important to underwriters and sellers of credit securities because they identify the type of market to which these will be sold. Part of the market might be global, but a good chunk will be local. This makes it even more important to target the right population of clients—and these clients will want, in all likelihood, to get factual, documented opinions from investment bankers.

This raises another issue: Are there any conflicts of interest in advising on investments in credit derivatives? Conflicts of interest might exist in *fairness opinions,* when a board of directors hires an investment bank to advise on whether shareholders are getting a fair price with emerging instruments (as contrasted to emerging markets).

Investment banks receive a success fee if the deal they are advising on goes through; they get a much lower fee if the deal collapses. Conflicts of interest might also exist when an investment bank securitizes the loans of a retail bank, but at the same time acts as financial advisor to institutional investors who buy the new financing instrument. It is always wise to watch out for cases like that.

2. INSTITUTIONAL INVESTORS, NEW MONEY, AND HEDGE FUNDS

According to estimates by cognizant financial analysts, in early 1997 in the UK alone funds under management by institutional investors were well in excess of £2 trillion ($3.32 trillion), two and a half times

Britain's gross domestic product. There has been a steep rise in the amount of managed money as shown in Figure 5.1.

British bankers believe that part of this steep rise in asset management cash flows to the UK, during the last few years, has to do with the fact that London is the world's financial capital. Funds managed on behalf of overseas clients have shot from £146 billion in 1992 to £530 billion in 1995 and the industry as a whole generates £1.7 billion a year by way of value-added operations.

Another interesting statistic is that each fund manager in Britain is now responsible for an average of £300 million. Pension funds, insurance companies, unit trusts (mutual funds), and investment trusts currently command some 90 percent of funds under management in the United Kingdom. As in all industries,

- About 50 firms account for more than three-quarters of this total, and

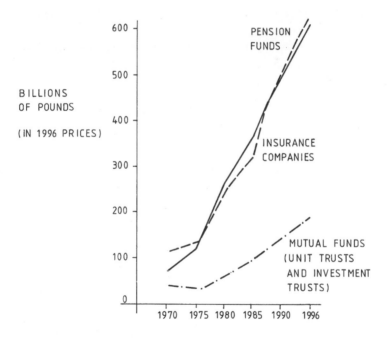

FIGURE 5.1 BRITAIN'S GROWTH OF INSTITUTIONAL INVESTORS IN A QUARTER CENTURY

- The 10 largest fund managers share among themselves 32 percent.

While this concentration is not as high as that in the United States, where Fidelity alone masters the 10 percent of capital invested in mutual funds, it is still impressive. The point is that a high concentration provides a basis for herdlike movements in the market and also places enormous power in the hands of a very small group of people.

Contrarians to the concentration of financial might look at such statistics as a bad omen for the free market. They say that the aftermath is that accountability and transparency are not of the highest, but fees can be heavy and they are structured in a way rewarding failure rather than success.

This large amount of money actively seeking ways and means to be invested sees to it that bankers who are active, or plan to be active, in credit derivatives don't have a quiet sleep. As Walter Wriston, the former chairman of Citibank, is rumored to have said, "The $3 trillion in savings accounts around the country don't let me sleep." But in order to be part of the action, the underwriters of corporates have to answer two key questions:

- From where will the expected big flow of money come?
- What sort of criteria and benchmarks are the fund managers using?

There are two main answers to the first question (the second query being answered in section 4). First, a large population of savers who finally understand that Social Security is bankrupt, no matter how you look at it, appreciate that they should not count on it for retirement.

- Each contributor to pension funds and mutual funds puts in a small amount of money at a time, but this makes a cash flow of about $20 billion per month in the United States alone.
- The U.S. government rewards the savers through deferred taxes via plans like Individual Retirement Accounts (IRAs) and 401(k)s, as discussed in section 3.

The other major party in cash flows has fewer players, but each is endowed with huge financial power. Nobody really knows how much money is flowing into the secretive, largely unregulated world of hedge funds, but it is in the billions, it is invested globally, and it usually represents speculative trades.

Estimates of the total amount of money in hedge funds range from $200 billion to $400 billion in more than 4,000 different funds. These numbers are strictly indicative, but even as an order of magnitude they carry a message because

- Hedge funds are able to liquify their holdings in a moment's notice, and no central bank has enough reserves to hold for long against a focused assault.

- Hedge funds target a 30 percent or more rate of return per year, though the results don't seem to be as beneficial to investors today as they were prior to the 1994 bond market crash.

There are, of course, exceptions. Some funds under Soros Fund Management beat the Standard & Poor's 500-stock index in 1998. Quota Fund gained 26 percent as of May 1998 versus 12.4 percent for the S&P 500. As a global macro fund, Quota tries to profit from changes in currencies and interest rates around the world by playing global macroeconomic trends. Some technology hedge funds also overtook the S&P 500's gain.

The majority of hedge funds, however, fell short of the S&P mark, some by a large margin. The high-yield sector, as well as market-neutral funds which try to cancel out market exposure with offsetting long and short positions, underperformed the S&P 500 by about 10 percentage points. As of mid-1998, Latin American hedge funds were down 12.2 percent, as were other emerging-market funds. Russian funds have been the worst hit. Also badly wounded are major U.S., British, and German banks as well as Soros.

Why is that so important in a discussion of credit derivatives? The answer is precedence. Funds that invest in the aforementioned instruments have been plagued by prepayments and are hurting. Just as poor are the results of those hedge funds playing the dollar–yen relationship which hit several snags in June 1998.

Wounded organizations, like wounded people, are more careful next time around. Yet, for underwriters of securitized corporates the position taken by hedge funds is very important. They have to be able to convince fund managers that betting on business loans has a better return than dollar–yen or dollar–mark relationships, and it also carries less risk. This is not going to be an easy sale.

3. RETIREMENT PLANS, 401(K)S, AND PENSION FUNDS

How much money should there be for retirement? The rule of thumb is that each individual needs at least 70 percent of preretirement income to maintain his established standard of living in retirement. This means that people should prepare for retirement or they will not be able to keep up their current living standards.

Precisely because of this concern, since the early 1980s American households have socked away hundreds of billions of dollars in tax-based savings-incentive plans such as 401(k)s and Individual Retirement Accounts. These contributions have stayed relatively strong, which puzzles economists because real wages are not growing the way they once did.

The 401(k) program was originally established as a long-term plan by the government to help people save for retirement. It offers advantages compared to traditional pension plans, with participation being set up by the employer. Employers are not required by law to offer a 401(k) program, but when they do it is a good offer.

Special tax advantages make the 401(k) appealing to employees since all contributions are made on a pretax basis, with the net effect that the participant's taxable income is reduced. An employee participant first decides the amount of money to be contributed to the plan, up to an established maximum, during each pay period. Then, he or she chooses where the money is to be invested from among the company's investment fund options.

The 401(k) program is very flexible, offering a number of investment options to choose from. Depending on the participant's future goals and objectives, the contributed plan money can be placed in either a conservative, relatively low-risk investment fund or an aggressive one that takes more risks but might offer higher gains. After participants decide how much and where the money is to be invested, they are not locked into these choices. They are free to alter the investment mix as their needs and retirement goals change.

Once plan contributions begin, periodic statements are sent to the 401(k) participant throughout the year to help track investment progress. All contributions and growth earnings remain tax-free until the money is withdrawn because of retirement or an emergency.

Since plan contributions are made on a pretax basis, the participant's taxable income is reduced, which in turn results in lower taxes. Tax-deferred income taxes are not paid on the contributions, or growth earnings, until the money is withdrawn from the plan.

As more and more American workers put their money into 401(k) retirement accounts, the old view of homes being the single best investment wanes. This is why credit derivatives underwriters might see the 401(k) market as one with good potential—provided they can offer high-quality securities.

Economists today speculate that if American consumers become accustomed to checking the value of their 401(k) plans as often as they calculate the balances in their checking accounts, their spending will become more sensitive to the state of the market— which might prove a plus or a minus for credit derivatives.

- The value of 401(k) plans surged from $525 billion at year-end 1994 to $640 billion at year-end 1995, with the bulk of the gains coming in equities.
- Over 1995, with a soaring stock market, someone holding $20,000 in his or her 401(k) plan's stock index fund would have seen an increase of $6,000 in value.[1]

But from where does the money *really* come? Is this cash flow sustained only through wages? A study by the Brookings Institution links the significant rise in 401(k) plan participation to an equally

---

[1] *Business Week,* December 4, 1995.

significant increase in mortgage debt over the same period. The results indicate that households have tended to shift savings away from tangible assets in the form of home equity to financial assets in tax-favored savings plans.

Employing nationwide household survey data, the Brookings study found that households with at least one worker eligible to participate in a 401(k) plan did accumulate significantly more net financial assets between 1987 and 1991 than similar households without eligible workers.

Eligible U.S. households took on substantially more mortgage debt than noneligible households. The inference can therefore be made that if these eligible households take mortgage money to invest in credit derivatives, they will essentially be leveraging mortgage loans through investments based on business loans.

4. IS THERE A CREDIT DERIVATIVES MARKET AMONG PORTFOLIO MANAGERS?

Insurance companies are an evident target of credit derivatives underwriters, not only because they have money to invest but also because they have absorbed mortgage-backed financing (MBF) instruments for their annuities—and MBF might be seen as a precedence. Some people think that banks, too, might be an interesting market for credit derivatives, though it is difficult to see why one bank would like to buy another bank's securitized loans.

Neither the potential market of insurance companies nor that of banks will be considered in this chapter. Instead, we examine the potential for credit derivatives among high–net-worth individuals, particularly through the interface of portfolio managers whom they have hired to look after their assets.

Fundamentally, portfolio management deals with credit decisions, buying and selling securities for portfolio accounts (if there are discretionary powers), collecting coupons and dividends, and doing inventory control and related activities. The goal is to optimize the risk–return trade-off across the aggregate of all transactions and positions taken. This includes

- Diversifying the holdings,
- Pricing to fair value,

- Evaluating profit and loss,
- Making risk assessment,
- Doing hedging activities, and
- Segmenting the portfolio and setting limits for each segment.

A portfolio can be segmented on the basis of criteria such as industry, geography, and product type. Or, it can be by type of instrument: bonds, stocks, currencies, precious metals, derivative products. For reasons of effective management, it is important to estimate the volatility existing within and between segments.

The estimates being made in analyzing an inventory of assets and liabilities are based upon an empirical evaluation of rating migrations and actual loss experience. The analysts look at asset volatilities; study equity, debt, and other prices; perform econometric modeling; and generally try to prognosticate future market movements.

Of course, the management of net worth is no recent development. What is recent is the amount of people who flock to private banking services (see section 2), a trend motivated by the affluence of the population to which private banking appeals and the need for property management. In the United States, for example,

- In the early 1970s, only 4 percent of the population was considered affluent.
- In the early 1980s, that percentage had grown to 12 percent.
- In the early 1990s, it had reached 22 percent and it still keeps growing.

Also known as asset managers, the administrators of private wealth see to it that the inventory under custody is structured with due regard to interest rates, currency exchange rates, equity prices, real estate prices, commodity prices, and so on. Each client who entrusts his net worth to a portfolio manager has an investment profile.

- There are risks to earnings from adverse movements in each of the aforementioned asset classes. These risks must be monitored and controlled at the level of each client.

- Risks are typically managed on the client's behalf by controlling money market positions, bond holdings, investments in shares, and so on.

Customers who have given their portfolio manager discretionary powers and have permitted taking positions including off-balance-sheet transactions may find in their portfolio interest rate swaps, forward rate agreements, futures, forwards, and options. In the opinion of asset managers, it is precisely these client accounts that present a market for credit derivatives.

Fair pricing would be a challenge, since portfolio managers must eventually justify their choices to their clients. A suggested method of pricing for the acquisition of such instruments is discounting cash flows computed on the basis of different scenarios depending on how the market goes from "here" to "there."

The use of scenarios helps to make transparent the likely changes in cash value of capital that would result from certain movements in interest rates and currency exchange rates. These changes must be compared with value-at-risk limits agreed upon with the client, and with exposures arising from the structure of assets and liabilities in the portfolio under management.

5. NEW BUSINESS OPPORTUNITY: MARKETING CREDIT DERIVATIVES TO PRIVATE BANKERS

The first thing a marketing plan for credit derivatives addressed to portfolio managers must do is to respect its mandate. The mandate is conditioned by the goals of investor(s). Such goals have traditionally been to maximize both the security and the yield of their assets (see also section 6). These two factors, security and yield, are up to a point contradictory, but they will remain the investor's primary concerns irrespective of whether he or she uses already existing financial instruments or chooses to bet on new products and emerging instruments.

Alert investors and portfolio managers know that reaping the benefit from any financial product requires constant observation of the markets and a level of information that normally exceeds the average person's capability. Therefore, the average investor expects the bank's asset manager to whom he or she entrusted the wealth to watch carefully the market and to prognosticate.

Not all accounts under management are a good market for credit derivatives. Only when the client issues the bank a *mandate* to manage his portfolio, after having formulated investment objectives on the basis of personal preferences, does the asset manager feel free to consider new products. Even then there are constraints.

Alternatively, the client may choose to use the bank only as a fiduciary and manage the assets by himself. The bank would then carry out, as per his instruction, the administrative chores. A fiduciary strategy can be lucrative to the custodian and trustee, but this is not a market for underwriters of credit derivatives.

Fiduciary fees can be significant. At the State Street Bank of Boston they now account for slightly more than two-thirds of revenues, and they grow an estimated 20 to 30 percent annually helped by the fact that other banks withdraw from this business. A custodian is not tempted to plunge deeply into the lending or securitization business, and does its best to avoid mixing two product lines such as underwriting and custody.

Instead of underwriting, a custodian may sell information technology services that are close to the fiduciary business and could be developed as another profitable product line. State Street has marketed a broad array of products related to its bread and butter record-keeping and safekeeping businesses—providing pension funds and others with the information they need about foreign exchange and securities markets, to coordinate investment activities around the globe.

Asset managers are a good clientele for information services because, whether the investor's goals are short- or long-term, the successful administration of assets depends on timely and accurate information that affects the portfolio's performance. Trading in shares, bonds, currencies, precious metals, other commodities, or derivative financial instruments can be successful only if (1) it is executed with professional know-how, speed, and precision and (2) it is steadily enriched by a flow of up-to-date information.

A successful asset management organization must be able to provide its clients with quick access to all of the world's financial markets, supplying them with the same kind of information available to its own financial analysts working in its global research network.

With this information in mind, while custodians will not be buyers of credit derivatives for accounts they have been entrusted with, the underwriters of credit derivatives have an interest in keeping them informed because custodians can help to disseminate information to potential buyers. A similar argument is valid about handholding with information providers like Bloomberg and Reuters.

Furthermore, a whole array of services, each with important information requirements, comes into play when private banking clients are setting up a new company, settling an estate, establishing a foundation or trust, or making inheritance provisions. Credit derivatives underwriters should not discount these potential opportunities, even if today the private banking market is not their primary target.

6. TAKING STOCK OF FOUR TYPES OF RISK AND MANAGING THEM

No matter to whom credit derivatives are being marketed, honesty is always the best policy. Knowledgeable customers understand there are risks involved in any type of investment. Therefore, a wise policy will be to identify these risks and explain how they have been taken care of—if this happens to be the case.

First is the risk of asset loss. With credit derivatives this connects to the possibility that the corporate loans underlying the bonds may go into default. In the general case, this is credit risk. Bankers are accustomed to the possibility of counterparty default, but the clients of credit derivatives (of whom we spoke in sections 2 through 5) want convincing arguments that the underwriter knows what he is talking about in regard to this exposure.

Second is loss due to fluctuations in interest rates and, possibly, volatility in currency exchange. Market risk, in simple form, is loss resulting from movement in market prices or rates. Many investors are acquainted with market risk, appreciating that it exists because commodity prices are volatile, but they don't necessarily see how securitized loans are affected by market risk. This has to be explained to them.

A third risk to be brought to the attention of potential buyers is that credit derivatives are leveraged instruments often traded over the counter, and their price movement can be disproportional to that of securities traded in exchanges. Therefore, it is not enough to say to the client that if there is no movement of substance in market prices, there will be no concern over market exposure.

A sound marketing practice is to assure that who buys leveraged products also knows how to manage them. This is one of the reasons why in the preceding sections I said that private bankers may be a good market. They are professional managers.

Fourth, there is the risk of wrong pricing. This may be due to plain error, but the reason may also be adverse volatility as well as a volatility smile. There are many types of pricing insufficiencies. Price risks that cause capital gains and losses to investors have not yet been thoroughly analyzed; neither have they been meaningfully addressed by supervisory authorities.

Volatility smiles are a default in pricing, which has a great deal to do with traders' commissions. The pricing of an option, for example, must account for volatility in the price of the underlier. Other things equal, if volatility is low, the price will be moderate; but because there is no limit to the losses the writer will suffer if he is asked by the option purchaser to perform, the price of options increases significantly with higher volatility.

- Everybody understands that it is much more difficult to sell a high-priced product than a low-priced one, and
- Every trader appreciates that since his commissions are in direct relation to his sales, he can better convince management that future volatility will be smiling, even if in this way the bank takes a far greater risk.

All risk domains examined in the preceding paragraphs require contingency reserves and the determination of an optimal size of *capital at risk*. They also call for steady watching of exposure along with the will to take corrective action. Because of their novelty, credit derivatives are a challenging project to anyone.

An analysis focused on capital at risk will consider both the new commitment and the cumulative exposure at portfolio level. Risk capital is not linearly additive across individual loans and securities.

- The incremental capital assigned to a new transaction is indivisible from the effect that transaction has on the bank's overall portfolio exposure.
- This overall exposure is studied through Value-at-Risk (VAR) analysis (see Chapter 15).

By means of a value-at-risk model, the banker, treasurer, and investor can examine his entire portfolio of assets and liabilities, value the different positions, estimate confidence intervals, and determine how changes in particular positions affect portfolio value—hence capital at risk.[2]

Through the simulation of risk and return, risk capital becomes an imputed quantity using rules that permit us to calibrate elementary risk premiums. With the securitization of loans, the problem becomes more complex, particularly when the portfolio includes loans with embedded options and loans with currency risk and country risk.

7. COULD CREDIT DERIVATIVES BECOME ANOTHER EXERCISE IN JUNK BONDS?

One of the definitions of junk bonds is that of risk capital masquerading as debt finance. Technically *junk bonds* is the name Wall Street has attached to high-yielding, often unsecured debt graded BB or lower by independent ratings services.

Junk bonds are bought by investors willing to ignore substandard credit ratings in exchange for better yields. They also bet on a permeability between the BB and A compartments of debt financing, but without considering the downgrading possibility.

---

[2] D.N. Chorafas, *The Market Risk Amendment: Understanding Marking-to-Model and Value-at-Risk,* McGraw-Hill/Irwin, Burr Ridge, IL, 1998.

- In one year, 1985, an estimated $4.6 billion of junk bonds moved up into the investment-grade category.

- However, during that same year double that amount, $9.1 billion, of higher-grade bonds slid down into junk.

"The market with credit derivatives might become 'FUBAR' [fouled up beyond all recognition] if there are many bankruptcies in manufacturing and merchandising," said one analyst during my research. "There is considerable speculation over if and when this will happen; but it might happen."

Japan provides an example of gearing in merchandising and manufacturing that has led to a bubble. Daici, the country's biggest supermarket chain, took on debt to expand and is now in trouble. Auto companies did the same. Alex Kinmont of Morgan Stanley points out that the domestic overcapacity in Japan's car market is equivalent to Britain's total car production.[3]

Plenty of companies are in this perilous situation of huge debt and overcapacity. Some financial analysts are worried that their loans might find their way into the credit derivatives food chain. In the simplest of terms, the trouble with highly leveraged companies, whether through junk bonds or through loans, is that they owe too much and own too little. Japanese firms, for example, are deeply indebted, with an average debt/equity ratio of 4 to 1. This situation might be bearable if everyone did not know about it, but it is wretchedly hard to fix the numbers while the investors watch.

In the United States, the unraveling of weak companies in the financial industry started in 1985 with the collapse of firms such as Drysdale Securities, Lombard–Wall, E.S.M. Government Securities, and Bevill, Bresler & Schulman Asset Management. While the bankruptcy of these brokerage companies menaced the apparently safe world of government bond trading, hundreds of millions of dollars have been lost by banks, cities, and state agencies under the impression that they were making perfectly safe investments backed by government securities.

---

[3] *The Economist,* August 29, 1998.

In the more staid world of commercial banking, equally disturbing events have taken place. A small Oklahoma bank, Penn Square, was able to persuade large, reputable institutions such as Continental Illinois and SeaFirst to acquire enough bad loans to result in the collapse of these institutions that did not pay attention to the fundamentals.

- The common thread running through such stories is the failure to assess risk on the part of institutions and fiduciaries eager to perform.
- There would have been no junk bonds if there were no investors acquiring them because they carry higher interest rates—never mind the risk of default.

What worries some financial analysts and regulators is that junk bond jitters are coming back. The prognostication is a possible repetition of April 1989 when, unlike previous lapses of confidence at the market, no single cause was to blame. Instead of a smoking gun there was a variety of negatives from rising interest rates to rumors of huge withdrawals from bond funds.

Nervous markets practically always drive down prices of financial paper, particularly low-quality bonds. In 1989, several junk bond mutual funds saw investors withdrawing more money than they were putting in. At the same time, thrifts were said to be selling off big chunks of their junk portfolios in expectation of new regulations that would require them to raise the quality of their assets.

It is evident that such precedents are of considerable concern to fund managers who consider adding credit derivatives to their portfolio. What distinguishes one asset manager from another is how much potential junk they own and how they offset it. By extension, a major caveat to buying credit derivatives is that no one knows how they will do in a recession. In a serious recession, defaults, which would already be increasing (see Chapter 8), could spike up. This would leave investors with large losses of principal, and the credit derivatives market might collapse.

As prices plunge on investment-grade bonds, yields will be soaring to compensate for the additional risk that companies might not be able to meet their suddenly greater interest costs or their outstanding obligations. The potential assumption of more debt raises the prospect that credit rating agencies may lower the grades on the bonds, forcing sales by many institutional holders whose shareholders, clients, or the law forbids them to own speculative issues.

8. THE FLIGHT TO QUALITY WILL HAVE FAR-REACHING CONSEQUENCES

One of the investment themes for much of 1998 has been that investors should make the most of the yield advantage offered by high-quality securities. Spreads are wide between yields on high-rated corporates and municipals versus Treasury issues.

In early January 1999, when this text was written, a 10-year A-rated corporate bond yields about 140 basis points more than a Treasury, while off-the-run 10-year Treasuries yield about 8 basis points more than the most current issue. Also, yields on FDIC-insured CDs in the 2- to 5-year maturity are about 70 basis points higher than those on comparable Treasuries.

A year prior to the aforementioned references, in early 1998, the widening interest rate gap was one of the reasons that LTCM sank. The spreads on high-risk junk bonds nearly doubled between January 1998 and October 1998, while new issues of high-risk corporate bonds slowed to a trickle:

- The offer stood at $4 billion in August and September 1998 combined,
- This compared poorly with a monthly average of $15 billion earlier in that same year 1998.

Because the market for junk securities caved in, several new issues were postponed. From the end of August to the end of October 1998, spreads on mortgage-backed securities have tripled. A flight to quality saw to it that credit card companies and sub-prime lenders, which rely on selling bundles of old loans to finance their lending largely to the less creditworthy, have found few takers.

Such references are most significant to credit derivatives issuers because they identify a change in the market's mood. The liquidity squeeze of 1998 also affected the commercial paper market. The spread between top-rated and slightly riskier borrowing widened to a high level on any kind of debt that had a certain amount of credit risk.

Investor sentiment, Wall Street analysts suggested, was not just a flight to quality, but also a flight to liquidity within the same asset class. Investors' fear was not inflation, because inflation was running at an annual rate of 1.5 percent in the Unied States, and a little less than that in France and Germany. Investors, however, did remember that other risks were lurking.

- The sharp rise in volatility,
- The widening of spreads, and
- Concerns about growing credit risk.

From currency exchange to interest rates, volatility has been symptomatic of a crude and destructive unwinding of many of the major trades that have been put on lightheartedly by financial institutions trying to make a fast buck. On Wall Street, experts felt that it was highly unlikely spreads will return anytime soon to the levels that prevailed before early August 1998.

- Because global credit risk has increased,
- Yield spreads need to reflect that increase.

Credit spreads also tend to widen when economic activity slows. As the composite leading indicator of the global economy turned south and pointed to a significant slowdown in growth outside the United States, investors did not fail to notice that the economies in doldrums constituted roughly one-third of the world's total output.

Astute investors picked up these signals way ahead of the rest of the lot. Ten-year notes issued by Chase Manhattan are a benchmark for the financial services industry. In early 1998 they sold at a yield 70 basis points over Treasuries. Then the issue plunged in the first week of October as the market demanded a 230 basis point spread. "[The yield] shot up like a child's fever," said Robert V. DiClemente, chief economist at Salomon Smith Barney.[4] Even a month later, in early November 1998, the Chase issue yield was 150 basis points above 10-year Treasuries.

The point the careful reader will retain is that 10-year notes by Chase are not junk bonds. Therefore, the argument that what happens to junk bonds and what may be the case with credit derivatives are two different issues is not receivable. For an investor the examples that I have given are a fundamental reference, and no designer of financial instruments worth his salt should brush them aside.

The choice was deliberate to include two sections on the risks of junk bonds and of widening interest rate spreads as a conclusion to Part One. The objective is to focus the attention of issuers, fund managers, and other investors on the wisdom of being highly selective and very well informed (see Chapter 3) about both the underliers and the market's whims. By the time the 21st century rolls in, the market may be quite different than the one we know today—and we must be prepared for a much greater emphasis on quality of securities than the one that has characterized the last 20 years.

---

[4] *Business Week,* November 9, 1998.

PART

TWO

Credit Derivatives Instruments and Their Underliers

CHAPTER 6

Asset Swaps, Total Return Swaps, and Default Swaps

1. INTRODUCTION

The more popular credit derivatives instruments are asset swaps (see section 2), total return swaps (see sections 3 and 4), default swaps (see sections 6 and 7), credit spreads and other options, as well as credit-linked securities. Another is credit forwards (see Chapter 8). Chapter 1 made a brief reference to these products which the banking industry develops as state-of-the-art techniques for discharging the credit risk the bank classically carries in its loans portfolio.

Traded over the counter, these instruments are contracts outlining either a present or a potential exchange of payments. Figure 6.1 shows an example of a credit swap between two banks. In an exchange, at least one leg of the cash flows is linked to the performance of a specified underlying credit-sensitive asset or liability.

Like all derivatives, total return swaps, default swaps, and the other instruments rest on an underlying market which includes business loans, corporate loans, emerging market debt, municipal debt, trade receivables, convertible securities, and the like. These examples are credit-type exposures generated from loans and other financing, trade activities, warehoused financial paper, and so on.

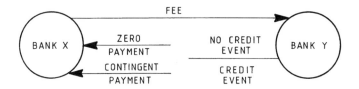

FIGURE 6.1 CHARACTERISTICS OF A CREDIT SWAP

What credit derivatives do is enable users to isolate, price, and trade credit risk specific to a given organization or pool, by unbundling a debt instrument or basket of instruments, meaning

- Dividing it into its component parts,
- Unbundling these parts, and
- Transferring each risk to the buyers.

As Part One has explained, banks profit from origination, distribution, and secondary trading of loans. They no longer hold the financial asset, but they can still capitalize on it. Today, credit derivative transactions are generally conducted between professional houses—there are few retail products. But as we saw in Chapter 5, this may change as retail products develop—provided the management of the instrument stays in professional hands because credit derivatives have many unknowns and need people well equipped to handle them.

2. ASSET SWAPS

Asset swaps can be seen as the precursor of credit derivatives. Many analysts consider asset swaps as being the first known instrument that permitted an investor to take *pure credit risk* rather than a mixture of credit risk and interest rate risk or some other market exposure.

In the following text we will consider asset swaps as the building blocks of credit derivatives, from which other products have evolved and are still evolving. With asset swaps, default swaps, and total return swaps, the assets and liabilities are underliers or reference securities. Asset swaps are tied to the asset of a balance sheet.

- They are designed to change one or more attributes of the cash flow from an underlying asset.
- An interest rate swap, for instance, converts a fixed interest rate into a floating rate, or one currency into another.

A good example are the internal interest rate swaps done by clearing banks in the United States and the United Kingdom, weeding interest rate risk out of the banking book and into the trading book. In Chapter 2 it was said that the Bank of England encourages this practice for internal management accounting purposes but not for regulatory reporting reasons.

An interesting aspect, for instance, of credit swaps is that companies that have available credit lines but are unable to lend or invest because of balance sheet constraints can sell default swaps (see sections 6 and 7). They do so using up some of the excess credit without breaching balance sheet limits.

In an asset swap one party makes payments equal to the actual cash flows on a credit-sensitive instrument, including principal and interest. The counterparty makes payments based on another credit-sensitive instrument, such as Libor. This model is valid both for internal management accounting reasons and for external asset swaps.

The block diagram in Figure 6.2 visualizes the mechanics of an asset swap. The example presented concerns a transaction consisting of putable bonds and an interest rate swap. This is in two stages:

- The investor buys the bonds, which are putable in, say, 2004.
- He simultaneously enters into an interest rate swap on the bond.

As a result, the investor receives Libor plus spread until the put date and then receives Libor plus spread plus 30 basis points until the bond matures in 2004. However, the bank might elect to repurchase the bonds at par and terminate the swap.

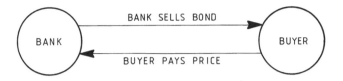

THEN THE CUSTOMER ENTERS INTO AN INTEREST RATE SWAP

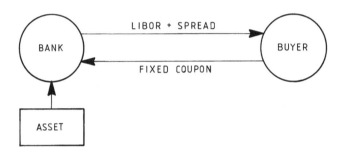

FIGURE 6.2 AN ASSET SWAP WITH PUTABLE BONDS

Like other credit derivatives, asset swaps are flexible instruments. Examples include corporate bonds, whether high-grade or junk, classical bank loans, sovereign bonds, Eurobonds, and Brady bonds. Three features are outstanding among the many characteristics of these instruments:

- Maturity,
- Amount, and
- Design.

Originally, maturities were in the three-to-five–year range, but recently there is a push toward eight years. Lengthening the time frame, however, tends to increase the embedded risk.

Originally, typical sizes of asset swaps were in the $5 million to $25 million range, but this too is changing. Corporate bonds push toward $100 million; sovereign bonds and Brady bonds push to $50 million; while Eurobonds tend to remain below the $10 or $15 million level.

The third important characteristic after maturity and size is design. To achieve the desired result in terms of credit, amount, and maturity, participants may simultaneously be buyers and sellers. In this manner, lenders and investors aim to (1) improve portfolio diversification and (2) gain exposure to credits, securities, and markets that may otherwise be difficult to access.

Some other characteristics can be seen in mortgage swaps, a derivative instrument replicating the flows found in a pool of mortgages. The mortgage swap is a synthetic structure offering the investor off-balance-sheet benefits of a physical mortgage-backed asset. It provides a fixed rate such as Treasuries plus a spread paid monthly in exchange for payment of a monthly floating rate, usually Libor.

The notional principal of the swap amortizes in a way emulating the MBF principal, which amortizes through repayments by the homeowner. The amortization rate of the mortgage swap is equivalent to the amortization level of a given MBF, and it can be calculated by means of an algorithm.

One more reference is the asset-linked trust securities (ALTS). These are special-purpose vehicles created by Barclays BZW, which make it feasible for investors to combine securities, loans, and other financial assets with a swap or other derivative product to produce a customized instrument.

- ALTS aim to transform one or more attributes of the underlying asset in a more sophisticated way than simpler derivatives.
- The objective is to enable investors to target geared risk and return without directly entering into a derivative transaction.

As this section has shown, there are many examples of asset swaps, instruments, and transactions providing investors with off-balance-sheet synthetic positions tailored to their individual requirements. Customization is one of the strengths of derivative financial instruments. But asset swaps involve exposure and risks must be managed.

3. TOTAL RETURN SWAPS

A total return swap is an agreement in which the total return of an underlying credit-sensitive asset, or pool of assets, is exchanged for some other cash flow. Usually this is tied to Libor or the return of another credit-sensitive asset(s).

As with other types of swaps, with total return swaps no principal amounts are exchanged and no physical change of ownership occurs. The contract specifies a notional principal amount and other conditions on which periodic payments will be based.

In a total return swap two parties periodically pay each other the total return on two reference assets or baskets of assets. The swap is a credit derivative when at least one of these reference assets is a credit-sensitive instrument.

- The structure of the swap allows the counterparties to effectively go long or short the reference asset.
- Therefore, a total return swap can be considered as a customized synthetic asset.

An example of a total return swap and associated arbitrage capital structure is shown in Figure 6.3. Typically two parties enter into this agreement in order to swap all the economic risks associated with a given security without transferring the security itself. The receiver in the swap

- Will bc long of the total economic risk of a security or portfolio and
- Will receive positive cash flows on that asset.

These cash flows may be interest payments, coupons, or dividends plus any appreciation in capital value. In terms of benefits, the purchaser of the swap will be paid some spread over a reference rate such as Libor as well as any depreciation of the capital value because of impairment of assets.

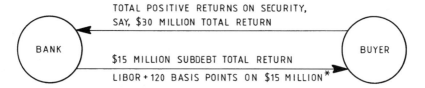

* In Essence, Libor + Margin + Losses on Security

FIGURE 6.3 TOTAL RETURN SWAP AND ARBITRAGE CAPITAL STRUCTURE

Total return swaps may incorporate puts and calls to establish caps or floors on the returns of the underlying assets. The financing leg of the transaction can be structured with caps and floors on a floating interest rate to control financing costs.

The maturity of the total return swap need not match that of the underlier, and the swap can typically be terminated at any time. At termination, the original agreement may permit the user to purchase the reference asset at its initial market price instead of doing a cash settlement for the swap.

A total return swap may involve mortgage-backed financing (MBF) in which an investor receives the total return on a principal only (PO) strip. The investor may purchase a cap on the financing leg of the transaction, protecting the return on the trade from adverse movements in short-term rates.

Another total return swap may involve corporate bonds. For instance, the buyer finances a BB-rated corporate bond, receiving the total return on the bond and paying Libor plus a spread. The structure allows the investor to finance an asset for which there is no traditional repurchase agreement market (see Chapter 7).

As these examples document, total return swaps are derivative instruments that permit an investor to receive, or oblige him to pay, the total economic return of an asset, without actually buying or selling the asset itself.

- One party is synthetically long on the underlier.
- The other party is synthetically short on the same underlier.

The underlying reference credit can be almost any financial asset, basket of assets, or index. Hence, return swaps are the synthetic equivalent of buying the asset and locking in term financing. Investors seeking to eliminate exposure to a specific asset or asset class can see total return swaps as the synthetic equivalent of selling the asset and locking in a return.

In the general case, total return investors are lenders who want to reduce their exposure to an asset without removing it from their balance sheet. By keeping the asset on their books, they may avoid jeopardizing relationships with borrowers and breaching client confidentiality, provided the documentation of the loan remains in-house, but buyers typically need this information.

4. TOTAL RETURN SWAPS, MARKET ANOMALIES, AND LTCM

Merging companies provide an opportunity for total return swaps, but there is no assurance that the assumptions underpinning the bet would turn out to be right. The market gyrations may decide otherwise and the losses suffered by the players could end up being quite significant.

Take the Citicorp/Travelers merger as an example. When it was announced, a highly leveraged investor could buy 2 million shares of Citicorp at, say, $150 and short 2.43 million shares of Travelers. Such a transaction would have capitalized on the fact that the shares of the two companies did not trade at the 2.5:1 ratio agreed by the two merging institutions for stock exchange.

- LTCM entered this game, to capitalize on what it perceived as a market anomaly in the pricing of Citi and Travelers stock.
- But because of the law of *unintended consequences*, the "anomaly" persisted and LTCM was run over by it.

In this sort of a transaction, instead of buying Citicorp stock, an investor, say LTCM, used a high-risk threshold buying a total return swap from firm "A," which agrees to pay him the total return on Citicorp stock. In exchange, LTCM (or any other investor doing the same sort of transaction) has to pay "A" a fixed-interest rate.

- To hedge itself in this transaction, LTCM shorted Travelers.
- It did this not with the same counterparty "A" but with another firm "B."

The way I heard about this event on Wall Street, LTCM's first counterparty "A" hedged itself by buying 2 million shares of Citicorp stock at, say, $153. This way, if Citi went up, its profits on the said shares offset its payments to LTCM. If Citi declined, the counterparty's share losses are offset by payments from LTCM since Citicorp's total return is negative.

The careful reader will appreciate that in the case of this transaction, and of many others, the concept of marking to market is hollow—because as long as it was running strong, LTCM *was* the market. The total return swaps that it did were so large, compared to those of other players, that market results obeyed one law: Murphy's. Anything that could go wrong, did.

With the financial markets debacle of September 1998, Citi's stock declined quite significantly. Under its swap arrangement, LTCM had to post an important sum of money (I was told $100 million) with its first counterparty to cover the losses. The risk has been that if LTCM defaulted,

- In this combination of credit risk and market risk, LTCM's counterparty "A" was left with its Citi stock, which had lost more than half its value.
- "A" had no offsetting short position in Travelers stock, since LTCM did the short trade with a different counterparty, "B."

Always on the hypothesis of LTCM's default, "A," the first counterparty, would be forced to dump Citi stock in a declining market for damage-control purposes—further aggravating its price. This is exactly what Merrill Lynch and other brokers feared in case LTCM had gone bankrupt. This is also what moved the New York Fed to act as broker in saving LTCM from bankruptcy.

- The total return swap was supposed to be an instrument for making profits.
- Instead, the counterparties ended by swimming in red ink.

That sort of unpleasant "surprise" evidently poses a crucial question about pricing total return swaps. The correct pricing of these instruments, as well as of other credit derivatives, depends upon the distribution of the future credit quality of the reference asset: for example, an underlying pool of corporate debt issues or projected equity prices as in the Citigroup example. But our estimates of future events are uncertain.

When we talk of prognostication we implicitly assume the probability of error. Though we will surely use our best judgment, this may turn out not to be good enough. Therefore, we should base our decisions not only on experience but also on analytics. For instance, for the fixed-income investor this will involve the movement and co-movement of credit qualities. The study of such movement necessarily involves credit volatility (see Chapter 1); requires the understanding of credit risk characteristics; and can be helped through credit ratings (see Chapter 10).

5. VARIANTS OF TOTAL RETURN SWAPS

As a matter of policy, swaps dealers use standard contracts that help define their transactions and normalize the clauses. The International Swaps and Derivatives Association (ISDA) is active in establishing bilateral contracts that serve as frameworks.

Cognizant executives in the financial industry believe that standard contracts reduce credit risks and facilitate bilateral netting agreements. If the contract is terminated early because of bankruptcy or liquidation, the netting agreement allows payables and receivables to cancel each other out, limiting the credit risk of the solvent counterparty to net exposures.

The problem is that in a global financial market, enforcing netting agreements is a job full of legal holes. Only slowly are bankruptcy judges establishing a decision making pattern that might become a standard.

One variation of total return swaps is the secured loan trust (SLT) notes offered by Chase Manhattan. This is a series of notes in which an investor leverages exposure to a pool of sub–investment-grade loans. Since Chase started marketing this total return swap in September 1996, it has passed an estimated $1.7 billion exposure of U.S. bank loans to investors.

Users of total return swaps would, however, be well advised not to forget that risk management is an integral part of any invest-ment—in particular, of a leveraged business. No product that allows buyers to use synthetic assets does so without assumption of expo-sure on their part.

The Chase secured loan trust, for instance, appeals to the lever-aged bank loan market. Theoretically, this includes institutional investors. Yet, as financial analysts suggest, of the more than $250 bil-lion in syndicated leveraged loans currently outstanding in the United States, only $20 billion to $25 billion is held by institutional investors.

Pros see an advantage in the fact that total return payers do not have to hold the asset on their balance sheets. Total return swaps can be a way to short an asset synthetically. As such, they may be appeal-ing to insurance companies, hedge funds, and corporate treasurers wanting to put their cash to work on a leveraged basis.

In some cases, investors also use total return swaps to arbi-trage perceived mispricing between bank loans and subordinated debt of the same issuer. The service provided to total return receivers is that of

- Locking in term financing rates and
- Creating repurchase agreements in markets where repos may not exist.

Another perceived advantage of total return swaps and their variants is that they avoid the clearing, financing, and execution costs associated with outright purchase. Pros say that for institutions with capital constraints they can provide a rather economic way of using leverage to optimize return on capital.

Still another perceived advantage is that their flexibility allows investors to isolate a spread of directional view and to take action in a single transaction. Investors also seek to benefit from differences in accounting laws and tax treatment in different countries, targeting higher after-tax returns than those available by outright purchasing an asset.

Because this section contains so many positive ideas regarding total return swaps, let me emphasize that these are the opinions I recorded from analysts and traders during my research. They are not necessarily my opinions. Though the ideas presented have merit, I would personally wait a few years and form an opinion based on the results rather than rush to judgment.

6. DEFAULT SWAPS

One of the first credit derivatives offered to the market were default swaps on a basket of corporate names. This came in 1992 from Bankers Trust. Such instruments were designed specifically to address the bank's own concentration of risk with certain counterparties.

Default swaps are financial products through which a periodic fixed payment or upfront fee from the protection buyer is exchanged for the promise of some specified payments from the protection writer. These are to be made only if a particular, predetermined credit event occurs. Under a standard default swap, a party with excess credit exposure on its book pays a counterparty a periodic fee in exchange for protection. Often, this periodic fee is a fixed number of basis points against a notional amount, while the counterparty's payment is a lump sum or periodic cash flow.

The counterparty's payment takes place if the underlying reference party defaults on an obligation. Typically, the transfer of credit risk through a default swap is multiyear, hence it is a long-term investment. It is also possible to enter into a default swap as a way of speculating on the likelihood of credit default by a given party. Essentially:

- The writer of a default swap becomes long on credit,
- While the buyer becomes short on credit.

As a medium-term derivative, default swaps provide the buyer with protection against the likelihood a counterparty or reference credit will not perform. The risk evaluation of a default swap is based on the floating payment the buyer pays the writer, and the potential payment the seller must make the buyer if the underlying reference credit defaults.

The case of large portfolios of medium UK corporates, which represent about 24 percent of the British loans market was mentioned as an example in one of the research meetings I had in the City. Banks enter into default swaps in their regard because they want to improve the efficiency of their portfolio, but handling leveraged financials has risks. Practical, the default swap buyer sets a claim against the writer's credit lines. A crucial risk is the trading level of the reference bond postdefault, which most likely will reflect expected recovery levels for creditors.

An analytical approach will use historical recovery statistics by class: secured, senior unsecured, and junior unsecured creditors. The aim is to estimate the value of the credit derivative postdefault. Because the end result is, by all likelihood, a concentration of credit risk in a few hands, another major determinant of the risk component is economic cycles. This has two aspects:

1. In the lows of economic cycles the number of corporate failures *rises,* accentuating credit risk,
2. But downturns in the economy are also accompanied by an increase in interest rates.

The analytical treatment should be thorough and comprehensive, as in a default swap the beneficiary pays the guarantor a fixed amount or an amount based on a generic interest rate. This payment is in exchange for the protector's promise to make a fixed or variable payment in the event of default on one or more reference assets. All payments should be subject to evaluation. The interest in this type of transaction comes from the fact that

- By selling default swaps industrial companies and banks with high funding costs can gain access to higher-quality credits, and

- A default swap's competitive advantage is that it does not require financing, unlike securities or direct lending.

Of course, high funding costs are associated with counterparties that have been given a low grade by independent rating agencies. Because their credit is weak, whoever enters into a default swap appreciates the amount of credit risk being assumed.

The mechanics of a default swap see to it that, by building on the basic default swap structure, investors can swap the default risk of one credit with that of another credit. Provided a risk management system is in place and functions properly, this may help companies diversify their portfolios while avoiding the transaction costs associated with buying and selling many individual securities.

Credit default swaps are typically cash-settled, but the agreement might as well provide for physical settlement through the delivery of a specific asset or basket of assets. A default swap can be structured on a single credit name, but it can also be structured on a basket of names.

A properly chosen structure can link the contingent payment to any or all credit events pertaining to the basket of reference assets. Alternatively, the chosen design can limit any exposure for the protection seller to the first *credit event* taking place, among those specified.

- A credit event is a default, which would include bankruptcy, insolvency, credit downgrade, or failure to make payments on the reference asset.

By mining its database for historical recovery statistics (for instance, regarding senior unsecured creditors), the banker, treasurer, or investor can estimate the value of the instrument involved in the transaction postdefault. This helps in calculating the payment due to the counterparty buying the default swap.

The flexibility of the instrument attracts attention, since the credit event may as well be different types of indebtedness manifested within a predetermined period of time. In the general case, however, the credit event must be a material and objectively measurable default. Technical types of defaults are not covered. By swapping payments for contingent credit events, participants in effect create synthetic loans or securities that separate default risk from market risk.

The contingent default payment may be structured in different ways. For instance, it can be linked to the price movement of the reference asset at a predetermined level as a binary payoff, or it may be in the form of an actual delivery of the reference asset at its initial price.

In these transactions, the investor makes periodic payments to hedge exposure to default by a reference credit. Alternatively, he receives periodic payments in exchange for accepting that exposure.

- If, during the term of the swap the reference credit experiences a credit event, the seller pays the buyer what is needed to cover the loss. Usually this is 100 percent of the final price of the reference asset, but there might also be other solutions.
- If no credit event has occurred by maturity of the swap, the counterparties end their obligations to each other.

In these examples, the default swap makes feasible transferring credit risk from one swap counterparty to the other. For instance, a regional bank could purchase a default swap on a local company's loan, and sell a default swap on a loan from another region or industry.

The idea behind this exchange is diversification of risk, but general-type references can be misleading—particularly since every trade can be different. Let me add that a similar type of default swap can be performed on portfolios using a default basket, with the default protection applying to each of the constituent securities or loans.

7. CAN DEFAULT SWAPS BE EXTENDED TO COVER COUNTRY MELTDOWN?

Designed with the hindsight of experimentation, default swaps and default baskets seem to provide an efficient means of diversifying risk. The pros think that they might as well reduce administrative costs while permitting a more customized portfolio hedging. Market experience is still too thin to validate this statement.

Regulators are also evaluating whether the current distinctions among credit derivatives (which this chapter follows) make sense. In June 1997, the Bank of England abandoned the distinction between credit default swaps and total return swaps—which had meant that credit default swaps should be held on the banking book, rather than on the trading book alongside total return swaps.

The same thinking seems to prevail at the Federal Reserve Board. Most financial analysts believe that this integrative trend toward credit derivatives will probably result in lower capital charges for credit default products. But other analysts suggest that the die is not yet cast.

Because the concept underpinning credit default swaps is flexible, analysts think that they can be tailored to specific needs. The keyword is *customization,* with the reference asset being any loan or security, or basket of loans and securities, that can be provided in any currency at the buyer's choice.

The customized swap can match or be shorter than the time frame of the reference asset, with the periodic payment depending, in large part, on the reference credit. Can this characteristic be used to extend the default swaps market in a way covering country meltdown?

The Asian crisis, for instance, has brought home the need to manage credit exposure resulting from country risk. To this end, the standard credit derivatives contract is a default option on emerging market sovereign bonds. Such default options allow the investor to assure against the risk of default or bankruptcy in exchange for a fee paid to the counterparty. The payment is often equivalent to the risk spread between the bond and its underlying benchmark. Typically, if the offering is denominated in U.S. dollars, the underlying benchmark is U.S. Treasury bonds.

This solution is not too different from buying options. Investors who buy options are really purchasing volatility to protect against market fluctuations—or to speculate. The greater the turbulence in the market, the greater the wave of flight capital and an economy's collapse. In early September 1998, flight capital from Brazil amounted to $1 billion per day.

This is written in appreciation of the fact that few debtor countries these days are willing to treat debts from the standpoint of ethics and equity instead of from that of convenience and politics. In the early 1980s, for instance, flight capital siphoned off an estimated 50 percent of Mexico's borrowed money and one-third of Argentina's.

In July 1998, it was rumored that the money landing in the pockets of former crony capitalists around Indonesia's President Suharto and his family was equal to the IMF loan of $43 billion. In August 1998, new rumors suggested that another quarter of the loans given by the IMF to redress the Indonesian situation landed in secret private accounts. This is the way easy money goes. Some people think that it grows on trees.

From the crisis of the Latin American debt in the early 1980s to the East-Asia meltdown of 1997–98 and the Russian disaster of 1998, there has been significant turbulence in the market of sovereign debts and of private and public companies operating under crony capitalism and shielded by the state. In mid-1998, this led the Hong Kong Authority to suggest that the World Bank issue bonds to guarantee sovereign debt.

I don't think that such approaches have any future. Bonds have to be serviced. Who will pay the interest (and administrative charges) if a supranational institution issues bonds to provide itself with funds for sovereign default? This sort of free-lunch thinking flourished in the 1970s after the two oil crises when Latin America and other countries misinterpreted the loans they got from money center banks as a new form of U.S. aid program in disguise.

To the contrary, the capital market might be interested in sovereign default swaps if the price is right. The less is the creditworthiness of the country (to be judged by independent rating agencies like Standard & Poor's and Moody's), the stiffer will be the clauses of the contract, and the larger the margins, to satisfy the investor's appetite for risk.

This concept can be carried further to include loans given to sovereigns as well as to local companies, whether denominated in local currency (where credit risk rating might be higher) or in a foreign currency (where a premium should apply for foreign exchange risk). Had this been the case in the 1990s, overexposure in

Indonesia, Thailand, and South Korea would never have reached a high two-digit number in billions of dollars.

By becoming a precondition for foreign investments, a default swaps strategy might be instrumental in checking the huge transnational money flows toward emerging countries and back because the cost of the default swap would apply a haircut to profits from such flows, commensurate with country risk and currency risk. The market will be the criter.

8. POSITION RISK AND DEFAULT RISK

The probability of default does not exist only with new transactions. It is also embedded into the bank's portfolio. Yet, position risk is not always considered today, or it may be taken into account only rudimentarily—even if it is a vital statistic and it should definitely become one of the moving gears of the risk management system (see Part Three).

As a matter of definition, position risk is assessed as the sensitivity of the position in each transaction that has already been confirmed and inventoried. Position risk exists in the bank's own and its counterparties' accounts and is due to the volatility of instruments such as currency, interest rate, or equity. This sensitivity regards changes in market parameters from which no portfolio can escape.

The best strategy in facing position risk is flexibility and polyvalence as well as interactive computation, permitting the control of exposure to be carried within established limits. By means of worst-case evaluation, the limits for each risk class can be converted into risk capital or derived from the risk capital allotted.

But after the discussion on default swaps, the careful reader should appreciate that there exists a hedging option. This will not be so different from the interest rate swaps policy practiced today by many banks.

- Internal interest rate swaps exchange fixed interest rates in the banking book with floating interest rates, carrying the interest rate risk into the trading book.

- Internal default swaps could do the same for credit risk, switching it out of the banking book and into the trading book.

In both cases the exposure stays with the bank. Therefore, such internal transactions should not be undertaken without a thorough experimentation on the effects of transferring assumed risks. A real-time internal management accounting system will facilitate the comparability of results derived from the above risk swapping, per risk class, doing so both in absolute figures and in relation to the ear-marked economic capital (see Chapter 4).

A different way of making this statement is that position risk should be steadily tested proactively from market risk and default risk viewpoints. This amounts to a cultural change because in the large majority of banks default risk is taken into consideration only in a case of realized loss. Yet, default risk is a permanent feature of all transactions. Therefore, it is correct to account for it through a virtual insurance policy.

Default swaps might play a role in such policy. A more linear alternative is accounting for default risk by means of a risk premium to be deducted from product-related income (see Part Three).

Once approved through a decision by the board, this strategy of default swaps or insurance premium becomes fairly simple to implement. In many banks standard risk premium rates are centrally determined per credit rating category or country rating by the division responsible for counterparty risk. Supplemented by the published opinion of independent rating agencies, risk scores can form the basis for special provisions. In the case of reinsurance a risk premium should be determined by those responsible for counterparty risk. With the default swap approach, the trader can execute online the algorithm and apply in real-time the appropriate conditions.

Notice that during the mid- to late-1990s the reinsurance fund culture has become a second nature among tier-1 banks. On this concept rests the risk-adjusted return on capital (RAROC) method originally developed by Bankers Trust (see Chapter 14). An internal accounting management information system sees to it that this extra premium is credited to the counterparty risk account, while losses due to defaults are debited to that same account.

Default risk premiums must be delivered by the operative units responsible for products and transactions to those responsible for the management of exposure. With a risk premium, the department accountable for risk control looks after the creation of provisions that are sustained through the credited risk premiums.

In a similar manner, with default swaps hedges can be done for credit rating, country risk, or other exposures as part of an overall risk management system. One of the handicaps in applying this strategy is that in the majority of banks today credit risk and market risk are managed by two totally different organizations, but top-tier institutions are changing this structure by unifying the management of risk and making it real-time.

Let me close this chapter with a couple of remarks that are applicable to most instruments presented in Part Two. As a buyer of credit derivatives, an investor is making a payment in exchange for a potential payoff. If he buys credit protection, then he gains in case the underlying reference credit defaults.

- In this transaction, the investor shorts the credit and benefits if the credit deteriorates.
- The underwriter sells the credit protection; therefore, he becomes long on the credit risk and benefits if the credit improves.

CHAPTER 7

Credit-Linked Instruments, Structured Notes, and Credit-Enhanced Ventures

1. INTRODUCTION

The definition of credit derivatives is not cast in iron. Some financial analysts tend to include under this term more instruments than others: credit-linked notes, credit options, yield spread options, currency convertibility products, collateralized bond obligations, and so on.

There are hybrids as well. Examples include packages of corporate loans bundled into a credit-linked loan. This solution offers investors a credit risk instrument in a specific sector of the economy where they may not have direct access but still possess credit expertise for risk management.

Some of the instruments in the market oblige the bank to keep a certain percentage of the underlying loans, while trying to obtain a reduction in its risk concentrations either in total or in specialist sectors. Generally, hybrid credit-linked instruments are niche markets while customized credit risk profiles appeal to specialized market segments.

The wider opinion is that the securitization of credit has the potential of offering to derivatives players an efficient, low-cost alternative to the underlying cash markets. Some analysts believe that the use of credit derivatives bypasses the need for incorporating covenants into loan agreements. But others think that this is not true.

Do these differences in opinion matter? Yes, they do. But even more important is the need to appreciate that in any process of collateralization and portfolio diversification or outright sale of the underlying exposure, what comes out is not much different than what comes in.

- The transformation of credit exposure through a derivative instrument sees to it that the output is more geared than bread-and-butter derivatives.
- Therefore, investors using credit derivatives must have first-class internal controls and risk management systems sensitive to changes in likelihood of default.

Only when these prerequisites exist and are steadily kept up can it be said that credit derivatives might become innovative risk management tools that hedge credit exposure from an economic perspective, without affecting the balance sheet in an adverse way. The reader may wish to keep in mind this reference when reading the examples that follow.

2. CREDIT-LINKED NOTES

Credit-linked notes are debt instruments issued by a bank or other institution, typically one that is highly rated. Essentially, such notes are loans or securities with a relatively standard coupon as well as standard redemption and maturity provisions.

- The instrument can be used by borrowers to hedge against credit risk or to achieve higher yields.
- The coupon or price of the note is linked to the performance of a reference asset or index.

The redemption value of the credit-linked note is directly dependent upon the market value of the reference asset(s). Chase Manhattan's Secured Loans Trust (SLT) Notes, a proprietary structure, is an example (see also the discussion of SLT in total return swaps in Chapter 6).

Unlike standard notes, the performance of a credit-linked note is expressed as a function of the performance of the underlying reference asset(s) plus the performance of the issuer. This sees to it that the coupon of the note is not a linear function of a single variable.

In spite of the nonlinearity, some financial analysts believe that credit-linked notes may be easier for investors to understand than naked credit derivatives. However, it is no less true that they have the potential to present new complexities in terms of design, execution, and follow-up in terms of exposure.

Credit-linked notes may be investment-grade debt obligations, but they have leveraged returns relative to a diversified portfolio of senior secured leveraged bank loans. For example, a bank might issue a note that provides for principal repayment to be reduced to a certain level below par. For instance,

- If the external sovereign debt of an emerging market country defaults at or near to maturity of the note,
- Then the investor finds himself selling credit protection to the issuer, for which he receives a higher-than-normal yield.

Pros say that investors can use these instruments to guard against credit risk losses. A fund or annuity holding a corporate bond might purchase a note from a bank providing that the amount of principal payable on the note's maturity will be increased if the total return of the corporate bond falls by a certain amount. This way, the investor is hedging credit exposure to the corporate bond.

How difficult is it to sell credit-linked notes? Opinions are not uniform. Personally I subscribe to the school that thinks that there may be both positive and negative surprises in terms of market potential because this market is not yet tested. An example is the way borrowers reacted when investment banks started moving into syndicated loans, announcing their intention to sell a basket of loans, retaining a few on their own book.

At the time, contrarians predicted that borrowers would lack confidence and stay away from the issues. But as defaults were rare, the market eventually developed in a satisfactory way.

Citing this as a precedence, proponents of credit-linked notes suggest that they should appeal to investors seeking higher yields, because they carry above-market coupons. Buyers can also achieve better returns by taking on synthetic exposure to a borrower via a credit-linked note, rather than by buying the same borrower's debt in the cash market.

A similar argument can, of course, be made with catastrophe derivatives (see Chapters 9 and 10). As insurance companies need to tap the resources of capital markets because of a fast-growing amount of risk, the push is toward a merger of two branches of the financial industry with the likely result of some quite interesting derivatives products.

3. STRUCTURED NOTES AND INVERSE FLOATERS

Some financial analysts consider structured notes to be a sort of toxic waste, a class with risks similar to collateralized mortgage obligations (CMOs). Structured notes, however, are among the securities of the moment because of their customized qualities. While the structured characteristics make these securities hard to define in a generic sensc, two issues are outstanding:

- There is usually an embedded option structure, and
- Cash flow is generally dependent on an external index or benchmark.

For instance, the external index may be Fed funds. How far can this market go? In four years, these securities boomed from a total issuance of $18 billion in 1990 to $84 billion in 1994 (a 466 percent increase), while in the mid- to late-1990s, the market continued growing, albeit at a slower pace.

Customization sees to it that there are many types of structured notes, and diversity increases because they are designed to meet the requirements of different investors. Two products in particular have been the focus of comment in the securities lending business (see sections 5 and 6):

- Range notes and
- Inverse floaters.

The concept behind such instruments is that in stable–interest-rate markets, they pay an enhanced coupon over prevailing interest rates, for each day the daily fixing of interest rates remains in a range. When interest rates fall, inverse floaters make a lot of money as the coupon is fixed at a rate minus a floating-rate reference index.

Inverse floaters, however, are leveraged instruments. When interest rates rise, not only do they lose their attractiveness, but also investors may lose big money—as the Orange County bankruptcy shows. One of the problems is that their relatively illiquid nature amplifies the price fall.

In the general case, investors who get burnt are the ones who did not understand the product and thought that they represent a risk-free yield enhancement. Unsophisticated investors typically buy range notes at the wrong time, not appreciating that complex derivatives instruments are inherently exposed to market swings—as I never tire of repeating.

An investor could make profits with structured notes if he has the ability to break them apart and see how they would react in different forward-rate yield curve environments. This is not a skill commonly found in financial institutions, and let's not talk about the rank and file.

While bankers are supposed to know better, most institutions employ people who are not really capable of evaluating anything more complex than an overnight repo. Yet, in spite of their complexity and risk, during the 1990s structured notes have been popular, though some recent surveys show a fall in their usage.

- In 1993, some statistics indicate, 49 percent of fund managers invested in these products.
- But after the events of 1994, the proportion has been down to 38 percent.

Let me add that all these figures are estimates. Two problems with surveys are the statistical dependability of the sample and the skill of the surveyors. It should therefore come as no surprise that other studies have shown no fundamental change in the number of managers using structured notes (see also section 4).

4. STRUCTURED BONDS

The attraction of structured deals is that they can be tailored to cover almost any view an investor takes of the market. They also permit him to establish the level of risk he wants to assume, provided he has sorted out his priorities and understands the instruments he writes or buys.

Superficially, structured bonds appear to be the same as other bonds—a fixed income instrument. In reality, however, structured bonds are firmly rooted in the highly leveraged derivatives market and present significantly different characteristics than the more classical types of bonds. There are two main types of structured bonds (real bonds and guaranteed bonds), but several others also exist.

Real bonds are issued by governments or by corporations. They typically offer a fixed income for a period of years. What varies is the price at which the investor buys the income stream. The typical way to calculate the yield is to divide the cost of buying the bond by the price, accounting as well for the time left to maturity. This yield is compared to interest rates on bank deposit accounts and other investments competing for money.

Guaranteed bonds are usually offered by mutual funds that invest in derivatives contracts, promising that the investor's or treasurer's capital will be returned after a number of years. This is the sense of the guaranty. But there is an unspoken credit risk—the counterparty may fail.

Because credit risk, market risk, or both are always present, with many derivative instruments, hedging is a way of talking. This is particularly true as an increasing number of players use structured bonds for speculation rather than for risk control, while other investors buy the instrument without full appreciating its risks.

Part of the problem in comprehending what structured bonds offer and how they work is due to a certain amount of confusion about the difference between a classical bond and the use of derivatives called a bond. This has been heightened by the recent trend for new fund launches to be sold to "bond investors."

The so-called guaranteed bonds (funds) coming onstream are seeking to tap the liquidity of the huge bond market. "High income" and other qualifications are misleading because they are just names invented by marketing people to persuade investors that they are buying something that has the assurance of a real bond (see also Chapter 5's discussion of junk bonds).

That is why serious traders and financial analysts warn individual investors to educate themselves on the nuts and bolts of credit derivatives, as well as on their many diverse if not contradictory characteristics, before entering the structured bond market. But few people listen.

Some of the reasons for this discrepancy between knowing and believing have to do with history. Structured bonds were originally designed to protect corporate treasurers against adverse movements in financing costs. If a company needed to hedge a loan against a possible rise in interest rates, a bank would be called upon to structure a bond whose income grew when interest rates rose.

The contribution offered by structured bonds was to use the cash from standard fixed-income securities to gain exposure to highly geared derivatives. But cognizant analysts advise that this involves laying out more money than going directly into derivatives, and contrary to what dealers say, it does not cut the risk—particularly in the case of sharp market movements.

An example may be instructive. In the United States, the Democratic Party political consultant James Carville recalled, "That day the 30-year bond rate dropped another 11 percent ... I was beginning to understand real power." As he told the *Wall Street Journal,* "I used to think if there was reincarnation, I wanted to come back as the president or the pope or a 400 baseball hitter. But now I want to come back as the bond market. You can intimidate everybody."

The point many people do not follow is that the high gearing of structured bonds can quickly turn significant profits into huge losses and these losses will leave scars that last several years. As a matter of fact, a number of huge losses made by the treasury departments of large corporations in the 1990s raises fears that many investors are taking risks in this complex derivatives market without fully understanding what they do.

5. REPURCHASE AGREEMENTS

Repo is an acronym for sale–repurchase agreement, a process for securities lending in financial markets. Specialists look at repos as a low-cost way of raising money. Because the securities act as collateral, the rate at which money is borrowed is usually lower than the rates banks charge on unsecured loans.

In a repo transaction, the holder of a security sells it to a counterparty, but he simultaneously agrees to buy it back at a predetermined date. The counterparty deposits with the original owner an amount equivalent to the full price of the securities. This serves as collateral and is paid back when the securities are returned to their initial owner.

Asset sale and repurchase agreements are made both for trading and for treasury management purposes. They are becoming more common as lending is increasingly securitized. When the asset in a repo is certain to come back to the original owner at some predetermined date, the credit risk on the asset sold essentially remains with the initial owner. But an additional credit risk arises from the possibility of the counterparty's failing to fulfill the repo.

The potential size of this counterparty exposure depends on the type of security involved, the form of the agreement, the maturity of the repo, and movements in market prices. The exposure is the cost of replacing the particular asset should the counterparty default.

Because during a repo transaction the legal owner is the borrower of securities, coupons are paid to him if they fall due during the repo period. When this happens, a cash amount equal to the coupon has to be paid back to the original owner—a process known as a *manufactured payment*.

Borrowing and trading are not the only reasons for repos. Participants in this type of transaction can take advantage of a tax loophole connected to the preceding example. In most markets, domestic holders of bonds receive dividends on which withholding tax has already been levied, but foreigners are paid gross coupons and this provides an arbitrage opportunity.

Therefore, it is tempting for bond holders to repo out their bonds to a tax-exempt counterparty just before a coupon payment and receive a manufactured payment. This feature of the repo market is known as *coupon washing*.

Another reason for repurchase agreements is that fund managers use repos to increase their performance. When a security is in demand on the repo market (becoming *special* in market jargon), borrowers are willing to pay a premium to obtain it.

Borrowers may also be eager to obtain securities through repurchase agreements because they are speculators engaging in short-selling. Short-selling puts downward pressure on the market, in the expectation that stock prices, indices, or bond prices will fall. If this fall occurs, speculators can purchase the securities they sold for less than the price at which they sold them.

Some governments do interfere with the repo market, but without much success. Indeed, the policies of governments and of regulators vary widely in regard to repos. For instance, in Malaysia, short-selling was allowed under certain circumstances until the government banned it in late August 1997 in an attempt to prop up a falling stock market. The restrictions caused Malaysian stocks to plunge further as foreign investors present in the market became infuriated at the change of rules. The government's decision to enforce the short-selling law then kept new foreign investors away from the Malaysian market.

The Malaysian government further erred by singling out a foreign company to penalize for a relatively minor offense. The market revolted. While the law of the land varies by country and also changes with time, both investors and speculators tend to capitalize on the prevailing conditions. Sudden changes in legal and business conditions can lead to the loss of both money and confidence.

6. RISKS ASSOCIATED WITH REPOS

Some analysts think that repos make markets more efficient because they allow traders to go short. They can sell securities that they do not own, thereby inducing their counterparties to inject liquidity into the market. Not everybody, however, agrees with this—particularly because of the exposure involved with repos.

Few repo players appreciate the size of risks associated with repurchase agreements until the time they have to lick their wounds. As Orange County has shown, there is a significant market risk with repos because of gearing.

There is also a temporary loss of ownership risk. When securities are given out in repo, the owner cannot sell them. In a falling market, this is a source of losses as the lender knows it is committed to buying them back at the original price.

This sort of risk is not easy to hide as, in most financial markets, repos are marked to market. Because the price of the securities is calculated daily,

- If the price falls, the losses are immediately visible.
- If it rises, the counterparty has to increase the cash collateral by an equal amount.

Credit risk also exists because of the possibility that the counterparty might not be able to return the securities specified by the repurchase agreement at the end of the transaction. Even if the lender keeps the cash collateral, he may have significant losses in a booming market. Other costs of a default are

- The administrative and legal headaches,
- Transaction costs of buying the securities from the market, and
- The risk that prices might move during the time it takes to repurchase the securities.

Outright forward purchases are less common than repos, but the full credit risk remains. Therefore, it is not considered prudent to offset forward sales against forward purchases in assessing credit risk, unless the transactions are with the same party. Even then, there may be legal issues to be considered.

Regulators tend to take a close look at these different risks. "A mutual fund or unit trust is a trustee organization," said a senior executive of the Financial Services Authority in the UK. "We want the trustees to judge the collateral, and to think of the risk."

I was told during one meeting that an answer the regulators get, when they insist on this vital issue of exposure management, is "This costs money . . ." and they ask in return, "Is thinking costing money?" Because board members are accountable for the exposure assured by their firm, they will do well to keep this brief but focused query always in perspective.

Regulators also pointed out that a great deal in terms of prudential supervision has changed after the effect of Robert Maxwell's actions and their aftermath on credit risk—but, even so, many trustees are not doing very clever things. As a result, they are exposing both themselves and their institutions. "If a trustee knew the risks, he would not be a trustee," a central banker suggested.

Counterparty risk is minor only when governments are the most active users of the repo market. For instance, repurchase agreements are a main instrument of the Bundesbank. To make the banking system more liquid, the reserve bank enters into repo agreements. It is taking securities from banks, and it is giving them the cash they need to invest or lend to clients.

By contrast, to drain cash from the market, the central bank executes this operation in reverse: It takes money from commercial banks and gives them government securities as collateral, on a repurchase agreement basis. This is the secure type of repo which is part of the central bank's monetary policy.

7. CREDIT-ENHANCED VENTURES AND STRUCTURED INVESTMENT VEHICLES

The concept of a credit-enhanced venture (CEV) rests on the simple notion that a high rating (especially a stable high rating) by the counterparty is instrumental in closing financial transactions. The problem is that the supply of unsecured or natural AAAs in the banking industry now comes from only one institution, Rabobank of the Netherlands.

Credit-enhanced ventures aim to close the gap between wishful thinking and real life. The need for CEVs is best illustrated by the fact that, until a few years ago, while a dozen banks worldwide were rated AAA by both Moody's Investors Service and Standard &

Poor's, as mentioned before, this species managed to drive itself to near extinction.

Of course, ratings change. Due to total rating downgrades outpacing rating upgrades during the 1990s, a number of major derivatives dealers sponsored some 15 derivative product company subsidiaries, creating a $2.5 billion industry in terms of initial capital. These are the CEVs.

- They are separately capitalized than their parents or backers.
- Their goal is to achieve an enhanced rating as a counterparty or debt issuer.

Financial analysts tend to look at credit-enhanced ventures in a larger context, as a natural extension of structured finance. They believe that CEVs put together the best features from the successful mortgage-backed securitization:

- A battery of coverage tests and payout triggers to protect a specified asset pool,
- The ability to issue AAA debt based on principles of credit support, and
- The facility of separating, in a legal sense, the derivatives from the underlying.

For operational reasons, credit-enhanced ventures must have the features necessary to become going concerns. In fact, only then can they be successful if they are active counterparties with operating flexibilities, such as the ability to originate, trade, and manage a portfolio.

Seen under this perspective, the CEV is a combination of a structured special-purpose vehicle and a traditional operating counterparty. Provided through appropriate capitalization separate credit support helps to protect against losses, while traders deal on the company's assets and risk managers handle the exposure. One could distinguish two types of CEV:

- The derivatives products company (DPC) and
- The structured investment vehicle (SIV).

DPCs are considered to be narrowly defined CEVs. SIVs are essentially credit arbitrage vehicles for investment managers. The concept originated with the launch of Alpha Finance Corp. in 1988; there are now half a dozen rated SIVs.

In 1991, Merrill Lynch created its Derivatives Products (MLDP) subsidiary. By endowing it with $500 million the broker proved that it was possible to engineer an actively trading independent business unit that could:

- Qualify for a coveted AAA rating, and
- Take on credit-sensitive counterparties with impunity.

Following the DPC of Merrill Lynch, a deep-rooted argument developed in the market over the relative values of capital and rating. This argument persists till today, as the Merrill Lynch venture has been joined by other DPCs in the 1990s, and market participants have become accustomed to structures designed to maximize credit ratings.

By now DPCs are a rather routine part of the derivatives landscape. Somehow the counterparties tend to forget that the DPC's increasing notional volume, and their hundreds or thousands of derivatives trades, may well exceed in terms of exposure—which in some cases runs into billions of dollars—their meager $500 million capital.

Salomon Brothers' Salomon Reinvestment Company (SARCO) has also been a credit-enhanced venture that sells investment agreements and repos to municipal and corporate clients. But there is also a countertrend. In 1996, Australia's Westpac closed down Westpac Derivative Products, its AAA DPC, on the grounds that the parent firm's return to AA status was enough to satisfy its customer base.

Let's also take note of a hybrid or dual DPC structure launched by Bear Stearns in 1996. This has a termination program to suit counterparty preference after a sponsor downgrade. "Bankers and brokers have decided that if they don't join the DPC mini-revolution, they will be run over by it," suggested an investment banker on Wall Street.

For its part, the structured investment vehicle is also an assets-and-liabilities management operation, but an especially focused one set up to realize the positive spread between selected lower–investment-grade assets, usually corporate securities, which rate at least BBB by S&P or Baa2 by Moody's. The careful reader will notice that credit derivatives—the instruments—and CEVs and SIVs—the vehicles—do not eliminate risk. They simply move it around. But

- Both the instruments and the vehicles might create additional risk. How much this will be depends on the gearing involved in their operations.

Like credit derivatives at large, CEVs and SIVs have two effects: leveraging and the switching of credit risk between the parties entering into the transaction. While credit derivatives are the means of securitization of credit risk, CEVs and SIVs are the agents—and sometimes the counterparties.

Their backers set them up because of the premium in interest rates they could master. Other companies deal with them because they believe that they have a better financial staying power than their parents.

8. CRITICAL QUESTIONS WITH CEVs AND SIVs

Collateralized programs and processes of the nature we examined in section 7 have another particular characteristic. Counterparties can supplement their internal capital with surety bonds from financial guarantors, using them as collateral.

Structured investment vehicles are examples of the implementation of a collateralized program. They redeem liabilities if they fail to maintain required capital from the sponsor or third party investors, calculating this capital in terms of excess assets over liabilities, through both leverage tests and marking to market.

The pros of credit enhancement ventures point to statistics that their sponsor base seems to be expanding beyond investment banks. For instance, in insurance, SunAmerica Life Insurance has established AAA venture SunAmerica National Life Insurance. Its mission is writing guaranteed investment contracts.

Not all ventures of the CEV, DPC, and SIV types are AAA. They can as well act as AA-rated sponsors for enhanced risk and capital management when the parent company's rating is a single A. There is also talk in the industry that we might see below–investment-grade sellers or sponsors in the asset securitization market.

Why are financial institutions interested in creating and owning such credit-enhanced firms? The answer is they seem to have several virtues. I have already mentioned the advantage of transacting or borrowing as a AAA or AA. Through this, they give the lower-grade sponsor

- An enhanced reputation,
- Additional business, and
- Higher spread profits.

Typically, the credit-enhanced vehicle will win business from credit-sensitive counterparties whose own investment policies require a high rating level. Credit-sensitive institutions believe that through these ventures credit risk is reduced and the diversification of the sponsor's overall portfolio improved. This, however, is not a self-evident truth.

Even less obvious is the expected general increase in profitability. The hypothesis is that there are synergies between transactions done in a CEV and other business that can bring higher profits. Theoretically, this is correct. Practically, the outcome will depend on

- The reputation of the parent company,
- The level of exposure being taken, and
- The way the parent company manages the new venture.

At the end of the day, the equation the sponsor will have to resolve includes the investments, the trades, and the risks the new affiliate is going to take on over the years. As with any other vehicle, there are trade-offs and choices to be made in structuring a CEV. One crucial decision is the type of credit support required:

- Whether it is sourced directly from the parent or from third parties and
- Whether it is in the form of equity capital, collateral, or insurance.

Another basic decision concerns the time horizon of the credit-enhanced vehicle, as the exposures that it takes accumulate. This means preestablishing the size of the window between a trigger event (such as sponsor default or capital shortfall) and the remedy. The remedy, for instance, may be termination and settlement. Other things being equal, shorter exposure windows can reduce aggregate market risk and credit risk. At the same time, shorter windows might introduce other negatives, like liquidity stress.

Still another fundamental decision concerns the protective triggers to be built into the new venture's operating guidelines. These are necessary to reduce exposure related to counterparty default and market risk. Because the assets put into a CEV are essentially risk capital, still another critical decision in setting up a credit-enhanced vehicle is the building of firewall(s) to ensure that there is legal separation between mother and daughter. Firewalls should include security of capital from a lower-rated parent or sponsor.

Finally, credit-enhanced ventures and structured investment vehicles require operating guidelines commensurate with the fact that they mitigate risk by adhering to a blueprint of exposure management. Sound risk control would see to it that there are limits on the vehicle's activities as well as carefully structured coverage tests, ratios, and triggered remedies like payout.

Not only do these basic functions have to be built in, but also there should be clauses about termination or sponsor replacement including thresholds and triggers. These must be put into effect upon sponsor downgrade or other adverse development that might endanger the new company's reputation and survival.

CHAPTER 8

Credit Spreads, Credit Options, and Debt Options

1. INTRODUCTION

As Chapters 6 and 7 have demonstrated, with credit derivatives the investor gets a foothold in an expanding credit market. The pros say that better known instruments like bonds and equity need a complementary product for reasons of diversification and for a more flexible product design.

Bonds can differ significantly in yield compared to a loan from the same issuer, even a loan of the same seniority and maturity. Because highly rated industrial firms can now address the capital markets and fund themselves through a bond issue at lower cost than a bank loan, some analysts look at credit derivatives as a way to close the loans-bonds circuit. This can be done through total return swaps (see Chapter 6), attracted by the relative premium of loans over bonds.

- With a credit derivative, it is as easy to take a short position as a long one, and
- Good loans might be securitized as well as loans that are not top grade.

An often cited example with investment-grade loans is NatWest's securitization of $5.0 billion in October 1997. This was followed by Sanwa Bank's disposal of $240 million of bad property loans. Other examples of loans-based derivatives come from France and Switzerland.

Few people would doubt that, since this market is just starting, there can be room for innovative instruments like credit spreads and credit options. Some specialists furthermore believe that some of the instruments being developed can be applied to a broader range of markets and products—not only credit derivatives. The concept behind total return swaps is an example.

This polyvalence in the implementation potential of new instruments is important because in a derivatives market that in notional principal amounts is well beyond $130 trillion worldwide, credit derivatives today don't represent anything big. I write this in full understanding that existing surveys of market volume do not cast much light as to how far the credit derivatives market can really grow without creating systemic risk.

Many supervisors and a growing number of financial analysts are nervous not just because of market risk but also because credit risk is on the rise. We may now be in a situation not unlike that of the 1980s with the junk bonds euphoria (see Chapter 5). Therefore, before discussing credit spreads, credit options, and other credit instruments, let's take another look at the potential of credit risk.

2. CREDIT RISK IS ON THE RISE

On March 22, 1997, Comptroller of the Currency Eugene Ludwig told the annual convention of the Independent Bankers Association of America, in Phoenix, Arizona, that at year-end 1996 his examiners had found credit risk on the rise at nearly a fifth of all community banks. At least some of this growth was a result of weakening in underwriting standards, where banks feel pressured to continue booking loans in an increasingly competitive business environment.

Mr. Ludwig suggested that now is not the time for any bank to cut corners on its underwriting standards or its internal controls. In fact, in mid-March 1997, OCC had issued a strongly worded advisory letter to its regulated banks to warn about the importance of internal controls, underwriting standards, and credit policies.

A policy is set by the board as the means for avoiding repetitive decisions on the same or similar issues. Therefore, only the board of an institution can set sound and lasting credit policies, while senior line management and the Auditing Committee should watch that the board's policies are scrupulously observed.

Credit policies do not only concern the granting of new loans but also the definition of the processes and rules governing problem loans. Regulators advise that credit policies should deal both with the rules and with exceptions to the rules—if and when there are exceptions. They should also specify under which conditions and under whose responsibility exceptions might be allowed. When this whole framework of credit policies is wanting, credit risk rises.

Of course, corporate business and clients are not the only at fault in the context of a growing credit risk. Banks have also experienced significant losses because of emerging markets debt—even if in some cases loans were guaranteed by the government and the taxpayer foots the bill. Apart from the low creditworthiness of some countries, many losses are due to restructuring and therefore to lengthening time scales.

- Over the 1992–97 time frame, the average maturity of emerging market debt has moved from 4 to 10 years.
- At the same time, the amount of money outstanding in emerging markets has skyrocketed, as Figure 8.1 shows with an example from China.

Far from being a spike, what Eugene Ludwig said in March 1997 proved a forerunner of things to come. In October 1998, when this text was being written, one-third of the world economy was in or about to enter a steep recession, and typically in a major recession credit risk rises sharply. Japan is going to shrink by 2 percent, Hong Kong by 4 percent, Indonesia by 15 percent, South Korea by 6 percent, and Russia by 5 to 7 percent or worse. All this indicates a higher risk of credit quality deterioration. In the books of Japanese banks alone nonperforming loans stand (as of October 1998) at the

$1.2 trillion level. This pitiful financial status is reflected in the move upward in the "Japan premium," which is about 800 basis points over U.S. banks, therefore amounting to junk status.

Some big Japanese banks are all but bankrupt, staying alive because of the domino effect. The Long Term Credit Bank (LTCB) is an example. It is sitting on some Yen 50 trillion ($365 billion) in derivatives obligations which, if LTCB fails, will default, creating a tsunami of counterparty failures.

It is a deliberate choice to discuss these issues in the middle of Part Two. We have already examined some of the current credit-derived instruments like asset swaps, default swaps, and total return swaps. We are going to discuss credit spreads and credit options. But the reader must also be aware of where high leverage has led the economy. The message is that

- The financial instrument will never succeed or fail all by itself.
- It needs a framework, and this is provided by credit policies and procedures.
- Credit risk is on the rise every time the framework is found to be wanting.

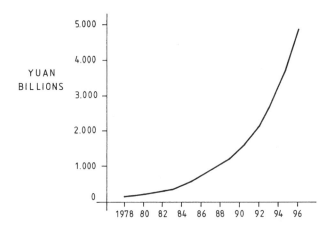

FIGURE 8.1 LOANS BY CHINESE BANKS IN BILLIONS OF YUAN, 1978–1996

Not only issuance but also risk control policies are needed with any type of securitization (see section 7). The public offering of credit card receivables has proved a boon to young, small, and regional issuers who have found that its ability to dissipate default risk has enabled them to compete with major lenders. But according to the Federal Deposit Insurance Corporation, American banks lost a total of $4 billion on loans in the first quarter of 1997, and the lion's share of these losses, in the above time frame, has been in credit cards.

Although the U.S. banks remained profitable because of the higher spreads charged on well-behaved debts, the losses have shown serious procedural weaknesses. Therefore, they should retain senior management's attention. In business the "could not happen to me" notion is fake.

As the consumer credit boom continues, with nonpayment reaching record levels in almost every consecutive month of 1997 for which there exist statistics, many issuers struggle to maintain adequate spreads on their credit card and loan securitizations. While no credit-card–backed securities have yet defaulted, some backed by auto loans have.

This rise in credit risk is no U.S.-only phenomenon by any means. In Switzerland, where a weak economy has pushed banks into losing some $29 billion on domestic loans between 1991 and 1996, both Swiss Bank Corporation (now United Bank of Switzerland), which took a $2.9 billion charge in 1996, and Credit Suisse have declared radical shifts in their approaches to provisioning against such losses.

- Rather than make provisions after the fact of loan impairment, they set provisions in advance (see Chapters 11 and 12).
- To do so, they estimate future losses on a portfolio basis, using the probability of default by category of borrower.

In North America this practice is followed by Bank of America and Bank of Montreal, in the United Kingdom by Barclays, and in Australia by Westpac. Several banks have started making provisions in a proactive fashion. The securitization of corporates can ease the strain of such provisions.

Increasingly, commercial and investment banks are paying attention to credit risk exposure through a modified value-at-risk (VAR) model, which became a regulatory standard for market risk (see Chapter 15). Besides modeling approaches' contribution in terms of analytics and methodology, they raise senior management's awareness of the need for proactive solutions in a context of growing credit risk.

3. CREDIT SPREADS AND CREDIT OPTIONS

Many of the classical-type options and their more sophisticated follow-ups can be applied to debt, equity, currency, and other commodities. Credit options, however, are a special class of derivative instruments. They are applicable only to risky debt; therefore, they are speculative.

A *credit option* is essentially a default option. It is a derivative instrument many analysts see becoming an integral component of an expanding financial market. Credit forwards could be looked at in a similar way. Investors' and speculators' objectives with these instruments are

- To profit from credit spread movements and
- To use them as a way of hedging credit risk.

A *credit spread* is a spread in which the value of the option purchased exceeds the value of the option sold—or vice versa. The credit spread itself is a function of the grade of the asset being handled, compared to some other grade that serves as a reference and is usually of high standing.

Knowledgeable readers are familiar with the concept underpinning this discussion, because the notion of credit spread is not alien to bond holders. It is associated with bonds that are priced and traded at a spread over a benchmark instrument of comparable maturity.

- Most bonds denominated in U.S. dollars are priced at a spread over the current yield on 30-year Treasuries or other U.S. government bonds with similar maturities.

- Expressed in basis points, the yield differential, or spread, represents the risk premium the market demands for holding the issuer's bonds.

The existence of 10-, 20-, and 30-year yield curves which serve as a frame of reference for a given currency is evidence of maturity in financial markets. Most emerging countries and their currencies don't have long-term yield curves like the ones for Germany's DM and the ECU shown in Figure 8.2.

Pricing financial instruments from bonds to credit options can be much more accurate with the availability of yield curves. For instance, options can refer to spreads over British Gilts, German Bunds, U.S. Treasury bonds, or other benchmark credit in the Group of Ten countries.

Both long-term and short-term yield curves are important. Credit spreads associated with credit options usually have maturities of between six months and two years. The contractual conditions they imply can be settled in cash or through physical delivery of the underlying bond.

The credit option's payoff is based on the improvement or deterioration of a reference issuer's credit quality. The instrument can be structured in price or spread terms, with spread-based derivatives being somewhat more popular.

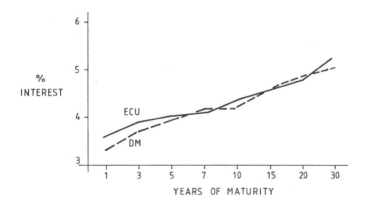

FIGURE 8.2 BOND YIELD CURVES FOR THE DM AND ECU, AUGUST 25, 1998

A banker, treasurer, or investor who purchases a credit option is primarily focusing on the maximum movement of the underlying reference credit spread during the life of the option. Significant risks are involved in the movement of the credit spread, to an extreme point prior to default by the option writer. Therefore, information both on credit standing and on volatility is at a premium.

Spreads-based credit options are negotiated over the counter. Their appeal lies in the fact that they can be customized to meet the specific credit-related requirements from hedging to other investment objectives. As with all transactions involving options, a credit call (put) option gives the purchaser the right, but not the obligation, to buy (sell) an underlying credit-sensitive asset or credit spread at a predetermined price for a predetermined period of time.

For instance, an investor could purchase a credit spread put to hedge the risk of widening spreads because he has written some notes. At the same time, however, different credit options provide the basis for building more exotic credit structures and with them comes a larger amount of risk (see also section 5).

Investors use options on credit spreads to take a position on the relative performance of two different bonds, without actually buying or selling either one of them. The design of the instruments strips out interest rate risk to focus on pure credit risk.

Theoretically at least, options on credit spreads permit investors to isolate credit risk from market risk and to take a position relative to an asset's credit risk profile in the future. In this way, credit spreads can be used to

- Buy securities on a forward basis at favorable prices,
- Earn premium income at higher level of risk, and
- Profit from spread tightening or widening.

On the option's exercise date, if the actual spread of the underlying bond is lower than the strike price, the option expires worthless and the investor pays nothing. If it is higher, the writer delivers the bond and the investor pays a price whose yield spread over the benchmark equals the strike spread.

Purchasing credit options enables investors to participate in price or credit spread movements while risking no more than the option premium. This is not true of writers. While selling credit options can be a source of credit-related fee income, it also carries with it unlimited risk.

In contrast to credit options, *credit forwards* are single derivatives targeting the appreciation or depreciation of an issuer's credit quality, in either price or spread terms. The investor expresses a view of an issuer's credit by entering into a contract with an institution having the opposite view of that same credit.

- The buyer contracts with a writer to purchase a given reference bond at an agreed forward date and forward price.
- If the underlying credit improves, the bond price rises and the buyer profits.

A similar reference is valid with a credit forward targeting a credit spread rather than a bond price. However, if the underlying credit deteriorates, it is the writer who realizes a gain while the buyer suffers a loss. The concept underpinning credit forwards has been applied not only to credit but also to equity, debt, currencies, and other commodities.

4. DEBT OPTIONS

Debt options used for trading are of two kinds: price-based and yield-based. The distinction is fundamental and should be understood by investors because the characteristics of debt options, like those of practically all derivatives financial instruments, are not cast in iron.

Price-based options are those that give their holders the right either to purchase or sell a specified underlying debt, or to receive a cash settlement based on the value of an underlying debt. *Yield-based options* are cash-settled, based on the difference between the exercise price and the value of an underlying yield. Therefore, as with credit options, the investor should appreciate the relationship between rates and yields.

Rates and yields are different ways of expressing return on debt securities. Coupon interest rates of a debt security express return as a percentage of the principal amount of the security at par value. Yields express return (or projected return) as a percentage of the amount invested.

Prices of debt securities move inversely to changes in interest rates. In the general case, declining rates on long-term bonds or money market instruments will cause prices of outstanding debt securities to increase. In contrast, rising rates across a particular maturity will cause the prices of outstanding debt securities of that maturity to decline.

The rise or the decline will be more pronounced the further out the maturity is. Long maturities are a means of leverage in the bond market, but the average investor does not appreciate this fact.

The designated maturity of the Treasury security from which the underlying yield is determined is a standardized term of every yield-based option. The specific Treasury security having that maturity is not fixed, but the underlying yield is derived from the outstanding security of the designated maturity that has the longest remaining life.

The aftermath of this condition is that newly auctioned securities having the longest remaining life will replace old issues on the first trading day following their auction. Therefore, the specific Treasury security from which the underlying yield is derived may change during the life of the option.

Many of the risks associated with debt options result from (1) the character of the markets in which the underlying debt instruments are issued and traded and (2) the distinctive characteristics of the instruments themselves. There exists an important difference between the stock market and the debt market:

- Stock quotations are all keyed to a 100-share round lot.
- But the basic unit of trading in debt markets typically involves much larger amounts of money.

For most dealers in Treasury securities a lot is, at a minimum, $1,000,000 of notional principal amount. On money market instruments such as short-term Treasury bills, the lot can be larger. This sees to it that most deals are oriented toward doing business with large institutional customers or other dealers, rather than directly with private investors.

Debt options that are U.S. Treasury securities require delivery of the underlying financial paper upon exercise of the option. The exercise prices of these price-based options are expressed in terms of the prices of the underliers.

The price of the underlying debt instrument, relative to the exercise price of the option, is the ultimate determinant of the value of a price-based debt option. With yield-based options, the value of the option is determined by the difference between the yield or yield complement of the specified debt securities and the exercise price.

In assessing the effect of a change in interest rates or yields on the price of a debt product, it is always necessary to remember the nature of the relationship between an instrument's price and its interest rate. As we have just seen, this relationship is expressed by the fact that prices of debt instruments move inversely to changes in rate or yield.

5. RISKS WITH DEBT OPTIONS

One of the risks, or constraints, with debt options is that the hours of their trading may not conform to the hours during which the underlying debt instruments are traded. To the extent that the options markets close before the markets for the underlying instruments, significant price and rate movements can take place in the underlying market that cannot be reflected in the options market.

Any risk control procedure should account for the possibility of such movements, relating closing prices in the options market to those in the underlying market. A risk is that debt options may be exercised on the basis of price movements in the underlying security after the close of trading in the options market, when writers are no longer able to close out their short positions.

Furthermore, since trading in Treasury bonds and notes tends to center on the most recently auctioned issues, the market does not continually introduce options with new expiration months to replace expiring options on specific issues. Instead, the options introduced at the commencement of options trading in a specific issue are allowed to run their course. However,

- Options trading in each specific issue of bonds or notes will be phased out as new options are listed on more recent issues, and
- There may be options trading on more than one issue of bonds or notes at any given time, making feasible selection.

Option contracts that are identical except for principal amount are not interchangeable. If a market lists different contract sizes on a particular issue of bonds or notes, a holder of a given number of smaller contracts could not close out his position by selling a lesser number of larger contracts with the same exercise price and expiration date, even though the amount of the underlying bonds or notes might be the same.

Exercise prices for Treasury bill options are based on annualized discount rates, the discount from par at which a hypothetical 360-day Treasury bill could be purchased or sold. Exercise prices are expressed as complements of discount rates: 100 minus the annualized discount rate, for reasons of consistency with other kinds of options.

Exercise settlement values for yield-based options whose underlying yields are derived from Treasury securities are based upon the spot yield for the security at a designated time on the last trading day of the option, as announced by the Federal Reserve Bank of New York. The assigned writer of a yield-based option is obligated to pay the exercising option holder a settlement equal to the difference between the exercise price of the option and the exercise settlement value of the underlying yield.

The reference time is the last trading day before expiration, as reported by a designated authority. This difference is multiplied by the multiplier for this option—but different yield-based options may have different multipliers.

One of the special features of yield-based options is that when the underlying yield is expressed in terms of a yield indicator, this indicator will represent a yield or discount multiplied by 10. When the underlying yield is expressed in terms of the complement of the yield, the yield complement will be simply stated as a decimal.

Given that exercises of yield-based options are settled in cash, option writers cannot fully provide in advance for their potential settlement obligations by acquiring and holding the underlying interest. Furthermore, the principal amount of Treasury securities needed to ensure that an options position is fully covered will generally not remain constant throughout the life of the option, but will fluctuate as a result of changes in yields and remaining time to maturity.

6. STRIPS

STRIPS is an acronym for the separate trading of registered interest and principal of securities. Interest and principal are seen as different components of a conventional bond; therefore, they are divided from one another and traded as distinct securities.

A 10-year Treasury bill, for example, is strippable into 10 yearly coupons and one final redemption. The result is a series of 11 zero-coupon securities, with maturities of one, two, and three years and so on.

STRIPS can be useful instruments for some market participants. Unlike bonds that pay annual or half-yearly dividends, the total return on a STRIP is known at the time of purchase. This is not the case for conventional bonds, because investors never know in advance the interest rate at which they will be able to reinvest coupons.

The value of a STRIP, however, is predictable only when the security is held until maturity, at which time the investor receives the whole notional amount. In the short term, their prices fluctuate more sharply than those of conventional bonds.

In the United States, where STRIPS have been available since 1985, they have become popular among people planning their own pensions as well as home owners with an interest-only mortgage and a lump-sum payment in the future. They are also used by institutional investors with long-term liabilities, such as pension funds.

Investors should, however, take notice that in most markets STRIPS usually offer lower yields than the bonds from which they are derived. There is a cost in stripping and managing several series of new securities, and this has to be charged to the users.

Among the risks faced by the user of STRIPS is that all the cash flows are concentrated at the end of a STRIP's life. As a result, the effects of changes in interest rates or in inflationary expectations are amplified. In contrast, the price of a conventional bond is less affected by changes in interest rate projections or in market conditions. The silver lining is that with STRIPS inflation is partly offset by expectations that interim payments will be reinvested at higher rates of interest, while generally inflation erodes the value of all future cash flows, affecting the bonds' coupons and final redemption.

STRIPS investors also benefit from the fact that because governments are the largest issuers of debt, government bond stripping results in instruments that are more liquid than corporate zero-coupon bonds. This makes it both easier and cheaper to buy and sell large amounts.

Finally it is worth noting that the broker, too, takes a risk with STRIPS as smart traders can misrepresent earnings while senior management may lack the knowledge or will to control the traders. Losses of some $300 million in STRIPS and other instruments brought down Kidder Peabody when General Electric decided that it was better to exercise damage control and merged the company with PaineWebber.

7. TERMINATION OPTIONS AND RISK CONTROL

One way to structure credit derivative transactions is through termination options. These permit the bank to make a noncollateralized transaction in exchange for the opportunity to exit this transaction at a future date if the counterparty's credit quality deteriorates.

There is a pricing problem with termination options not unlike that present with all options and it concerns timing. It is absolutely necessary to adjust the price of an option to the expiration date.

- With exchange-traded options, the interval is usually equal to one year.

Most options, particularly those that are exchange-traded, have less than a one-year life span.

- To the contrary, OTC interest rate options have long maturities.

OTC maturities can run up to 10 years and in cases beyond this.

- Termination options can have all types of maturities, making more complex the job of setting the right price.

Two-way issues introduce another pricing factor. Though most termination options are one-way, they can also be two-way. This primarily takes place when counterparties of equal credit quality enter into long-term transactions. For instance, two banks may negotiate the right to

- Terminate a transaction at specified points in time and
- Do so without a detailed explanation of their reasons to the counterparty.

Even if the implicit understanding may be that the termination clause specifies downgrade, saying, for instance, that the option is only exercisable if a credit rating agency downgraded a given counterparty, other reasons too might trigger the use of a termination option.

For instance, instead of a downgrade by an independent rating agency, the derivatives instrument may be structured to terminate based on the deterioration of financial conditions, such as a given index or ratio falling below a defined threshold. This has similarities with some covenants used in loans.

As these examples help to document, we can look at termination options as tools for risk control in bilateral agreements when a bank perceives that its counterparty is turbulent and may no longer be able to perform. This can happen both to companies and to sovereigns when they are headed for a very steep economic or financial downturn and there is no evidence that the management (or government) is able to bend the curve's sharp slope.

As section 2 relates, mounted credit risk amplified by irresponsibility at the top management level makes an entity's counterparties nervous. It is therefore no surprise that the measurement and management of credit risk have become key issues for financial institutions. Also, because default rates are expected to rise in the near future, exits are being attached to bilateral deals.

The more deals are done OTC, the more top-tier banks feel the need to work on innovative strategies and techniques to internally measure their credit risks—as well as on instruments that permit damage control. Current methods include

- Fair value assessment of nonliquid assets and liabilities (such as bank loans),
- The securitization of assets and debt through credit derivatives,
- Analytical estimation of loss reserves, with prognostication as the goal, and
- Pricing of both public and privately placed debt in a way providing protection through reinsurance.

The use of sophisticated methods, tools, and options to manage credit risk permits one to effectively attack a whole spectrum of counterparty problems. Among the components of rigorous credit risk measurement are intraday data streams,[1] database mining, and other approaches leading to a more objective evaluation of credit risk, including ratings by independent agencies.

---

[1] See D.N. Chorafas, *How to Understand and Use Mathematics for Derivatives,* Volume 1, *Understanding the Behavior of Markets,* Euromoney, London, 1995.

CHAPTER 9

Credit Derivatives and Catastrophe Insurance

1. INTRODUCTION

A complete list of instruments that could fit under the credit derivatives umbrella would go well beyond the most popular, which have been covered in Chapters 6 through 8. In principle, every transaction with a *credit* reference to it could be subject to repackaging and selling in the capital markets.

The securitization of insurance products is an excellent example on derivative financial instruments that may be coming onstream, even if the financial markets have not yet discovered its full potential due to the changes taking place in the insurance industry. This is particularly true in connection with catastrophe insurance (CAT). In fact, the Chicago Board of Trade (CBOT) introduced CAT futures and options in 1992 (see section 3)—which most likely is the tip of the iceberg.

Several investment analysts believe that catastrophe derivatives are part of insurance industry consolidation which is taking place for years. As the market advances and innovates, there have been developments like "superCAT bonds" which are no bonds at all.

- Investors in CAT derivatives operate at a disadvantage to insurance companies because they do not benefit from float.

- Warren Buffett says that float comes to an insurance firm at a negative cost; that is, a cost of less than zero.

One of the most important innovations in the insurance industry with evident effects on derivative products is the redirection of supervision toward solvency control. The new supervisory rules are better focused, roughly amounting to the abolition of substantive insurance supervision, as was done in the past. One of the fundamental changes is that prices and conditions can be freely agreed between insurer and insured.

The obligation to obtain prior authorization, which had been normal practice in many countries up to 1997, no longer applies. This could be described as a far-ranging deregulation that might bring along a number of insurance-based financial products.

In a practical sense, solvency control could replace price and product regulation if some kind of minimum standards substitute for direct financial supervision. An example is standards relating to the calculation of the type and spread of assets, as well as regarding the level of technical provisions.

Once this has been done, the way is open for a framework within which innovative financial products can be developed and sold, with global competition playing a key role and acting as a regulator of sorts. Experts in the insurance business believe that there will be a lasting effect on the structure of the insurance industry because of the deregulation of supervision and the opening up of markets to foreign suppliers.

This might well be accompanied by a revolution in insurance products. Vague generalizations, however, cannot do justice to the complexity of the case. Therefore, in this chapter and in Chapter 10 we will look into natural and man-made catastrophes, examine the potential of securitization in the insurance industry, define what this industry represents in economic terms, and explain some of the instruments that might be of interest to the capital markets.

2. INSURED AND UNINSURED LOSSES FROM NATURAL AND MAN-MADE CATASTROPHES

In 1997, *insured losses* from natural and man-made catastrophes reached the level of $6.7 billion. This amount is large, yet it is about half that in 1996, mainly because no extremely costly catastrophes occurred over 1997. As the reader will appreciate in Figure 9.1, based on statistics from Swiss Re, the most recent quarter-century time frame, 1973–97, divides into two parts:

- In the 15 years from 1973 to 1987, natural and man-made catastrophes kept a low profile, albeit with an upward trend.
- But in the 1988–97 period, both the means and the variance of costly catastrophes have been beefed up, in particular in connection to natural disasters.

Insured losses and total losses due to natural and man-made catastrophes are not the same thing. In 1997, the estimated total losses from catastrophes amounted to $28.8 billion. This is more than 400 percent larger than insured losses. Approximately $24 billion of the $28.8 billion was due to natural hazards.

- As the name implies, *natural hazards,* or *catastrophes,* are events caused by natural forces.
- Usually these result in many single losses involving various insured parties and insurance contracts.

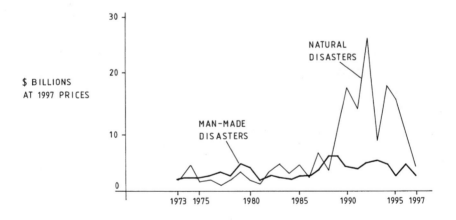

Used by permission of Swiss Re, Sigma *No. 3/1998*

FIGURE 9.1 INSURANCE LOSSES FROM NATURAL AND MAN-MADE CATASTROPHES IN $ BILLION, OVER 25 YEARS

Natural catastrophes in 1997 accounted for insured losses of $4.1 billion, out of a $6.7 billion total. The single event that caused by far the highest single loss, $940 million, was the extensive flooding in Eastern Europe. In America, insurance losses of $3.1 billion were mainly due to storms and floods.

- The extent of damage caused by a catastrophe depends on the severity of the natural forces involved.
- It also depends on certain human factors such as the efficiency of disaster protection measures.

Another significant issue is whether there is material damage alone or also personal injury. For many natural hazards (for instance, earthquakes), much depends on the time of day the event happens.

In connection to natural catastrophes, among the top claims in 1997 were high water levels following persistent rains in Poland and the Czech Republic; storms with wind speeds up to 160 km/h in the United Kingdom; tornadoes, hail, and flooding in the United States; flooding caused by melting snow and major fires in the U.S. and Canada; flooding along the Ohio River in the U.S.; and still other events involving tornadoes, hail, heavy rain, flooding, snowstorms, and wind speeds up to 130 km/h in the U.S.

Another example of natural hazards, the media-covered El Niño, dominated global meteorological events in 1997 and 1998. Yet, in these years El Niño caused considerably fewer losses than the powerful El Niño in 1982–83. The media perception of a devastation in 1997–98 was essentially due to the availability of detailed information and its visualization.

Natural catastrophes can be divided into categories such as floods, storms, earthquakes, tsunami, drought, bushfires, high waves, extreme cold, frost, hail, avalanches, and landslides. Some of these catastrophes (like China's extreme floods in August and September 1998) have at their origin man-made events like deforestation. To my thinking, such events should be reflected in the risks taken by the insurance policy, and their risk should be embedded in derivative instruments based on insurance contracts.

- *Man-made disasters* are those directly connected to human activity and its aftermath. Examples are fires, explosions, and aviation, shipping, road, and mining accidents.

Heavy damages, often involving loss of life, result from the collapse of buildings and bridges and from explosions due to gas leaks and fires as well as from acts of terrorism. Many man-made disasters are created because of negligence—or sometimes because of human ingenuity—though purely accidental conditions also play a role.

An example of a man-made hazard that was neither planned nor purely accidental, but stemmed from negligence and lack of foresight, is the year 2000 problem (Y2K),[1] which put the insurance industry on alert, leading to the incorporation into contracts of a clause terming the failure to correct Y2K by the insurer as a case of gross negligence.

Man-made catastrophes tend to be insured much more frequently than natural catastrophes. Therefore, it is not surprising that a good 40 percent of insurance losses in 1997 were due to man-made disasters. It is also interesting to note that roughly a quarter of the losses suffered by insurers for man-made reasons originated from three fires (in a silicon wafer factory in Taiwan, an aircraft hangar in Belgium, and a spinning mill in Japan) and from an explosion at a gasworks in South Africa.

Another big disaster was the premature shutdown of the proton booster, which caused loss of the AsiaSat 3 satellite in space. This sort of software-related man-made accident is on the increase, as our society gets more and more technologically sophisticated (see also this section's earlier discussion on Y2K).

It is not necessary to explain that information is crucial to loss estimates. But information also magnifies the perception of losses. "More information" contributed to a higher estimate of losses than previously assessed from natural and man-made catastrophes, another big factor being the higher damage potential. This is due to

- The rising density of population all over the globe,
- More insured (and uninsured) assets in hazard areas, and
- A significant concentration of assets in the Group of Ten nations.

---

[1] D.N. Chorafas, *Cost-Effective IT Solutions for Financial Services,* Lafferty Publications, London and Dublin, 1998.

All these factors have led to a drive for more consistent scientific knowledge and assessment of *future risks*. Climatic changes, for example, result in an increase in claims, but also bring a higher level of uncertainty related to claims, which eventually translates into losses.

Dispensing with these claims against insurance policies makes possible a relatively early assessment of the insurance year. Early assessments, however, can lead to an underestimation of the costs of accidental events. At the same time, limits with respect to personal injury as well as to physical losses allow the reduction of money outlays in connection to insurance cover.

What has just been said about insurance is valid for the reinsurance industry, which must take into account a higher average claims burden, as well as the fact that this burden will show substantial fluctuations from year to year. This will lead to higher premium rates, but it will also call for burden sharing by the capital markets, as long as investors see a gain in such coverage. It is at this point that the impact of credit derivatives, to be issued by insurers or by investment banks on their behalf, will be felt.

Prior to closing this section, I would like to bring the reader's attention to a loophole in financial reporting regulations. FAS Statement 133 is a well-studied document that pays attention to detail. However, at a time when catastrophe derivatives are starting to take off, and traders believe that they have a great future, it contains one major loophole. It states that contracts that are not traded in exchanges are not subject to its reporting requirements *if* they address a climatic geological or other physical variable. That's exactly the target of catastrophe derivatives.

3. TOWARD A SECURITIZATION OF INSURED CATASTROPHES

In the Group of Ten countries, regulators keep an open mind about catastrophe derivatives while they study their aftermath. During our meeting an executive of the German Federal Banking Supervision Bureau suggested that: "It is a good idea to introduce catastrophe derivatives, to spread insurance risk to the investors. But it is very important to study the risks this would involve and this needs long time series."

Several of the commercial banks I met had a similar attitude. At the Deutsche Bank, a proposal has been made to the board on catastrophe derivatives. The decision is pending. Allianz Insurance, which owns 21.4 percent of Dresdner Bank's shares, while Dresdner owns about 10 percent of Allianz, has asked the senior management of Dresdner Bank for a catastrophe derivatives product line. Here again, the decision is pending.

One may wonder why credit institutions are both interested in the catastrophe derivatives market and, at the same time, slow in making a decision. The reason is that there exists both business opportunity and a potentially major risk. Therefore, prudence is recommended.

In the 1990s, the insurance industry has been hard hit by a large number of natural catastrophes. The costs involved in these events have raised several questions, one of them being the *limits* of insurability, bringing to center stage the issue of credit risk.

Potential losses from storm, hurricane, and earthquake risk in the United States currently exceed the available coverage capacity in the insurance and reinsurance markets. An analytical approach, however, shows that the cost of these events, though high, is smaller than the daily volatility of wealth in the American financial market.

- No doubt this is behind the emergence of derivative instruments related to insurance products like CAT futures and options, and index-linked policies where the *loss index* is the underlying instrument of the future's final value.
- Insurance futures currently trade in quarterly cycles with contract months March, June, September, and December, each covering losses from events occurring one quarter earlier—but being settled three months down the line.

These contracts, and those that will develop in the coming years, compete for a share of invested wealth that can be tapped through capital markets. Wealth invested in the United States alone amounts to about $19 trillion. On average, its daily volatility is roughly 70 basis points—which means some $133 billion. At least theoretically, this exceeds the maximum possible insurance loss that might arise from a truly big earthquake. This reference is important because

- The largest U.S. catastrophe risks include earthquakes in California and hurricanes in Florida, Georgia, and the Carolinas.
- Simulation done by some companies has quantified probable maximum losses for these events between $50 billion and $100 billion, depending on the scenario.

Such cumulative potential losses are currently matched by stated capital and reserves of the entire American property and casualty insurance industry to the amount of $200 billion. About 10 percent of this belongs to the U.S. reinsurers. This, however, does not mean that available money more than covers a worst-case scenario, particularly if the globalization of the insurance and reinsurance industries is kept in perspective.

The reason for this discrepancy between worst-case claims and available resources is that the capital and surplus of insurance companies must as well be available for a variety of other obligations, such as the consequences of aggravated American product liability. Therefore, experts believe that the traditional insurance system currently faces a significant capacity gap in the area of natural catastrophe risks.

Experts are also of the opinion that only the capital markets can cover supercatastrophes (superCATs) in an effective manner. Behind this argument lies the impressive capitalization of the financial markets and their ability to absorb large shocks without system breakdowns.

Without doubt, this is a necessary condition for mastering major losses from natural catastrophes. Only time will show if this can provide a sufficient basis for the growing catastrophe problems.

Already the search for new capital sources has led to the prospect of trading insurance risks not only within the traditional insurance environment but also by transferring them to the broader financial market. As mentioned earlier, at the end of 1992 the

Chicago Board of Trade launched futures on catastrophe loss indices and related options.

The loss index consists of losses reported to the Insurance Service Office by about 100 companies, though the office selects only some of this information based on diversity of business, quality, and, of course, size. The index is therefore weighted, with weights corresponding to percentages of estimated premiums earned per line and state in the United States.

The careful reader will notice some parallels with other derivatives products. Fifteen years prior to the aforementioned reference to the loss index, in 1977 CBOT had launched what was then a new instrument, U.S. Treasury bond futures. Twenty years of statistics presented in Figure 9.2 shows that trading volume in U.S. Treasury bond futures grew fairly fast during the first decade but then tapered off. Can these statistics be seen as a prognostication of catastrophe derivatives?

Only the market will tell, and for this the market must be tested. The salutary effects of market response is that products do not remain static. In the elapsed years after the launch of U.S. Treasury bond futures, these contracts have significantly improved, while

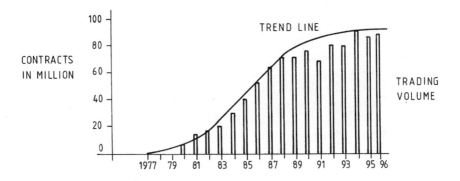

Used by permission of Swiss Re, Sigma *No. 5/1996*

FIGURE 9.2 IS THE DEVELOPMENT OF TRADING VOLUME IN U.S. TREASURY BOND FUTURES ON THE CBOT A PROGNOSTICATOR OF CAT DERIVATIVES?

newer instruments came along like the STRIPS (see Chapter 8). At the same time, similar products have been listed in more exchanges.

The pros in the securitization of catastrophe insurance will not fail to remind us that not long ago came to life a new exchange in New York more relevant to our discussion than CBOT, because it specializes in catastrophe risks. This is the Catastrophe Risk Exchange, or CATEX, which will be discussed in section 4.

The careful reader will appreciate that to face the challenges posed by new financial instruments in terms of risk and return, investment banks develop models that assist in pricing and in sales. This gives a further push to the market, increasing product demand, because it helps in the insurance industry's evolution from mainly a liability orientation to its being an important segment of the global financial industry.

Investment banks have been gaining experience on the securitization of catastrophe risks in cooperation with insurance companies. The goal is to place such risks directly with investors, assisted through assets/liabilities and risk capital modeling—marketing them as securities.

The principles underpinning securitization of insurance liabilities can be further illustrated through the example of a specially structured bond to cover earthquake risks in California. Known as the Earthquake Risk Bond (ERB), it is part of a state insurance program of the California Earthquake Authority (CEA) and it is expected to contribute toward solving the current capacity crisis in the Californian market for earthquake cover.

4. WHAT'S THE FUTURE OF A CATASTROPHE RISK EXCHANGE?

Whether securitized or in another form of derivative financial products, catastrophe risks might establish themselves as a new assets and liabilities class. Investors, however, will be well advised to study the operational features of the new instruments in a detailed manner, whether they come from inside or outside the insurance industry and whether they are traded OTC, in an established exchange, or in a new exchange.

As its name implies, the Catastrophe Risk Exchange is a special exchange for catastrophe risks. Its aim is to realize a reciprocal risk transfer mechanism enabling licensed risk takers, insurers, reinsurers, and insurance brokers to exchange baskets of specific catastrophe risks with each other. This could be done

- On a regional basis according to loss category or
- On a global basis by loss category or index.

At the opening of trading, CATEX provides a set of benchmark exchange rates based on historical loss distributions and the latest realized rates. With trading, these relative prices adjust to the current market forces.

For any practical purpose, the insured are not affected by the risk transfer targeted through packaged instruments traded in the exchange, because no insurance policy portfolios are changing hands. This is similar to many other credit derivatives deals. What changes hands is the cash flows.

- The system expands the insurance perspective through the inclusion of risk takers who were so far no part of the traditional insurance business.
- But the establishment of fair insurance premiums as well as of loading—and the handling of claims—continues being performed by insurance companies.

The pros say that in addition to providing an above-average yield potential, insurance-based derivatives instruments are attractive because their performance does not correlate with other financial instruments and their risks. Some analysts think that securitized natural catastrophes promise an interesting diversification effect, but not everybody agrees that catastrophe risk exchanges might prevail over OTC deals.

On the practical side, from both investment and insurance perspectives, the possibility for alternative risk transfer through derivative insurance instruments has promise. The early issuers of such security products anticipate that over time there will be an influx of risk capital to cover U.S. catastrophe risks.

- Calculations through a portfolio optimization model have shown benefits for potential investors.
- However, only real market tests can provide firm evidence on the size, trend, and clients of such transactions.

For the time being, projected market size is not that large. Early information suggests that the amount may be in the $30 to $40 billion range. This represents between 0.5 and 1 percent of the U.S. stock market capitalization, which is a drop in the bucket for the capital markets.

Major questions of course remain and nothing is yet set. A key query for which the experts are looking for a documented answer was posed in the opening paragraph of this section:

- Is it possible that someday insurance derivatives and securitized catastrophe risks will evolve into a significant new assets and liabilities class?

To answer this question one has to address another issue:

- What makes such contracts attractive from an investment standpoint?

One answer is the potential market of the instruments. Figure 9.3 shows three curves projected by Swiss Re. In their background is a scenario for direct securitization and exchange trading in insurance derivatives. Notice that the securitization curve rises faster than that of over-the-counter deals promoting the concept of catastrophe exchanges—but then it bends.

The pros also say that, after all, this market is not revolutionary because investors have always participated, albeit indirectly, in catastrophe risks. They have done so by buying insurance. However, despite similarities the new investment vehicles display major differences compared to classical insurance and reinsurance solutions.

Let me iterate in one paragraph the message sections 2, 3, and 4 have brought to the reader. The potential of credit derivatives linked to catastrophe insurance comes from their ability to function as a flexible complement to other instruments.

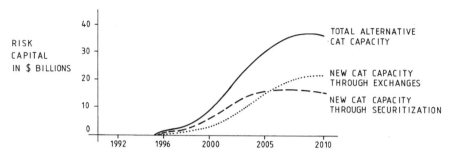

Used by permission of Swiss Re, Sigma *No. 5/1996*

FIGURE 9.3 A SIMULATION MADE BY SWISS RE OF THE POSSIBLE RISK CAPITAL MARKET FOR CATASTROPHE (CAT) INSTRUMENT

What is still to be established is how much the risks embedded in these different insurance-based products correlate. Until this is done in a convincing manner, investors will not rush to CAT securities because diversification is not proven.

Also to be tested through a real market response is the attraction presented by investment vehicles whose returns are determined directly and solely by the loss pattern related to natural catastrophes. Such products will offer an above-average yield potential but in all likelihood will have high volatility and a still unknown pattern of risk.

5. CONTRARIAN OPINIONS TO THE SECURITIZATION OF CATASTROPHE INSURANCE

One of the reasons why some financial analysts think that it is not possible to design catastrophe insurance instruments with practically zero correlation to other financial risks is that major natural catastrophes influence market psychology. By extension they could affect the behavior of the financial market as a whole.

Other analysts (contrarians to the idea of credit derivatives based on catastrophe insurance) suggest that when major earthquakes and hurricanes hit, the nerve of the investors for securitized catastrophe insurance will wane. This is, however, without regard to the stamina of investors like Warren Buffett.

After the troubles-plagued Lloyds of London withdrew from the California earthquake market, Berkshire Hathaway stepped in. When asked the probability of an earthquake hitting California, Warren Buffett answered that this is not a probability, it is a certainty. The question is simply when. But while waiting for the day of the apocalypse, Berkshire gains a very good cash flow, and in a worst-case scenario the losses will represent about 1 percent of Berkshire's net worth—which is affordable.

Warren Buffett's argument makes sense. Indirectly, it also suggests that the parties interested in credit derivatives will principally be large institutional investors who can afford the aftershocks of a major bankruptcy. At least, this is the market at present targeted by the pros. Such investors already participate, or plan to participate, over the counter in certain catastrophe risks (for instance, buying bonds whose interest or principal payments depend on the loss pattern).

As section 2 suggested, a basic issue behind securitized insurance policies is that a significant cover gap in traditional earthquake risk exists because there are limits to insurability. Through simulation, major insurers have calculated the theoretically best weight of catastrophe risks in an efficient investment portfolio, for various target returns, and the results seem convincing.

Swiss Re published a well-done study that brings into perspective an interesting parallel to the securitization process in the banking sector.[2] Based on this concept, Figure 9.4 helps in answering contrarian opinions about the issuance of catastrophe securities via the capital market.

The pro faction argues that from both viewpoints (insurance and investments), there are good long-term prospects for alternative means of transferring catastrophe risks to the financial markets. Contrarians answer that this is an optimistic judgment that has as much to do with current challenges in insurance as with future investment potential.

---

[2] Sigma Press No. 5, 1996, Swiss Re, Zurich.

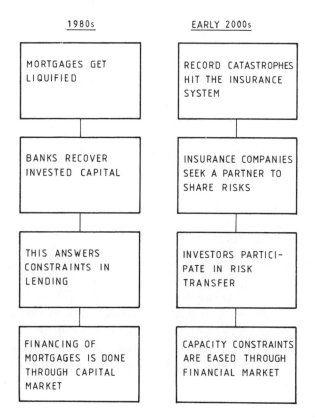

1980s · EARLY 2000s

| MORTGAGES GET LIQUIFIED | RECORD CATASTROPHES HIT THE INSURANCE SYSTEM |

| BANKS RECOVER INVESTED CAPITAL | INSURANCE COMPANIES SEEK A PARTNER TO SHARE RISKS |

| THIS ANSWERS CONSTRAINTS IN LENDING | INVESTORS PARTICI-PATE IN RISK TRANSFER |

| FINANCING OF MORTGAGES IS DONE THROUGH CAPITAL MARKET | CAPACITY CONSTRAINTS ARE EASED THROUGH FINANCIAL MARKET |

FIGURE 9.4 PARALLEL PROCESSES: THE SECURITIZATION OF MORTGAGE-BACKED FINANCING IN THE 1980S AND OF CATASTROPHE INSURANCE IN THE COMING YEARS

Contrarians also point out that the investment level required to share the risks of major catastrophes will not emerge overnight and eventually it will taper off. Swiss Re, however, has reached the conclusion that before tapering off, this market will reach a respectable volume in number of contracts and invested money.

To my judgment, there is a market for the products under discussion but how big this market might become will depend not only on salesmanship but also, primarily, on the risk profile of catastrophe and supercatastrophe derivative instruments. Along this line of reasoning, financial analysts are getting busy to study

- The volatility-induced risks and the (historical) returns of the asset classes that will be proposed to investors, and

- The correlation structure among the individual securities that will provide a pattern of independent market behavior.

This brings us back to our discussion of correlation. If the pattern being studied suggests that stocks and bonds don't correlate with CAT and supercatCAT derivatives, then the inclusion of catastrophe risks as a new alternative investment opens opportunities for portfolio management. Asset managers always look for a portfolio mix through either of two criteria:

- A higher return for each level of risk or

- A lower risk for each level of expected return.

The keywords in investment today are *return, security,* and *diversification.* As section 6 shows, nobody should expect an exaggerated engagement in insurance derivatives or securitized catastrophe risks. The major investors are quite sharp in choosing instruments that promote return on investment while lowering the total risk.

6. BANKERS, TREASURERS, AND INVESTORS MUST ALWAYS BE CONCERNED ABOUT DIVERSIFICATION

Among the few relatively reliable predictions about the way financial markets may evolve is that both the kind and the degree of adjustment will depend primarily on how the different players act and react to risk diversification and exposure management. Credit risk is an integral part of this reference, and insurance customers may have more to say than the insurance companies themselves regarding the guarantees to be obtained from the capital markets.

Globalization will also play a major role. It is expected that the abolition of market barriers to domestic and foreign insurance companies will mean the appearance of new key players wanting to take advantage of the additional entrepreneurial freedoms.

The empirical evidence from industries that are already largely deregulated, like banking, supports this view. But insurance customers may also wish to see some sort of prudential supervision and legal clauses to guarantee that their claims will be honored.

Banking is a good example of an industry where the lack of a legal framework (for instance, in emerging markets) amplified the crisis, while effective supervision has given confidence to investors, particularly in connection to credit risk.

A strong regulatory framework and a first-class legal system that is independent of government interference are pluses for the globalized market. The assessment of an insurer's solvency is not only done by supervisory authorities but also by rating agencies, brokers, customers, and others. Usually, this centers on the adequacy of the insurer's capital funds and the ethics of its management. Even from an internal company viewpoint, it is important to have the necessary capital and a watchful board (see also Chapter 10 on solvency control).

Every factor mentioned in the preceding paragraph has a role to play. One of the problems with evaluations made in a broad sense is that many people confuse the action by a supervisory authority with management responsibility exercised by the board and by senior executives.

- The management of a firm (not the regulators) is responsible for running its day-to-day and longer-term business.
- Supervisors do not get into the insurance company's operations management. They set the rules and watch to be sure that they are observed.

To run any business in an effective manner, the board should keep exposure under lock and key. Senior management must understand what is happening and why it is happening, in every corner of the enterprise. It must also be sure that it made a well-documented decision by evaluating the aftermath, then rethinking the basics of the original decision and learning a lesson from the results.

Years ago I was a consultant to the chairman of a large financial group who was more concerned that the presidents of his banks made factual and documented decisions than that they were always "right" in their choices. The rationale has been that the market changes and while, at its time, a given decision may be correct, over time it may prove to be the wrong one because the market may turn on its head.

What I just said about insurance companies and banks is equally valid with investors. All parties should care about the diversification in their portfolio holdings. A golden rule is no more than 5 percent of assets in any one investment, no matter how promising it is. The market for credit derivatives based on catastrophe insurance comes from the fact that there are not so many distinct asset classes around in which to invest, and a low one-digit number in percent share might be an acceptable level.

Institutions should diversify their investments in a way that they feel safe with the distribution of risks. Let me take as a practical example what one of the major Swiss banks stated about the risk distribution in its lending portfolio.

- Banks and other institutions accounted for 53 percent of the lines of credit.
- Commercial borrowers accounted for 36 percent.
- Private borrowers accounted for 6 percent.
- The remaining 5 percent consisted of public-sector entities.

How diversified is this distribution of credit lines? A critic would suggest that the institution in reference was overexposed to correspondent banks. Lending and investing more than half the assets in one single sector of the economy is not a prudent policy. To the contrary, the 6 percent level allocated to private borrowers was underweight in an overall sense.

If the institution in this example wanted to diversify the 53 percent level, credit derivatives based on catastrophe insurance might have been one of the bets. While this should be done on a thoroughly calculated basis, and even then it would not diminish the 53 percent a great deal, it still would amount to a reallocation of resources—probably bringing the percentage referred to a little below 50.

This is not unreasonable inasmuch as many banks have entered the insurance business, either only by selling insurance policies in their branches or through equity in insurance companies—the merger of Credit Suisse and Winterthur as well as Citibank and Travelers being two examples. Provided they are not highly leveraged, securitized CAT policies are a reasonable extension of what already takes place.

Diversification should characterize not only instruments and counterparties but also policies on time brackets. In the case of the above mentioned Swiss bank, senior management was sensitive to time limits: Three quarters of the risk exposure expired in less than one year; 18 percent in one to five years; and 7 percent in more than five years.

The geographical distribution, too, is important. In the case of the institution in reference, Swiss borrowers accounted for 18 percent of the credit lines utilized; 41 percent was drawn by borrowers in other European countries; 25 percent and 2 percent, respectively, by counterparties in North and South America; and 14 percent by clients in East Asia—which is a big share.

The criteria of a distributed portfolio that I used in this example (counterparties, instruments, time brackets, and geography in a global market) apply hand-in-glove to credit derivatives at large and, more specifically, to catastrophe derivatives. Within the percentage of assets allocated to this new instrument there should also be diversification. Therefore, the investor is well advised to add to the inventory of products that he examines, prior to commitment, more alternatives such as those to be presented in Chapter 10.

CHAPTER 10

New Derivatives Instruments, Hedging Policies, and Credit Rating Agencies

1. INTRODUCTION

Chapter 9 asked whether securitized catastrophe risks could evolve into a significant new assets-and-liabilities category. This chapter follows up by posing the same query in connection to instruments with a different underlier, like weather derivatives and energy derivatives.

In comparison to owning the assets of companies in the insurance and energy business, investment vehicles whose returns are determined directly and solely by a certain event, such as a given weather pattern, offer opportunities. As we already saw, the inclusion of credit derivatives based on some type of catastrophe risk provides new possibilities to investors who know how to keep exposure under control.

Besides the financing of major risks, insurers have other reasons to be interested in a market for catastrophe derivatives. The 1990s have been characterized by falling prices for catastrophe coverage. This is an indication of excess insurance capacity, which leads to

- All sorts of offers by insurers, designed to defend or expand their market in a globalized economy, and

- The consolidation of the industry, which aims to weed out over-capacity while swamping costs.

The dual challenge for insurers is to achieve globalization while saving on costs rather than incurring new ones. Costs matter, and important savings will be instrumental in preventing a deterioration of underwriting results.

The securitization of insurance policies is seen by insurers in a positive light because it brings a big chunk of the administrative costs to somebody else. But to appeal to different market segments, the offering of derivative instruments must be focused. Weather derivatives and energy derivatives will be examined from this perspective.

2. THE SENSE OF WEATHER DERIVATIVES

One of the basic tests for an insurance contract is that a future uncertain contingency has to occur. In this sense weather derivatives can be considered as contracts of insurance because an event needs to occur before the contract is activated.

- As long as payment must be made on the basis that a party has suffered a loss, the contract is a form of insurance.
- A reasonable paradigm is the reinsurance for catastrophic property and casualty (P&C) risks, as it is practiced today.

Weather derivatives are among the instruments showing that financial products are in full evolution. If an investor can buy a derivatives contract based on an index, why not do so with one that has as underlying the *probability* of a hurricane? In fact, since 1997 an investor can buy or sell a contract whose value depended entirely on events such as fluctuations in temperature and accumulations of rain or snow.

Weather derivatives based on rain probability pay out, for instance, if the amount of rainfall at a specified location ranges between 30 and 50 centimeters from November 1 through March 31. By writing such contracts, the insurer helps himself by providing for future claims by policyholders.

Other weather derivatives contracts might be written by farming enterprises that suffer from extreme weather conditions. Whichever the purpose of hedging by the writer, such contracts should be based on rigorous analysis and the offer to be made must be examined from many angles by means of mathematical models.

Major farming enterprises, particularly in the United States, are by now well acquainted with derivative financial instruments used for hedging. The agricultural industry has been very hard hit by a record number of natural catastrophes from floods to droughts, which have raised the question of the limits to survivability. Potential losses from severe storms and flood risks can be effectively hedged within the traditional system of derivative products— but new instruments focus on credit characteristics by guaranteeing, under certain weather conditions, the loans the farmer has taken from the bank.

The best way to look at weather derivatives is that they are becoming part of the business of custom-packaging securities to provide price insurance or credit insurance against events that may be financial or strictly physical (for instance, excessive rainfall in the wrong season, an unexpected off-season hail, or temperatures well above or below normal).

Events may also be mixed in both physical and financial senses because extreme weather conditions create a severe drop in income so the agricultural enterprise or single farmer can no longer face its financial obligations.

In the past insurers have offered some form of protection, but the way people think about risk and return becomes more sophisticated while (as shown in Chapter 9) insurance companies are poised to tap the capital markets as a guarantor of their risks. This will not happen without challenges.

On the one hand, there is always the risk of mispricing, which exists with all products, financial or physical. But on the other hand, because of their internal information in estimating risk events, insurers have latitude in figuring their underwriting risks and results. This second factor makes it difficult for investors, who are not privy to the information the insurers have, to calculate the true risks taken by the underwriter and the costs he tries to recover.

- Some estimating errors may be innocent, but others may be intended or even excessive.

- When estimating errors sneak in, the consequences go directly into earnings.

These two bullets have a message for both parties: the clients and the underwriters. Sharp financial analysts might be able to detect pricing errors but, in general, investors cannot do so—being obliged to accept or reject what is presented. If they accept, they may eventually discover that virtually all surprises in insurance are unpleasant ones.

Section 3 will bring this argument forward by paying attention to hidden costs. Let me, however, make a general statement prior to that discussion. An often mentioned example is the bankruptcy of Barings because of gambling with the Nikkei Index of futures and options. But a general condemnation of derivative instruments based on such cases is similar to the decision of a judge placing the blame for cancer from smoking on the tobacco industry as a whole.

3. RISKS ASSOCIATED WITH HURRICANE DERIVATIVES

As their name implies, the value of hurricane derivatives is linked to hurricane events. These are a new financial instrument that can be dangerous to investors unfamiliar with the insurance business at large and, most specifically, with natural catastrophes. Section 2 already suggested that pricing risks magnify the chance of unpleasant surprises.

Investors interested in hurricane derivatives bet on the fact that there are good years and bad years in insurance. The premium covering hurricane events is high, but the aftermath of this natural hazard involves both property damage and corporate damage or even deaths.

Part of the interest in this instrument comes from the fact that the potential market for hurricane derivatives is bigger than the insurance business currently contracted for extreme weather events, because the large majority of these losses are not insured.

Analysts think that hurricane derivatives might dramatically increase the coverage ratio and the risks. If hurricane derivatives are sold to the public, rather than only to institutional investors, this will recreate a sort of "names"—the names of unknown, relatively small underwriters—on which Lloyds based its financial strengths.

Credit derivatives designed for the hurricane insurance market aim to shift the risks to those better able to absorb them. They also expand the pool of risk coverage to encompass those not traditionally involved in catastrophe insurance—which is becoming a necessity.

While prevention measures are now available and insurance companies ask for higher deductibles, as Chapter 9 has shown, the number of natural and man-made catastrophes rises because of the steady increase of population density and a greater concentration of assets in industrialized nations.

In the 1990s, a succession of hurricanes and earthquakes hit areas where property values were high and insurers lost money. From Hurricane Hugo in 1990 through the Northridge earthquake in southern California in 1994 to Hurricane Bonnie in late August 1998, insurance companies worldwide have sustained billions of dollars of claims.

Insurance companies have insufficient capital to cover the mounting risks of natural catastrophes—and this can lead to deteriorating credit.

The rapidly increasing cost of insurance coverage is shown in Figure 10.1, which compares nine years of the 1970s to nine years in the late 1980s and early 1990s. Statistics show that both the mean and the variance of insurance costs have increased significantly, posing evident problems to the P&L of insurance firms.

We are in an epoch of climatic change, leading to an increase in the uncertainty related to the level of claims. Hurricane derivatives, and the insurance industry as a whole, must take into consideration the possibility of a higher average claims burden with substantial volatility from year to year. The likelihood of an uncertain event is high. This requires better accident knowledge with assessment of future risks because of suspected climatic changes, while at the same time it alters existing risk/returns ratios and leads to higher premium rates.

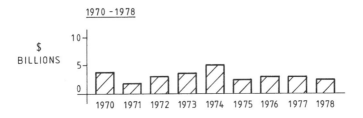

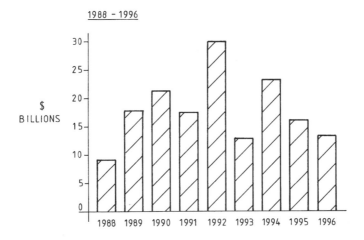

FIGURE 10.1 THE RAPIDLY INCREASING COST OF INSURANCE COVERAGE ($ BILLIONS IN 1996 PRICES)

To appreciate the pricing decisions that enter in the setting of rates, it is proper to recall that insurance losses comprise not only cash flows and disbursements but also ways and means to control what must be paid out. Claims are sometimes extravagant and, at an increasing rate, differences are settled in court.

Precisely, because of the complexity of the instrument, its risk, and its return, investors in hurricane derivatives who rely on representations of salesmen, rather than on underwriting knowledge of their own, can awake with rude surprises fairly equivalent to that of the "names" in London's Lloyds. To my judgment, investing in derivatives of extreme events should be done only through risk capital.

The pros suggest that hurricane derivatives would not be a first for the "innocent" investors. Some of them have already come into the reinsurance business without exact knowledge of what they obtain, by means of purchasing catastrophe bonds—which is a misnomer. A true bond obliges the issuer to pay, but catastrophe bonds are contracts that lay a provisional promise to pay on the *purchaser.*

This is one of the convoluted arrangements that took on, so to speak, a life of its own because the promoters of the contracts wished to circumvent laws that prohibit the writing of insurance by entities that have not been licensed by the state. Another benefit for these promoters was that calling the insurance contract a "bond" led unsophisticated buyers to assume that these instruments involve far less risk than is actually the case.

Calculations involving monster hurricanes and earthquakes are rather fuzzy, and the best one can do is to estimate a range of probabilities for such events. Because of the rarity of these catastrophes, the lack of precise data plays into the hands of promoters who may employ an expert to advise the potential buyer about the probability of losses. The expert usually receives an upfront payment no matter how inaccurate his predictions and his assurances.

As these examples document, whether they recognize it or not, investors have a major problem: Outstanding risks do exist in many contracts if they are not properly priced. Thoroughly read contracts prior to commitment. A particular characteristic of hurricane derivatives, and of catastrophe insurance at large, is that mispricing may not be discovered for a long time—until it is too late.

4. WHAT'S THE USE OF ENERGY DERIVATIVES?

Energy derivatives may be in the margin of discussions on new financial instruments involving credit risk. Some analysts believe that energy derivatives will offer investors a way to take advantage of the differences in credit pricing in the multiple sectors of the energy industry.

Before taking a look at this subject, a word of caution. As with all financial products, risk measurement and management connected to energy derivatives is key to long-term success. Damage control functions become more important with instruments that are new (so experience with them is thin) and whose default rates could rise significantly, wiping out the benefits of a great return.

Credit derivatives, catastrophe derivatives, and energy derivatives benefit from the fact that sophisticated tools to manage risk not only are available but also are reaching general acceptance (see Part Two). There is no lack of tools and methods. The need is for cultural change in the way in which investment professionals use innovative models to measure and manage their credit risks.

As we have seen with other financial products, the estimation of loss reserves and correct pricing are most crucial. This is also true with both publicly offered and privately placed energy derivatives. Measures of assessment of potential exposure include off-balance-sheet market risk as well as the analysis of counterparty risk employed in derivative contracts through an in-depth portfolio risk evaluation.

Like the insurance market, the electricity and other energy products market may not be an easy nut to crack because it requires fundamental knowledge leading to deeper industry understanding. But as electricity markets are deregulated throughout the world, a real business opportunity might be in this sector.

According to some fairly reliable accounts, in the early part of the 21st century, electricity may become one of the largest commodity markets in the world. Some analysts make a similar statement regarding gas and oil markets. As an example of energy market valuation,

- The U.S. wholesale gas market stands at about $30 billion, and domestic oil amounts to $50 billion.
- Electricity accounts for $95 billion, 1.2 percent of U.S. gross national product.

At present, derivatives in the electricity market are less developed than those in the insurance market, even though, according to some estimates, the electricity market stands to become larger in the long run. Hence, it is no wonder that many analysts currently work to unlock the wealth that may be hidden in the energy derivatives box.

New electricity derivatives, the experts say, are a function of the deregulation of the cash market for electricity. A freely operating cash market will be a great boost for derivative financial instruments.

The companies best placed to take advantage of this market are those having a long horizon. General Electric, a manufacturer of power producing equipment, is one of the big firms taking the long view. Over the past decade it has weathered plenty of unforeseen events in many of its product lines. Any large global company is used to some market somewhere either underperforming or overperforming—and the same is true of institutional investors.

Knowledgeable financial analysts consider energy derivatives to be a better hedge than insurance derivatives because the correlation with other financial instruments is trivial. This does not mean that there will be no surprises (as evidenced by the energy crisis in the 1980s), but it does mean that there are managerial prerequisites to be met.

The board and senior management of a company well tooled to reap business opportunities in the coming years will be well advised to take a rigorous attitude to analytical studies. Another precaution is to have some cash cows that financially sustain the long-term move. Investors in the financial markets are never fans of long-term pain, no matter what justification there is for it.

5. NEW PRODUCT DEVELOPMENT FAVORS CREDIT DERIVATIVES

Despite negative press reports on risks associated with derivatives, customer demand keeps climbing. Therefore, arguments that the market for this or that type of derivatives has become decreamed or even saturated appear overblown. This includes the markets for credit derivatives, weather derivatives, and energy derivatives.

If anything, the appeal of virtual financial instruments seems to grow, which is one of the factors attracting new capital into what could be seen as a self-feeding cycle. While American banks are still the leaders, many continental European banks have stepped up their presence in the derivatives market, some going through acquisitions of investment banks in London, while others bid up the price of specialist personnel.

Aggressive specialist acquisition is one of the gears behind this self-feeding cycle. It sees to it that dealers in the OTC market work hard to make effective use of their capital base and to gain big commissions. They are leveraging their existing capital by using collateral and netting agreements widely, developing their business through aggressive marketing.

Contrarians are not convinced that this is a wise policy. They particularly resent one of the arguments with insurance derivatives that the addition of catastrophe risks to a portfolio increases the potential return while simultaneously lowering risk.

Using order of magnitude statistics, Figure 10.2 visualizes the aforementioned idea by contrasting a portfolio of stocks and bonds

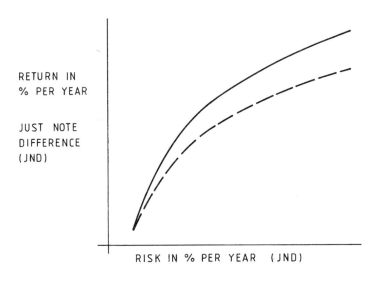

FIGURE 10.2 PORTFOLIO RETURN UNDER TWO INVESTMENT HYPOTHESES, SUGGESTED BY AN INSURER

to one that includes a reasonable amount of catastrophe risk. This graph is "right" only when the associated risk factor is also shown—which many financial reports don't do. Even if it is shown, these exposures are not right for private conservative investors.

The value of the graph in Figure 10.2 comes from the fact that big deals in derivatives are done among an exclusive club of large companies, whose number dwindles as a result of mergers and acquisitions. This turns our discussion back to the opposite viewpoints expressed in Chapter 1, as in the bottom line there is concentration of counterparty risk.

Analysts who subscribe to this school of thought don't fail to point to the existing evidence: the greater demand for collateral in the OTC market as well as margining. But there is an opposite shift in market emphasis found in the extension of maturities in OTC deals. As late as 1994, it was difficult to strike a deal with a maturity beyond 10 years. Now it is not uncommon to see maturities of 20 years, with 30 years also on the horizon.

Still another interesting switch in market behavior is that, more than ever before, dealers are focusing effort on new product development, where higher margins can sometimes be obtained. With this comes emphasis in the emerging products—rather than emerging markets—where derivative structures are being used to allow investors to

- Confront counterparty risk more efficiently than otherwise possible,
- Circumvent restrictive trading or ownership rules, and
- Overcome difficult custody or settlement arrangements.

Not only banks but also treasuries of manufacturing and merchandising companies confront credit risks. The primary means of distribution of most personal computer vendors, for example, are third-party resellers. In its 1996 annual report, Compaq noted that in monitoring and managing the credit extended to resellers, it limits credit risk by

- Broadening distribution channels,

- Obtaining security interest, and
- Utilizing risk transfer instruments.

Manufacturing companies are less exposed than agricultural firms to natural catastrophes, but they are not alien to risk transfer solutions. Treasurers in the manufacturing industry are very sharp on hedging market risks like currency and interest rate exposure, as well as credit risks.

Counterparty exposures connected to manufacturing and merchandising might one day become an underlier. Any manufacturer's business could be adversely affected in the event that the condition of third-party resellers worsens. For instance, upon the financial failure of a major reseller, a PC manufacturer could experience both disruptions in distribution and loss of the unsecured portion of outstanding accounts receivable.

Globalization (particularly the expansion of manufacturing operations in emerging countries and the expansion of sales into economically and politically volatile areas) subjects the manufacturer to a number of economic and political risks:

- Currency control measures,
- A debt moratorium (as in Russia in August 1998),
- Expropriation of local investments, and
- Financial instability among resellers.

Compaq notes that it has generally experienced longer accounts receivable cycles in emerging markets—in particular, China and Latin America—compared to U.S. and European markets. In the event that accounts receivable cycles in these markets lengthen further or one or more of the large resellers in these regions fail, the manufacturer is adversely affected.

This underlines the wisdom of steadily evaluating business operations, taking measures to limit credit risks, but also using new financial instruments for hedging. Prudence dictates that boards and senior managers should err on the side of caution. Many business conditions are under Murphy's law: Anything that can go wrong will do so.

6. THE ROLE TRADE ASSOCIATIONS AND RATING AGENCIES PLAY IN CREDIT RISKS

Chapter 9 told how regulators' actions give confidence to the financial markets because investors feel that excesses will be checked through prudent supervision. Insurance supervision in America is by the individual states. Regulators increasingly concentrate on solvency control, while they continue checking material aspects of the insurance business.

The National Association of Insurance Commissioners (NAIC) has been instrumental in obtaining a reasonable degree of homogeneity in rules. Its activities aim at stricter solvency control and also facilitating individual state licensing and supervision.

This issue of stricter solvency control needs attention. Solvency control is assured under NAIC's new risk-based capital regulations, whose goal is to determine the amount of minimum capital requirement on the basis of underwriting risks, investment risks, credit risks, and derivatives risks.

A second important development is that in a manner similar to policies followed in the banking industry, insurance companies are now coming under the scrutiny of independent rating agencies. At present, 13 of the 100 biggest reinsurers worldwide have an AAA rating. There is, however, a selective choice of rated insurers. Only companies expecting an advantage from voluntary ratings submit to this procedure, for which they pay.

Qualified solvency ratings are also nonvoluntary ratings based on a standard statistical evaluation of ratios taken from the annual reports to the supervisory offices. In the United States, these are drawn up in accordance with Statutory Accounting Principles (SAP). Nonvoluntary evaluations are carried out at the company level, but (unlike voluntary ratings) they do not benefit from internal information.

For qualified solvency ratings in the insurance industry, only three categories have been used so far. Of the 100 biggest reinsurers worldwide, 84 are rated by Standard & Poor's as *secure*, which means BBB or better. The financial strength of nine other companies is BB, while four are classified as vulnerable and three companies are not rated.

Three independent agencies (A.M. Best, Moody's, and Standard & Poor's) are active in rating insurance companies. A.M. Best, the oldest agency for insurance ratings in the United States, was established in 1899. Its ratings, produced at the request of the insurer being rated, are based on publicly available information as well as on internal meetings with senior management. Besides U.S. insurers, foreign companies operating internationally are also rated. For both American and foreign firms A.M. Best uses standard ratios regarding profitability, capitalization, and liquidity.

These are supplemented with qualitative information on spread of risk, reinsurance, quality of investments, diversification of investments, loss reserves, adequacy of equity capital, and capital structure. Quality of management also plays a key role.

Moody's financial strength ratings are made mainly on demand with the agreement of the insurance company being rated. The results are published. As with A.M. Best, Moody's ratings are based on publicly available information and on additional internal meetings with senior management.

Moody's assessment reflects an analysis of the competitive situation, regulatory trends, adequacy of equity capital, investment risks, profitability, liquidity, group interrelationships, products, distribution channels, and quality of management.

Standard & Poor's offers three types of ratings: claims-paying ability ratings (CPA), qualified solvency ratings, and Insurance Solvency International (ISI) ratings. ISI used to be an independent firm, but has been an affiliate of S&P since 1990.

ISI ratings are nonvoluntary. They are assigned to non-U.S. companies without a CPA rating. These ratings are done on the initiative of S&P and based solely on published information. This information is used to calculate standard ratios. Points and weighting factors are allocated based on these ratios. The evaluation also includes some qualitative factors.

The claims-paying ability ratings of S&P are produced worldwide at the request of the insurer being rated. The customer pays for the study. These ratings are based on (1) both quantitative and qualitative analyses of all publicly available information, (2) personal meetings with senior management, and (3) confidential internal information.

The analysis done by S&P for rating purposes considers industry risk, underwriting results, investment policy, interest rate risk management, capitalization, liquidity, and financial flexibility as well as management and corporate strategy and the results of a business review. This is a first-class reference because such information is vital in evaluating credit derivatives risks.

The careful reader will appreciate the distinction rating agencies make between voluntary and nonvoluntary ratings of insurance firms. The former are done on request, with the agreement of the rated company and at its expense; the latter take place without its agreement.

Voluntary ratings allow access to internal information and generally involve direct contact with senior management. But whether on a voluntary or nonvoluntary basis, each company is rated individually through a uniform procedure. This is a good basis that offers dependable results. It is the sort of basis that should be required for all derivative financial products.

PART

THREE

Models for the Evaluation and Management of Credit Risk

CHAPTER 11

The Art of Modeling Credit Risk and Its Analytics

1. INTRODUCTION

Rigorous mathematical analysis has revolutionized the management of market risk. Now it becomes fashionable to model credit risk, capitalizing on the market risk experience of the last few years. This is further encouraged by the fact that the use of credit derivatives leads to reshaping the lending culture—and this requires a great deal of analysis.

Banks get increasingly preoccupied with *risk-adjusted earnings* and with a rigorous evaluation of single-transaction exposure. Risk-adjusted pricing of loans and bonds, which accounts for counterparty risk and interest rate risk, aims at restructuring both concepts and algorithms used in connection to the supply and demand for financial services. It also requires revamping the pricing equation.

Another aspect of risk-adjusted earnings is the distinction increasingly made between expected losses, unexpected losses, and catastrophic losses due to credit risk. We will take a close look at this concept in sections 4 through 6 in connection with Actuarial Credit Risk Accounting. What underpins this approach is the ability to mark to model credit risk when marking to market is not feasible.

Marking to market and marking to model are new, important disciplines both for risk management and for substantiating a process of price formation, but models are only one of the pillars on which analytical solutions are based. The other is the system approach necessary for effective credit risk and market risk management:

- First appreciating that credit risk and market risk up to a point overlap, while credit risk is the long-term view of market risk.

- Then understanding what credit derivatives can do to long-term credit risk and why this is feasible.

In principle, a mathematical model for counterparty risk should take into account credit risk over an extended time frame, 10 years being a first step. The challenge to incorporating unexpected losses is to spot a developing risk and put a figure on that risk.

To help the reader appreciate what needs to be done and how to work with the tools at his or her disposal, this chapter starts with a brief reminder of the method that has classically been used in lending. Accounting for reserves is the way the banker always worked. It is also the new way by means of different, more sophisticated tools.

Let me add one more introductory remark to the modeling theme. No algorithm and no methodology will solve all of the risk control problems. Neither will a certain model, no matter how sophisticated, be ever "final" in its structure. New problems always show up and need to be attacked with an open mind.

The global bond crisis preceding the near bankruptcy of LTCM, in September 1998, turned out to be an 8-standard-deviation extreme event—a concept unknown to the usual normal distribution approach. The market for junk-bond-level corporates collapsed and their interest rates spiked to 570 basis points over Treasuries. This makes pricing of corporate loans haphazardous at best, and brings into the spotlight the likelihood of a severe loss in capital. No existing model would have handled that event.

The stock market, too, presents extreme events. In the crash of October 1987, the event was 15 standard deviations, almost double the bond market extreme event discussed in the preceding paragraph. Banks that now use 5 standard deviations for stress testing would have missed both these events.

2. ACCOUNTING FOR RESERVES

The literature of the accounting profession contains numerous arguments on the use of the word *reserve*. The most basic one is that appropriations of retained income should not be made or displayed in such a manner as to create misleading inferences, as those that can be hidden or put aside through an ill-focused financial reporting practice. For this reason, FASB and other accounting-standards–setting organizations have paid considerable attention to the issue of reporting on reserves.

Since 1949, the Committee on Concepts and Standards of the American Accounting Association has advised that the use of the term *reserve* be limited to reserves that constitute a part of stockholders' equity.

- The term *reserve* should not be employed in published financial statements of business corporations, and
- The *reserve section* in corporate balance sheets must be eliminated and its elements exhibited as deductions from assets or from liabilities, or as retained income.

In the general case, outside of accounting, a reserve is a fund of cash or other assets. According to my Webster's dictionary, the term means, in finance, funds kept on hand to meet demands. But financial reporting for corporations must use the term *reserve* the way regulators define it, rather than as Webster's does.

Accountants use the term *reserve* to caption a variety of balance sheet items including segregated retained income, segregated assets, asset valuation, asset amortization, and liabilities. Occasionally the term is observed on statements of operations, where it is used to warn the reader that an expense has been estimated.

The "reserve section" has been a common feature of published financial statements. It customarily appears between liabilities and capital. The items displayed vary from statement to statement, but in general they have been observed to represent

- Asset valuation and asset amortization items,
- Liabilities, including deferred revenues,
- Appropriated retained income, and
- In some cases, earmarked capital stock premium.

The classification in one section of such heterogeneous balance sheet elements can, however, be misleading. Most asset valuation and asset amortization amounts, established by proper charges to operations, are misclassified unless shown as deductions from the assets to which they relate.

Amounts reserved to provide for anticipated shrinkage in asset values—such as future inventory losses or other losses which, if they do occur, are clearly related to future (not current) operations—are not necessarily proper deduction-from-assets items. Such anticipated losses preferably are disclosed in footnotes to the statements. One of the main issues, however, is that of appropriations of retained income, which generally are of three types:

- Designed to explain managerial policy with regard to prospective or accomplished reinvestment of earnings,
- Intended to restrict dividends as required by law or contract, and
- Reflecting a possible shrinkage in the net resources, providing for anticipated conjectural losses.

Appropriations of retained income whose purpose is to reflect managerial policies relative to earnings retention are ineffective and frequently misleading, unless all retained income that has in fact been committed to operating capital is earmarked. Partial appropriation fosters the implication that retained earnings not earmarked are available for distribution as dividends. The classical approach is that

- Appropriations of retained income required by law or contract preferably should be disclosed by footnotes, and

- If required to be displayed as balance sheet amounts, they should be included in the proprietary section.

Appropriations of retained income reflecting anticipated future losses or conjectural past or present losses preferably should be disclosed by footnotes—particularly when it is not established by reasonably objective evidence that any loss has been incurred. If displayed as balance sheet amounts, such appropriations should be included in the proprietary section.

This is the traditional way in which accounting statements are established and presented. What changes with the prudential management of credit risk and market risk is that appropriations are formally made for longer-term losses and for outliers—which may correspond to a stress loss. As we will see from section 4 onward, this is an integral part of a new method for effective management of credit risk.

3. THE ART CREDIT DEPARTMENTS HAVE BEEN USING

Classically, credit departments have focused on the analysis of counterparty credit quality. Then, based on their findings, they proceeded to approve or reject the transaction and, in the case of approval, to monitor the exposure.

However, as top-tier banks appreciate, it has become increasingly important that credit institutions pay attention to more factors than a simple scoring, not only in order to use their financial resources in the most effective manner possible but also to gain a better understanding and control of counterparty risk. For instance, credit conversion factors are created utilizing simulation techniques.

Underpinning the new, analytical approach to credit risk is the concept that credit resources must be actively managed. There is no lack of means by which dynamic management of credit exposure can be accomplished. Examples are the use of

- Credit risk mitigation through credit derivatives,
- Models for experimentation on changes in exposure,

- Scenario analyses to determine credit quality and areas of potential credit concern, and
- The setting of limits to control different components of credit risk.

A limiting factor in applying analytical approaches is obtaining accurate, timely credit information. Given that lenders' acquisition of information about credit quality is much more problematic for small firms than for large firms, it is not surprising that the ways in which these two groups of clients obtain credit financing differ significantly.

Banks employ a variety of mechanisms to address the information-related problems associated with lending to small borrowers including intensive borrower monitoring and tailored loan contracts. But whether in the retail or in the wholesale loans market, financial institutions typically know how to measure simple risks, not complex risks. This is particularly true of medium-sized banks, corporate treasuries, insurance companies, and pensions funds.

Yet, practically all of these companies engage in complex risks. They assume exposure without the skill to study the aftermath and, as a result, they are often taken by surprise. One of the goals of the modeling approach studied in this chapter is to take away this element of surprise.

Another element that makes credit estimates complex is that up to a point loans, commercial paper, and corporate bonds are instruments competing with one another for the same clients. But the bank loan market differs from the corporate bond market in its emphasis on the lender–borrower relationship. Through the client link, banks may acquire private information over time and use this information to refine the contract terms offered to the borrower.

Increasingly, financial institutions employ data on loans and collateral requirements on lines of credit issued to businesses, to test their clients dependability as the relationship progresses. Then, provided there are covenants attached to the loan, they adjust the contract terms or reexamine prices and other conditions.

These are issues that enter, or at least should enter, into the credit models we examine in this and the following chapters. Failure to account for them makes the mapping of the credit world into the computer weak, because it is removed from reality.

A basic element to be factored into the model is that companies that establish a good, dependable credit record tend to pay lower interest rates. Some research projects estimate this differential at about 60 basis points over a 10-year relationship. Other research has documented that small businesses with long banking relationships are less likely to pledge collateral than those with short relationships.

Based on these premises, the hypothesis of *relationship lending* suggests that it is possible to limit the decline of bank lending, in spite of the fact that securitization and nonbank competition are reducing the share of loans held by banks. What we have so far seen in loan management suggests that lending is, by and large, an art.

- Modeling has the power to change this approach, making credit management as well as the prognostication of reserve requirements much more objective.

- Experimentation made on current and future credit risks can revolutionize the time-honored solution to reserve requirements described in section 2.

One of the novel approaches to the modeling of expected and unexpected credit risk is the Actuarial Credit Risk Accounting (ACRA), which we study in this chapter and in Chapter 12. ACRA is an example of advancements in credit technology providing a basis for legally accumulating reserves to face unexpected credit risks.

To date, when the law of the land and supervisory authorities allow, many institutions keep secret reserves for the rainy day—but so far this has been done largely by rule of thumb. By contrast, a model can offer a fundamental credit risk mitigation technique which is necessary to the financial industry.

This does not mean that ACRA and CreditMetrics, which lies in its origin, are the ideal credit risk models. Far from that, they are still relatively primitive (see Chapters 12 and 13), but they are first steps. For instance, as shown in Figure 11.1, a major shortcoming of

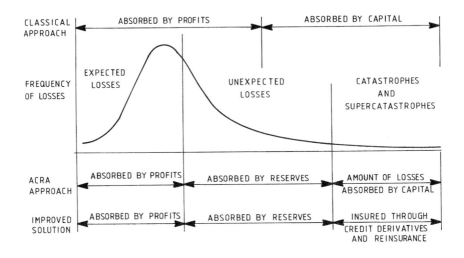

FIGURE 11.1 CLASSICAL APPROACH, ACRA APPROACH, AND AN IMPROVED SOLUTION TO UNEXPECTED AND EXTRAORDINARY RISKS

ACRA is that it does not consider credit derivatives and reinsurance for CAT and superCAT (we will see another major failure in Chapter 16).

A well-designed model will also account for the fact that in the context of credit risk, a growing number of commercial banks have been successful in pricing traditional loan products according to credit quality. Therefore, it will make rating and management quality critical factors (see Chapter 10). This policy is increasingly challenging for financial institutions, because it requires not only models but also accurate input data.

It is only normal that institutions active in managing credit portfolios in a dynamic manner employ an increasing array of credit risk models. These act as a magnifying glass when examining the counterparty's creditworthiness. This goes beyond credit proper, bringing into the picture the need for active management of the bank's financial resources.

In conclusion, dynamic credit risk mitigating solutions are necessary for many reasons including the fact that the rapid expansion of the derivatives market has led to an industrywide increase in credit-sensitive business. Parallel to this comes the introduction of complex financial instruments as well as products with long maturities.

4. MEASURING LOAN LOSSES ON A STATISTICAL BASIS

The concept that risk is inexorably associated with any loan is as old as the practice of loans itself. During the last four decades, scoring systems have been devised to give a hindsight to the dependability of a counterparty. In the 1980s, expert systems were introduced to help loan officers in screening applicants.

However, not until the first draft of the Basle Committee's Market Risk Amendment, in April 1993, did the banking industry see consistent attempts to measure and analyze the risk of losses on a rigorous statistical basis. While this work largely concerned market risk, the fact that the central banks of the Group of Ten stood behind it opened new vistas and provided tools that migrated into credit risk.

Derivative financial instruments and the globalization of financial markets have been instrumental in creating the new pattern that now develops in loans. The profits banks derive from lending have become subject to a very significant volatility year by year, making it difficult for investors and analysts to assess the efficiency of the bank. At the same time, significant provisions cannot be made without the supervisors looking the other way, as well as without consideration of banking secrecy. This leads to the need for new regulations and for the development and use of analytical models capable of estimating credit risk.

The quantitative thinking promoted by the Basle Committee of Banking Supervision has in the mid-1990s led to a quantum leap in the analysis of provisions necessary for problem loans. Loan losses have been examined under a new perspective that is quantitative and qualitative at the same time.

Like a good manager who asks himself, What are my alternatives?, bankers started to rethink their options. This process is the result of heavy loan losses due to a weak economic growth and cyclical lows, coupled with serious structural problems in individual industries plus the collapse of the real estate market in most G-10 countries.

We have already spoken of the rise in credit risk (see Chapter 8). The compound effect of this rise led to defaults by borrowers which significantly increased long-term provision requirements. The trend is dramatized in Figure 11.2. The same situation, however,

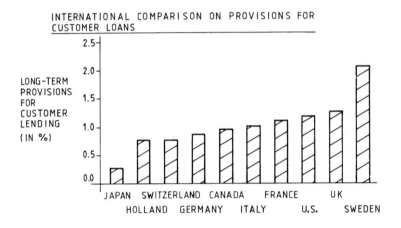

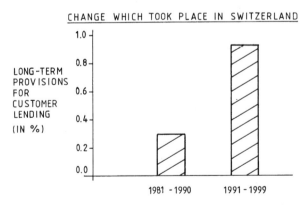

FIGURE 11.2 THE CHANGE IN CREDIT RISK PROFILE FROM THE 1980S TO THE 1990S AND LONG-TERM PROVISIONS IN GROUP OF TEN COUNTRIES

increased the interest of bankers, treasurers, and investors in analytical solutions.

The careful reader will observe that in spite of the problem loans that have hit the emerging countries from East Asia to Russia to Latin America; the G-10 countries also suffer. There is an earthquake in the Japanese banking industry, as Japanese institutions still score the lowest long-term provisions for loans. As a result, since 1995, there has been a "Japan premium" for interbank loans.

All these situations are important to the management of credit risk because they have been instrumental in ongoing cultural change. While deregulation and globalization have been welcome, during the last few years problem loans have seriously impaired many banks' profitability. The second half of Figure 11.2 gives an example from Switzerland.

Several commercial banks believe that the loan losses of the 1990s are a spike and that these levels will decline in coming years as the economy picks up again. But cognizant financial analysts are convinced that their average credit risk exposure will remain well above the figures experienced during the post–World War II decades of economic boom (see also Chapter 8). This fact closely correlates with the interest tier-1 banks express in modeling credit risk.

While only time will say which one of the aforementioned two hypotheses is right, prudent policies should see to it that provisions for loan losses are calculated dynamically—and that they are adequate.

My guesstimate is that provisions will most likely stabilize at a level considerably higher than the one experienced in the past.

- The growing interest in statistical analysis of loan losses is propelled by the fact that these are now taking new a dimension.
- Neither the size of wholesale loans nor the volatility characterizing interest rate risk can any longer be addressed with old accounting procedures.

This is what induced me to present in section 2 the old but still popular method of accounting for reserves. As we will see in the following sections, this approach is turned on its head as new more analytical techniques are introduced and used by institutions.

5. ACTUARIAL CREDIT RISK ACCOUNTING (ACRA)

The Swiss Bank Corporation (SBC), now merged into the United Bank of Switzerland, is one of the major institutions that revamped the standard used in the calculation of reserves—as well as in risk assessment—in connection to its lending activities. The model acknowledges that in essence the banker's job is not to avoid the risk of nonpayment. Rather, it is to manage the risk being taken in a professional way.

Part of the new philosophy in banking is that loan losses represent events with a statistical probability of materializing. This makes it feasible to apply a quantitative approach and to develop a loan default pattern. SBC chose to follow the strategy insurance companies established a long time ago.

Like insurers, bankers must quantify and manage the financial risks that they accept, using a discounting approach. For the insurer the risk comes from compensation claims; for the banker it comes in the form of loans that are not repaid.

In both cases, sufficient premiums must be received to cover the *expected losses*. The concept banking borrowed from insurance is that actuarial reserves are required to cushion volatility at the level of the effective size of *unexpected failures* or even *supercatastrophes* (see Chapter 9).

- Expected losses are classically assumed to arise as an aftermath of daily business activities.

- Unexpected losses are not unusual, but they fluctuate in time, and they represent bigger amounts of money.

Both expected and unexpected credit losses should be absorbed by the bank in the normal course of its business. However, the ability to distinguish between them is vital to profitability and capitalization. It also permits more accurate measurement of the consequences of decisions regarding exposure.

- Contrary to these two classes of losses, catastrophic losses are spikes (see also Chapter 16). They are improbable extreme scenarios for which there should be adequate provisions.

ACRA regards them as stress losses to be covered by capital. I disagree. Capital should never be put in the front line. Capital is, so to speak, the line of last defense. As I suggested in section 3, CAT and superCAT should be covered through credit derivatives and reinsurance.

Based on this relatively simple concept of cross-fertilization between insurance and banking, an institution can develop a statistically based, dynamic provisioning method that is an improved version of Actuarial Credit Risk Accounting. Among the issues to be found at the core of ACRA is the premise that expected losses can be determined over a period of time and for a specific loan portfolio.

By means of a statistical approach, the expected loss is seen as a reduction of gross income or interest margin. This reduction represents risk cost, and it has a parallel in the way earnings in the lending business are reduced by administrative and other costs (see also Chapter 12).

There is no single best way of calculating expected loss. The figure corresponding to the expected loss in the loan portfolio depends on the risk characteristics of each individual transaction and its counterparty. Like other solutions adopted in the banking industry, the ACRA model has three dimensions:

1. The risk that a borrower will not be able to meet his obligations,
2. The risk that the bank will face at that point in time, and
3. The amount (as a percentage) actually lost after realization of the security, or of bankruptcy proceedings against the customer.

Data streams corresponding to the first dimension can be effectively managed to produce the statistical probability of default by the counterparty. To quantify this risk, ACRA bases its assumptions on the data provided by rating agencies and other sources, which have tracked companies and their defaults over many years (see also Chapter 10).

Another factor affecting the first dimension is general economic data and their impact on bankruptcies. Both current information and prognostications are important, because we must always consider expectations for the future. The outcome is a statistical probability characterizing the likelihood of default.

A modeling procedure will be more accurate if it is focused on the stratification of customers. Each stratum will have a different curve than the one shown in Figure 11.1, because there are major differences between big, medium, and small counterparties (see section 3).

- Each large customer must be considered individually or as part of a one-digit group of similar cases.

If there was no other difference than special conditions and covenants attached to large loans, this would have been enough to justify what the bulleted item suggests. But other reasons too contribute to the heterogeneity of big loans.

- By contrast, loan risk connected to small customers can be treated through sampling and statistical inference.

Say, for example, that a bank observed and recorded loans behavior of 2,000 clients of roughly similar size and activity. Say also that on average, over a given economic cycle, 20 have defaulted on their obligations per year. With a statistical default risk of 1 percent, the chief credit officer could expect 1 out of 100 companies to go bankrupt—but he does not know which company this will be.

All the bank knows through this sampling inspection by attributes of client companies with similar sizes and activities is that it can expect that all of the 2,000 customers have individually a 1 percent probability of default. Assuming, for the sake of an example, that exposure is the same in all cases (for instance, $100,000) and the recovery rate is 40 percent for all of them, the result is an expected loss of $2.0 million per year. This has to be offset for the bank by a *credit risk premium* of $600 per customer.

In case the expected 20 loans go into default, the bank will lose $2.0 million, a fact taken into consideration during the described actuarial procedure. The credit risk premium, of which we will talk much more in the discussion of RAROC (Chapter 14), is essentially a way of buying an insurance policy. Once this system is in operation, the bank can use part of the money to get reinsured.

6. EVENT RISK, EXPECTED LOSSES, AND UNEXPECTED LOSSES

The case that we considered in section 5 made the hypothesis of a uniform loans environment. A more accurate approach would see to it that a population of client firms is stratified by *type of activity* and *size of loan.* Examples of activities include, but are not limited to,

- Mortgages for residential housing,
- Mortgages for business buildings,
- Commercial loans for medium-size companies in manufacturing, and
- Commercial loans for medium-size companies in merchandising.

Each of these categories can be further subdivided into a finergrain classification. For instance, medium-size companies in manufacturing can be separated into consumer products, home appliances, ferrous metals, chemicals, pharmaceuticals, and the like.

The more we focus on the type of company, the smaller becomes the population of companies falling into that class. The laws of large numbers no more apply. Therefore, we have to use distributions able to handle small populations (not just small samples), as we will see in Chapter 12.

No matter how big or how small is the customer class that we are addressing, the algorithm that will evaluate expected loss should definitely incorporate creditor quality. This has to be done when the loan is negotiated because it indicates the insurance premium to be assigned to the transaction (see Chapters 12 and 14).

But there is also a dynamic element to be integrated into this approach. Borrower quality might have changed since the last transaction because of a loan turning sour or *event risk.* If so, credit exposure has to be recalculated even for existing loans.

Nothing said so far about a statistical subdivision of loan clients should be terra incognita to the banker. But while our starting algorithm may be simple, we must keep in mind that a model can be raised to higher levels of sophistication. Let me give an example. A relatively simple way to express expected loss is through the equation

Expected loss = Expected default probability × Expected loss ratio × (Current exposure + Future exposure)   (1)

The basis for the estimates entering into the component parts of equation (1) can be found in publicly available statistics such as those in Standard & Poor's and Moody's. This algorithm talks of counterparty risk, but there are also other risks to be covered, such as transfer risk, which is not considered in equation (1).

Usually institutions use publicly available data. A more accurate approach, however, is to also employ statistics internal to the bank, which can be obtained through database mining. These are more representative of *our* particular bank's type of business, client base, and area of operations in connection to expected default probability and expected loss ratio.

Accuracy will be increased if we stratify the population of clients as it was already suggested. Accuracy will be further improved if, instead of *expected value* (that is, mean value), we consider the whole distribution and develop worst-case scenarios at the 99 percent level of confidence.

The careful reader will appreciate that while we have started with a simple generalized model, this can become more sophisticated as we focus on *our* problem. There is something in the difference between empirical values often used by loans officers and estimates of future expectations as well as projections made by financial analysts.

As a general principle, the greater the bank's experience in modeling, the more accurate the model and the data it employs. But there is also model risk. Therefore, it is a good policy to start with simpler models that everyone can understand—and to which everyone can contribute.

- If the models and their aftermath are not understood, they will not be appreciated by their users.
- If the models' output cannot be readily compared to real life, then the effort is deprived of practical value.

Another fundamental issue is management's resolve. Senior management must stand firm behind the model and its application as well as its underlying methodology. A model is inseparable from its implementation methodology. For instance, ACRA treats credit risk and associated losses in a way that separate account is taken of the *expected loss* and *unexpected loss*—hence of *volatility* (see Chapter 12).

Instead of the classical methodology of a lump sum for bad loans provisions, banks using this approach charge the consolidated profit and loss (P+L) statement with an amount that corresponds to the statistically derived expected loss for the institution's credit portfolio.

- The loss projection is based on assumptions about developments over the medium term.
- This amount is credited in the balance sheet to a newly instituted ACRA Credit Risk Reserve.

With the new methodology, the annual amounts charged to the income statement are credited to this account, which can fluctuate depending on economic cycles and the occurrence of loan losses. The output of this model suggests to the bank's Group Executive Committee the amounts necessary to assure that the volatility of unexpected loan losses is taken care of over the long time horizon on which the bank's economic plan is based.

CHAPTER 12

Building Improved Versions of ACRA and Other Credit Models

1. INTRODUCTION

From the viewpoint of modeling credit risk, the problems character-izing ACRA, CreditMetrics (from which ACRA is derived), and CreditRisk+ (Chapter 13); RAROC, CreditPortfolioView, and LAS (Chapter 14); and Value at Risk (Chapter 15) are similar. A key issue is that these models are fairly static and two-dimensional. They do not account for market dynamics and they don't have the notion of time embedded in them, which is important in mapping the market's behavior.

- Significant changes are taking place in the institution's portfo-lio day by day and intraday, not every few years.
- The profile of counterparties also changes, which impacts the institution's assumed credit risk.

Reflecting on the steady evolution in the inventory of assets and liabilities, and on the profile of the counterparties with which a bank is doing business, is an important element in determining the characteristics of the business we are modeling. An example of the impact of market dynamics on portfolio structure is when, within a certain class of loans or other instruments, the bank lends and trades with a limited number of counterparties. This brings up two problems:

- There is a credit risk concentration that should definitely be mapped into the model, and
- The hypothesis of a normal distribution is hard to sustain, because it does not work with small samples.

Models of the type currently available serve best when there is a diversity of credit exposures and the counterparty population is large and distributed. This presents less correlated default probabilities than would otherwise be the case, and might make acceptable the hypothesis of a normal distribution.

Savings and loans have this type of diffused clientele, but CreditMetrics, ACRA, and CreditRisk+ are not made for thrifts. For a wholesale institution like J.P. Morgan, the Swiss Bank Corporation, and Credit Suisse, the problem is totally different. Therefore, this chapter brings to the reader's attention the wisdom of using the chi-square distribution. Other things being equal, the model should be more sophisticated if in real life the distribution of credit risk has a skewed pattern.

Another significant improvement in credit risk modeling is the assessment of the expectation of changes in credit exposure, fair value, and cash flow during the time frame addressed by the computation. But the most common pitfall with all present credit risk models is that they have not yet effectively managed a three-dimensional representation to account for frequency, exposure, and time. We will return to this subject in Chapter 16.

2. USING ACCURATE DISTRIBUTIONS FOR CREDIT RISK

Chapter 11 said that small samples, which are often used in analytical studies, have a severe aftermath: a reduction in the dependability of the results. Estimating approaches based on twisting statistical theory to fit the problem result in high variance and are not dependable.

Examples of unreliable statistical estimates are normal distribution hypotheses with a sample of 4 or 5. This is often done with pools of corporate loans as opposed to the large samples of mortgages. Projections based on averages of small samples have zero value—and samples are small because of the need of accounting for differences among the members of a population: the enterprises and their loans.

Many people misuse the statistical theory. I recently saw a study where social scientists considered a sample of size one to be statistically valid. On this nonsample they based their conclusions, which shows how serious some people are in their work.

Let me restructure this argument. Because a mathematical computation of credit risk involving corporate loans necessarily rests on relatively small samples, we should be careful not to use the normal distribution. In statistical terms this would be an aberration, and it is even more so in regard to the financial viewpoint.

- Models that disregard the theory of statistics are increasingly offered as the messiah of credit derivatives.
- But credit derivatives are leveraged instruments and in the process they gear up the errors.

The mathematical problem with small samples is that there are only a few degrees of freedom and the resulting statistical distribution is by no means normal. Instead, it has the skewed form shown in Figure 12.1, which corresponds to a chi-square distribution with four degrees of freedom.[1]

ACRA and its kin could be significantly improved by adopting the chi-square distribution, given the corporate loans environment to which they primarily address themselves. One significant advantage of the chi-square model is that it makes it feasible to study unexpected losses as the long-term volatility of credit risk. This long-term volatility represents the uncertainty as to whether the expect-

---

[1] See section 3, and D.N. Chorafas, *How to Understand and Use Mathematics for Derivatives,* Volume 2, *Advanced Modeling Methods,* Euromoney, London, 1996.

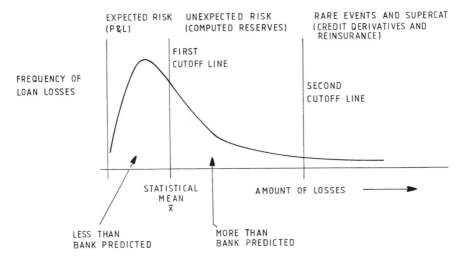

FIGURE 12.1 THE STATISTICAL DISTRIBUTION OF LOANS LOSSES CLASSIFIED INTO THREE MAJOR CATEGORIES

ed loss materializes or the effective losses are more than the bank had projected.

If we consider the area under the curve in Figure 12.1, the expected loss is more than the mode and, quite likely, the mean value of the distribution but below the first cutoff line. Less than this cutoff line is what the bank predicted as losses for the running year. More than the cutoff line is in excess of the losses from credit risk for the going year of operations. As Chapter 11 suggested,

- To absorb these annual fluctuations beyond the expected value of current losses, a bank needs capital.
- Up to a point, the reserves are capital put aside in the fat years.
- But beyond the second cutoff line, needed resources should be procured by reinsurance and credit derivatives.

While an institution can always keep an extra margin for extraordinary credit risk, most likely this will not be enough because stress losses are usually high. Reinsurance for CAT and superCAT makes sense, with credit derivatives both an alternative and a supplement.

The careful reader will appreciate that in contrast to market risk distributions, credit risk patterns for wholesale loans cannot be handled through bell-shaped approximations—a fact that should be kept in mind in connection to "credit VAR" (see Chapter 15). In the example from ACRA, the fact that the mode (peak) of the distribution is left of the mean (expected value) suggests that in the majority of years, the actual losses should be lower than the statistical projection of a cutoff. But the lower frequency of the area to the right of this line is more than compensated by much higher costs—and there can be spikes.

Some bankers look at the area to the left of the cutoff line as being representative of periods of economic growth in which the effective number of bankruptcies reported falls below the average. Empirically, this makes sense, but it is not a rigorous theoretical explanation. Only database mining, which capitalizes on a rich information content, can verify this hypothesis.

- One of the reasons why I recommend using time as a third dimension is to test these tentative statements, which should be subject to a verification mechanism.
- But the most important aftermath is to visualize change in credit losses over time with peaks and valleys (see Chapter 16).

Another tentative statement that sounds reasonable is that in economically depressed years the effective losses will exceed the expected losses. To document this hypothesis we must be ready to learn from the superposition of economic factors and failure statistics.

What can we learn? Figure 12.1 does not answer this query because it misses the time dimension. All it says is that the frequency of loan losses rises steeply and reaches the mode, before the mean value. Following this, there is a slow decline in the probability of occurrence of losses. As a general trend, that's fine, but it is not a basis for focused decisions.

What this model essentially suggests, and what ACRA advises, is that in years of economic growth and windfall profits, the bank should charge its income statement with an amount higher than the actual need for individual problem cases (the expected losses). Conversely, in years of economic crisis or minicrisis, the bank should still make provision for expected loss—but the actual size of losses can be much more severe.

The concept is based on the actuarial approach and, as I already mentioned, it is not altogether an unheard of practice. Major Swiss banks have been keeping extraordinary reserves (essentially retained earnings) for many years without the benefit of an analytical model.

This practice is not universal. Some central banks, like the Federal Reserve, question the notion of extraordinary reserves as disguised profits; and stock exchanges, like NYSE, look at this money as hidden, nondisclosed assets—which is not permitted under the Generally Accepted Accounting Practices (GAAP). The new strategy of analytical computational finance tries to legitimize the practice of keeping extra reserves, but I doubt that it will change the mind of the Fed or NYSE.

3. OPERATING CHARACTERISTICS CURVES, CHI-SQUARE, AND DEGREES OF FREEDOM

Three decades ago, numerical rating of counterparty risk was rare. Today most banks have introduced a rating scale with a number of grades to identify their counterparties' credit risks, and also use reports established by independent agencies. One way to express internally these grades is in a decimal scale, while rating agencies use a scale from AAA to B- or worse.

For the example presented in this section, we will use a numerical scale in rating counterparty risk. The grades vary from 1 to 100 and correspond to credit risk performance classes as well as expectations. A sophisticated credit risk system will see to it

- That each of the performance classes has a defined probability of default and
- That these probabilities increase in gradual steps from one grade to the next.

This is a linear system that can be significantly improved through probabilities. Tier-1 banks use an operating characteristics (OC) curve based on a rigorous statistical analysis of actual defaults within individual business segments.[2] The origin of OC curves dates back to World War II and the Manhattan Project—more precisely to the seminal work by Professor Uri at Columbia University.

The use of OC curves would be a major enhancement to ACRA, CreditMetrics, CreditRisk+, and the other models because it provides a crisp picture of the lenders' behavior. They can be drawn by industry, region, type of loan(s), or other segmentation criteria. The problem is that with big loans, segmentation thins out because the samples are small, making the estimates less reliable.

In order to use large samples and therefore steepen the OC curve, banks with experience in statistical analysis map all existing internal credit ratings. Some even add the bond-rating categories of major agencies to the new credit-rating scale. This improves the size of the statistical sample, but brings in heterogeneity.

The careful reader will never forget that while large samples help in terms of using tools that we know well, that respect statistical theory, and that are supported by statistical tables, with corporates we need to differentiate between individual counterparty risks in small samples.

- Small samples reduce the degrees of freedom (df), and the shape of the statistical distribution is skew.

The degrees of freedom inherent in a sample equals the size of the sample minus the order of the statistic being used—for instance, minus 1 if we use the sample mean $\bar{x}$; minus 2 if we use the mean and the variance s^2. Few analysts appreciate the major contribution of degrees of freedom in the study of a statistical distribution, yet the concept of degrees of freedom is of fundamental importance in modeling, as vital as the test of hypothesis, which (unfortunately) is rarely done.

---

[2] See D.N. Chorafas, *Statistical Processes and Reliability Engineering*, D. Van Nostrand Co., Princeton, NJ, 1960.

Section 2 said that credit risk analyses with small samples should use the chi-square (χ^2) distribution, but it did not explain what this means. Chi-square is a statistic expressed as the sum of the ratio of frequencies. Figure 12.2 gives an example of chi-square distributions with degrees of freedom varying from 1 to 10. It is

$$\chi^2 = \sum_{i=1}^{n} \frac{(f_i - F_i)^2}{F_i}$$

where

f_i = Observed frequencies in each of n categories of observations.

F_i = Theoretical frequencies for each category.

For instance, with the stratification of loans, along the chi-square distribution example, it will be

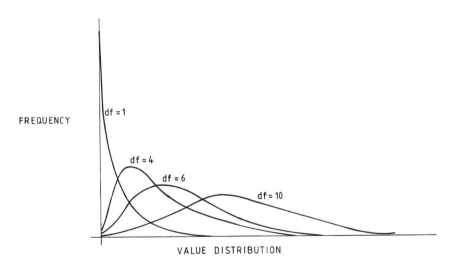

FIGURE 12.2 PATTERNS OF THE CHI-SQUARE DISTRIBUTION FOR 1, 4, 6, AND 10 DEGREES OF FREEDOM (DF)

$$\chi^2 = \sum_{i=1}^{n} f_i = n, \text{ and}$$

$$\sum_{i=1}^{n} F_i = n.$$

What we are essentially asking in a chi-square test is whether or not the practical observations disagree with the theoretical values F_i. The goal is to test the hypothesis that states the values of the theoretical frequencies.

It is proper to notice that the total number of observations does not enter chi-square except as the total of all f_i, or the total of all F_i. Another important observation is that the number of categories and not the total number of observations plays the critical role. In a chi-square test, if the sample size n is such that none of the f_i, F_i are less than, say, 6, the degrees of freedom will be df = 4.

As we see in Figure 12.2, even with df=10 the distribution is not bell-shaped. Rather, it is platokyrtotic. On the basis of the hypothesis being tested, this changes the frame of reference from the third momentum (skewness) to the fourth momentum (kyrtosis)[3] but still does not permit the use of normal distribution tables.

The choice of chi-square can reconcile the statements bankers make with the use of distribution of known statistical properties, given that, in this case, an approximation by the normal distribution is misleading. Some users of CreditMetrics say that in their applications credit risk is characterized by more or less four degrees of freedom. It is therefore important to provide the theoretical background needed to study this small sample.

Notice that the chi-square distribution can also help in the study of market risk in connection to OTC deals, where counterparty risk is a crucial factor, but most contracts are customized or nearly so. By contrast, exchange-traded contracts are standardized;

---

[3] D.N. Chorafas, *How to Understand and Use Mathematics for Derivatives,* Volume 2, *Advanced Modeling Methods,* Euromoney, London, 1996.

hence, they are characterized by a large population. Therefore, risk approximates a normal distribution, permitting the effective use of statistical tables and operating characteristics curves.

4. THE NEED TO INTEGRATE CREDIT RISK AND MARKET RISK BY IMPORTANT CLIENT

One of the failures of the current versions of ACRA, CreditMetrics, CreditRisk+, and other models in connection to counterparty risk is the lack of tools and procedures for the conversion of derivatives exposure into a risk that is equivalent to loans exposure. Yet, this is a prerequisite for the effective integration of credit risk and market risk by important client—to provide an integrated profile.

With relationship banking, assets management, and a variety of derivatives deals, a financial institution usually takes a long horizon with its customers—particularly those who are the most important in loans, trading, and portfolio handling. It is therefore inescapable that management is faced with the questions:

- How much total exposure the bank should have with each counterparty, and
- How it can steadily measure that exposure to make feasible an effective control of risk.

Fundamentally, this poses two problems that so far, in the vast majority of cases, have been handled independently from one another. The first is assessing the creditworthiness of the counterparty. The second is computing the exposure taken with the counterparty not only in loans but also in trading. In most cases, risks with loans and risks with derivatives are treated as separate problems. Yet, there is evidence that in the bottom line they are tightly coupled.

What the board and senior management should care about is total exposure by counterparty. Therefore, bankers and rocket scientists (see Chapter 16) should appreciate that the use of separate, incompatible approaches for credit risk and market risk is a half-baked solution.

Assessing creditworthiness is not new. The procedure is based on careful analysis of a firm's financial health. Credit models help in doing a better job. Still, the goal should be integrated exposure management.

Total exposure management is new and more mathematically oriented than credit risk or market risk management alone. We mine the database for credit ratings and market prices to evaluate our portfolio by major client—more precisely, to determine a risk distribution that we develop through simulation.

Monte Carlo simulation[4] is helpful inasmuch as it permits us to account for the fact that the counterparty's credit risks and market risks are not stationary. The problem is that very few financial institutions have ever used simulation. Hence they lack the necessary concept, let alone applications experience.

The goal is to find the worst-case loss if the counterparty forfeits, such computation being based at the 99 percent level of confidence. Through Monte Carlo simulation we evaluate the portfolio with a major counterparty over many runs—typically 5,000 or more.

Contrary to the classical look at creditworthiness, which provides a single number, the simulation's result is repeated for different scenarios permitting us to do "what-if" experimentation—for instance, how are our counterparty's credit risks and market risks distributed

- In the global sense,
- By type of commitment,
- By interest rate level,
- By currency,
- By country, or
- By maturity?

We may also target our own executives in terms of business done and assumed exposure. What's the pattern of our credits by credit officer? By branch? By foreign subsidiary? Is there any

---

[4] See D.N. Chorafas, *Chaos Theory in the Financial Markets,* Probus, Chicago, 1994.

abnormal number of "weak credits" or of over-the-counter derivatives deals? Is the same credit officer always dealing with the same counterparty? Other critical questions for what-if analysis are

- Are our credits diversified or concentrated in a few names?
- What's the trend in exposure taken by each counterparty?

It is a matter of good internal controls to analyze credits for risk management reasons, but the questions must be focused. Is the same dealer following a similar pattern in trades with the same counterparty? Why is *this* counterparty dealing in billions of dollars in swaps? Is the counterparty a steady user of OTC? What is its ratio between OTC and exchange-traded products?

The target of an individualized exposure analysis is to find the worst-case loss if the counterparty goes bankrupt, including the case of losing market gains. A case in point is the recent happening with J.P. Morgan and SK Securities of South Korea where the Morgan Bank is rumored to have lost over $400 million in anticipated profits.

The goal of an integrative global analytical exposure study, and of the tools that this can provide, is to compute the general worst case. Order of magnitude is sufficient, because in estimation and in prognostication the aim is accuracy rather than precision, as related in section 5.

5. EMPLOYING FERMI'S CONCEPT TO CALCULATE THE BANK'S EXPOSURE

The simulation of the entire portfolio provides a good estimate of true exposure, while simulating a contract independently of all the other commitments could lead to inconsistent assumptions about customer relationships and the effect of market prices. Fundamentally, however, both the risk taken with each individual customer and the comprehensive estimates are important to the board and to senior management for their decisions.

Regulators are moving in this direction. They want cumulative exposure results, VAR being an example, but they are also becoming inquisitive about major individual exposures. This is as valid for loans as for derivatives. Effective in 1996, the Swiss National Bank and the Federal Banking Commission require that the banks integrate into their balance sheet derivatives trades that have to be recognized even if they are not realized.

- Trades whose marking-to-market value is positive to the bank are reported as "other assets."
- Trades where the bank loses money at the time of their recognition are "other liabilities."

While all derivatives trades have a major market risk exposure, the "other assets"—largely over-the-counter deals—also incorporate a significant amount of counterparty risk. These are the profits the bank will be seeing some time in the future (1) provided the market does not turn against its best judgment and (2) depending on the counterparty's ability to pay as well as its willingness to perform.

The bank's own management should be even more demanding than the regulators. What is important to the board is to know *the order of magnitude* of this "other assets" and "other liabilities" exposure,

- Counterparty by counterparty and
- Instrument by instrument.

While theoretically a very detailed calculation would be the better strategy, in practice this is not doable at a rapid pace—particularly with the low technology of mainframes, geriatric Cobol programs, and batch processing employed by most banks. What is feasible is an order-of-magnitude calculation.

One of the best examples on how to approach an order-of-magnitude solution in connection to a problem with many unknowns comes from Enrico Fermi. Dr. Fermi asked his students at the University of Chicago, "How many piano tuners are there in Chicago?" Part and parcel of this question are

- The improbability that anyone knows the answer and
- The number of unknowns that an answer would involve.

This type of problem has no standard solution, which is exactly the point Enrico Fermi wanted to press. As a physicist, however, the great researcher and teacher knew that it is possible to make assumptions leading to an approximate but acceptable answer.

- If Chicago's population is 5 million, an average family consists of four people, and one-tenth of all families own pianos,
- Then there will be 125,000 pianos in the city requiring servicing.

If every piano is tuned once every five years, 25,000 pianos must be tuned each year. If a tuner can service four pianos a day, 250 days a year, this will make a total of 1,000 tunings a year. Therefore, there must be about 25 piano tuners in Chicago.

The answer Dr. Enrico Fermi gave shows a phase shift in thinking. A phase shift means a radical change in the characteristics of the way we look at problems and their solutions. Fermi's answer is not exact. The true number could be, say, as low as 20 or as high as 30. But as an order of magnitude 25 is the right answer.

In real life, in a surprisingly large number of cases, accuracy and precision cannot be obtained at the same time at a rapid pace and reasonable cost. When this happens it is better to be accurate than precise. Figure 12.3 explains what is meant by this statement and why it is so.

The metaphor of the piano tuners shows that even if at the outset an order-of-magnitude answer is unknown, we can proceed on the basis of different hypotheses and arrive at estimates that fall within an acceptable range. This is the secret behind the *Chorafas algorithm* briefly examined in section 6: the demodulation of derivatives trades to credit risk equivalence.[5]

- Fermi's message is that when we talk of an order of magnitude, errors in our hypotheses and in our calculations tend to cancel out one another.

---

[5] See D.N. Chorafas, *Managing Derivatives Risk,* Irwin/Probus, Chicago, 1996.

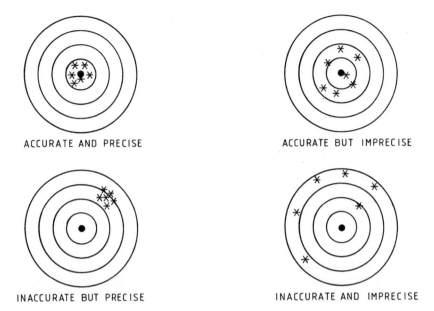

ACCURATE AND PRECISE

ACCURATE BUT IMPRECISE

INACCURATE BUT PRECISE

INACCURATE AND IMPRECISE

FIGURE 12.3 THE TRADE-OFFS BETWEEN ACCURACY AND PRECISION

- This happens because, as a whole, it is improbable that all of our errors will be underestimates or overestimates.

Deviations from the correct assumptions, in terms of estimating credit risk and market risk in connection to derivatives trades, tend to compensate for one another. Therefore, the final outcome will converge toward an order of magnitude that stands a good chance of being right—and once obtained it permits us to integrate *our* bank's total exposure with each counterparty.

6. AN ORDER-OF-MAGNITUDE CALCULATION OF DERIVATIVES RISK

Let's start with the fact that a derivatives deal involves a *notional principal amount.* This is a term borrowed from the swaps market— meaning money that is never actually paid or received, but it serves in *contractually* establishing a reference level. With swaps, the notional (not nominal) amount is used as the basis for calculating the periodic payments of fixed or floating interest. We will be using a notional amount for the calculation of derivatives exposure at an order-of-magnitude level.

The principle is that since the notional principal is a contractual obligation, we should be able to do something with this number to facilitate the construction of a frame of reference in credit risk and market risk taken with derivatives, in a way that is known and appreciated by bankers. The algorithm I am proposing fulfills this requirement.

A frame of reference that is generally understood will help us in estimating, always in order of magnitude, both market risk and counterparty risk. If we succeed in doing so, we will be in a position to integrate on–balance-sheet and off–balance-sheet exposure in compliance with the new rules promoted by the Group of Ten central bankers—most particularly, to help the board and senior management of *our* bank in their decisions.

- Dividing the notional principal amount by a *demodulator* permits us to derive a figure that is approximately equivalent to a loan's exposure in terms of capital at risk.

The challenge is to properly estimate this demodulator. When this is done in a factual manner along Dr. Fermi's notion, it leads to the creation of a *common denominator,* which simplifies the task of following up on different heterogeneous types of risk as well as that of estimating exposure to counterparties.

Demodulated notional principal amounts are among the best possible examples of *stress testing.* They make possible stress analysis of positions through a more rigorous approach than value at risk (VAR), which has been advanced by the 1996 Market Risk Amendment (see Chapter 15).

An order-of-magnitude calculation means that while preserving an acceptable degree of accuracy, we can accept a somewhat lower precision by taking a global demodulator for all derivatives exposure.

This is what many banks do today, in the aftermath of the Long-Term Capital Management near-bankruptcy. As a safeguard for credit exposure, they take 5 percent of the notional amount and apply it against the limit of the counterparty.

A similar strategy can be followed with an over-the-counter contract in regard to market risk. Say, for instance, that mining the database of FRAs with maturity between six months and one year we obtain a distribution with mean $\bar{x} = 3.65$ and standard deviation $s = 0.5$. At 99-percent level of confidence, for one-tailed distribution it will be:

$$
\begin{aligned}
x &= \bar{x} + 2.34s = 3.65 + 1.17 \\
&= 4.82
\end{aligned}
$$

Using this estimated risk factor as divisor, the notional principal amount of a $50 million forward rate agreement will be demodulated to a loan risk equivalent of $50/4.82 = 10.37$ million. A similar strategy can be used with all transactions and all inventoried OTC instruments.

As this brief example suggests, only part of the notional principal is at risk because of market volatility. The amount of money contracted has been reduced, or demodulated to pure market risk. On a 100-percent basis, the 4.82 percent risk corresponds to a demodulation factor of 20.74. This factor can be subsequently adjusted for other events, as we will see in the following paragraphs.

The process of demodulation can also be instrumental in connection to risk embedded in our whole trading book. Knowing the composition of *our* portfolio in derivative financial products we can periodically compute a weighted average risk factor that would need to be updated as the relative weight of different instruments and maturities change. Say, as an example, that the weighted average risk factor of our portfolio's pattern is 25, computed along the lines of the preceding example.

We can improve upon this factor by accounting for the nervousness currently prevailing in the financial market, using statistical quality control concepts and tables developed at Columbia University during World War II for the Manhattan Project.[6] These

---

[6] Which can be found in MIL-STAND 105, U.S. Government Printing Office, Washington, DC.

are associated to the notion of normal, tightened, and reduced inspection. *If* 25 were the demodulator for normal inspection, *then*:

- For tightened inspection it may be 20, and
- For reduced inspection, 30.

Reduced inspection characterizes the time when there are no failures in the banking systems, no systemic risk in "emerging countries," no LTCM-type meltdowns, and no major bankruptcies anywhere in the G-10. These are rare but plausible events.

Normal inspection typically corresponds to liquid markets with relatively low volatility—but while the banking system seems to be in control, there are some pockets of concern to regulators. Tightened inspection is necessary (1) when there are crises and panics or near panics and (2) during experimentation with stress scenarios.

These conversion factors, the demodulators, are used in conjunction with the notional principal amount of derivatives deals. The example taken with 20, 25, and 30 demodulators is essentially one of averages computed on the basis of a derivatives portfolio which includes

- Interest rate risk, representing about 50 to 55 percent of the total notional principal.
- Currency exchange risk, typically amounting to 40 to 42 percent of the notional principal.
- Equity risk at 5 percent and the balance of other risks of the total notional amount.

Of course, every bank has its own distribution of risks, and it should use its own rather than the averages I took as an example. A more precise approach would have required computing a demodulator for each one of the above classes, and then combining the outcome accounting for the relative weight of each class.

This is evidently feasible, but it requires supercomputers to be done on a real-time basis and, as I never tire of repeating, the majority of banks don't have that power available—in spite of billions of dollars they spend on computers, communications, and software. Also, borrowing a concept from industrial engineering, it is advisable that each bank estimates *its* demodulators in detail and then uses them in real-time interactive computational finance—as it is done with Method, Time, Measurement (MTM).

It does not take extraordinary brilliance to understand that the computation of a loans equivalent derivatives exposure is more precise if treated instrument by instrument, since each instrument has its own risk characteristics and therefore its own divisor. A still more precise approach is to break every major class—like interest rate risk—into smaller, more focused subsets accounting, among other factors, for maturity.

This being said, I don't advise that this be done every time. But it should be done periodically to calibrate the demodulator of total derivatives exposure. For an instantaneous real-time computation, Fermi's concept is the best also because a single demodulator permits us to handle in a homogeneous way

- Accounts of counterparties,
- Markets in which the deal is done,
- Maturity of the transactions, and other issues.

The principle is that either we focus on order-of-magnitude buying accuracy but selling precision, or we focus on precision. But we should be aware that by doing so we may be selling accuracy without knowing that we have done such an unfavorable trade.

CHAPTER 13

RiskMetrics, CreditMetrics, and CreditRisk+

1. INTRODUCTION

Institutions that do not have the in-house skill, the *rocket scientists* (see Chapter 16), to develop eigenmodels usually buy off-the-shelf software. This comes from two sources: (1) other banks that have developed models for their own use and market them for income or give them away for relationship banking reasons and (2) software vendors.

Banks that are ahead of the curve would not give away all their secrets. The model they offer is usually barebone, but it works. It may also be that senior management has decided to stop selling the model. This happened in the late 1980s with Risk Adjusted Return on Capital (RAROC, see Chapter 14), when Bankers Trust stopped selling it through DEC because other institutions that brought RAROC sharpened up their competition.

The policy of giving away a model starting with correspondent banks and treasuries of big manufacturers, and then enlarging this population, practically started with J.P. Morgan when it took its market risk management expertise outside. It did so by launching the RiskMetrics initiative in 1994. RiskMetrics involves measuring and analyzing market risk, including value-at-risk (see Chapter 15) and daily earnings at risk.

239

The Morgan Bank also collects and distributes historical data on rates and prices, including correlations, and it follows up its support with the development of more models. RiskMetrics was followed by CreditMetrics co-sponsored by Bank of America, Barclays BZW, Deutsche Morgan Grenfell (now Deutsche Bank Securities), Swiss Bank Corporation (see Chapters 11 and 12 on ACRA), and Union Bank of Switzerland.

CreditMetrics and its desktop implementation, CreditManager, measure changes in portfolio value due to upgrades and downgrades of its contents because of counterparty risk. The model's advantages are that it includes correlations among credit quality changes, and it makes it feasible to quantify the results of concentration and diversification within a portfolio.

In a nutshell, CreditMetrics presents three alternatives in connection to the estimation of risk. One is using historical default data as a guide. Another is calculating actual bond spread correlations on the relevant credits. Both necessitate the support of rich databases.

The third approach is inferring correlations from empirical studies of relevant equity markets. The problem is that the inference of debt correlations from those observable in the equity markets requires some hypotheses that, as experience demonstrates, are not always documented by the facts. This and the nonexistence of appropriate information in the institution's own database become limiting factors of the method.

Both CreditMetrics and CreditRisk+ can be seen as credit-oriented value-at-risk models aiming to provide quantitative results to manage assets and liabilities more accurately. They also permit experimentation on capital allocation, risk-mitigating decisions, and investment alternatives. But like all models, they are no substitute for sound credit risk management.

2. RiskMetrics AND THE QUALITY OF RISK MANAGEMENT

In November 1994, the Morgan Bank made RiskMetrics available free of charge via the Internet. This brought a modeling tool to firms that could scarcely afford to develop one of their own. J.P. Morgan says that within a little over half a year (November 1994 to May 1995), there were 17,000 downloads of the RiskMetrics data to investment managers interested in the effects of volatility and correlation to asset allocation.

Four months after it introduced the model, in March 1995, Morgan expanded RiskMetrics by adding commodities and extending the program's coverage to eight more countries. The target has been the handling of derivatives.

Will RiskMetrics give its Internet users a benchmark that lets them tell clients, "The portfolio I run has this much risk attached to it?" Through a value-at-risk estimate, the model measures the most that could be lost in a given period, assuming markets continue to behave as they have in the past. This should respond positively to the preceding query, but (because the large majority of bankers understand little or nothing about how models work), a more accurate answer is that cultural and algorithmic barriers can make the use of RiskMetrics (and of any other model) ineffectual.

Only if it is used in the proper way will this value-at-risk instrument permit us to (1) understand whether the portfolio is gaining or losing value and (2) examine how well the risks are diversified. For the average user, the mathematics is complex, though it should be comprehensible to expert financial analysts.

Precisely because, in the general case, the population of potential users has no skill in analytics, J.P. Morgan has been adjusting RiskMetrics to help banks calculate the impact of new central bank guidelines concerning trading risks and capital requirements.

Capital requirements for potential trading losses and the quality of the existing risk management system have an important impact on a bank's profits and competitiveness. However, the ability to use quantitative tools must be matched by the banker's sophistication in balancing risk and return.

Critics of RiskMetrics point to the user's need to mark to market all investments in a given portfolio. This is not as easy as it sounds since for many OTC derivatives (particularly the more risky ones), there is rarely an active market to use for pricing.

Critics also comment that the multidiversity of risk can rarely be studied through packages, particularly in connection to a complex portfolio. Investors who classically relied on bankers to provide information about their risks are now questioning the general model practice because they have been deceived too often.

It is difficult to say how fair or unfair this criticism is because the general level of experience with the model is not yet high. RiskMetrics does provide some estimates of volatility, which impacts asset value. The procedure it offers must be applied to each asset and then factored in a way that gains and losses on various assets could offset each other—if this is feasible.

Without doubt, the institutions and treasuries that will benefit most from RiskMetrics and similar tools are those that learned the lessons of the past few years. One lesson is the degree to which standard statistical and mathematical risk measurement techniques fall short of describing the real thing. An answer lies beyond modeling in database mining and real-time simulation of market data streams.[1]

For this reason J.P. Morgan is expanding the database currently included in the RiskMetrics system. Its goal is to make the model a gauge for measuring risk across major asset classes such as stocks, government bonds, short-term interest rates, commodities, and currencies for 22 geographic markets.

3. THE NEED FOR A METHODOLOGY TO IMPROVE OBTAINED RESULTS

One of the problems presented by the use of models obtained from a third party is that they correspond very little to the specific requirements of an institution. Another more severe problem is that, as with many packages, sophisticated software comes without the necessary methodology for a successful implementation. This can have a severe aftermath on both the accuracy of obtained results and end users' appreciation of these results.

Not only should the methodology serve the model's implementation and operation, seeing to it that it is accurately done, but

---

[1] D.N. Chorafas, *How to Understand and Use Mathematics for Derivatives*, Volume 1, *Understanding the Behavior of Markets*, Euromoney, London, 1995.

also it should provide support to senior management policy decisions (for instance, the strategy the institution follows in terms of market risk and credit risk measurements as well as the bank's ways and means to comply to regulatory standards).

This strategy should be comprehensive to include valuation of financial assets, assuring an accurate measurement of volatility and liquidity. Management policy should also see to it that all computer applications are available on an interactive basis, running on client servers and high-performance computers, not on obsolete mainframes.

Another sound policy is that the model gives a value-added output compared to what the bank already had. This is not a foregone conclusion when management chooses one model or another. Even after their search, some institutions find the output of a bought model to be wanting.

For instance, for risk management purposes some financial institutions adopted the Morgan Bank matrix of *zero-coupon equivalence.* Not all of them, however, found it to be satisfactory. Therefore, they switched to the cash flow method with a catastrophe curve set at two standard deviations.

An important consideration in terms of choice is the frequency of reporting. Some financial institutions with experience in risk management, both with the cash flow method and with RiskMetrics, comment that computation should be done on a day-by-day basis with overnight calculation. But others say that this is too little, too late.

The more technologically advanced banks opt for an *intraday* approach which they consider much more desirable. But high-frequency financial data resulting from tick-by-tick intraday data feeds require high-performance computing. It is not possible to dissociate models and methodology from the bank's information technology.

Institutions with experience in the interactive use of models add that an important advantage from intraday applications is the ability to focus on the trader level by establishing and maintaining trader profiles. This makes it feasible to control Barings risk as well as to closely follow the observance of limits.

These comments apply both to RiskMetrics and CreditMetrics as well as to any other bought or house-made software. There are other prerequisites too. The use of CreditMetrics (see section 4) presupposes the existence of a scoring system, since (1) it targets the probability that a particular credit or pool of credits will default and (2) credit ratings help in expressing the likelihood in a quantitative manner.

We have spoken of scoring systems (see Chapter 10), but let me add a word of caution. Many people think that once a rating agency has established a score, it will remain for a long time if not forever. This is wrong.

Table 13.1 shows increasing probabilities of average cumulative default rates over a 15-year time span. Notice that at the end of this period even AAA counterparty has a 1.40 percent probability of default, while the default likelihood of a B counterparty is slightly over 30 percent. Disquieting statistics, indeed.

Exposure to credit risk arises from the potential inability of counterparties to perform under the terms of the contracts. While every company attempts to limit its exposure to credit risk by dealing with creditworthy partners and also using collateral and various credit monitoring techniques, credit risk is always present.

Table 13.2 presents a different type of transition probability than Table 13.1. The time basis is only one year, but notice that even AAA counterparties have a probability of changing status: More than 8 percent might become AA. There is even a BB probability, albeit a low one. Let's keep in mind this transition matrix.

To appreciate the message in transition probabilities, we should understand the need for calculating the market value for each change in rating, taking into account the correlations between exposures. Transition matrices can be instrumental in estimating the distribution of losses for a given portfolio.

Some portfolios are very analogous to the sort of trade transition statistics Moody's and S&P deal with; others are not. Banks that have portfolios that are very different than those the independent rating agencies study should evidently develop their own models—provided that they have a rich database of historical default data.

Table 13.1 Increasing Probabilities of Average Cumulative Default Rates over a 15-Year Time Span (in %)

	Year 1	Year 2	Year 3	Year 4	Year 5	Year 6	Year 7	Year 8	Year 9	Year 10	Year 11	Year 12	Year 13	Year 14	Year 15
AAA	0.00	0.00	0.07	0.15	0.24	0.43	0.66	1.05	1.21	1.40	1.40	1.40	1.40	1.40	1.40
AA	0.00	0.02	0.12	0.25	0.43	0.66	0.89	1.06	1.17	1.29	1.37	1.48	1.48	1.48	1.48
A	0.06	0.16	0.27	0.44	0.67	0.88	1.12	1.42	1.77	2.17	2.51	2.67	2.81	2.91	3.11
BBB	0.18	0.44	0.72	1.27	1.78	2.38	2.99	3.52	3.94	4.34	4.61	4.70	4.70	4.70	4.70
BB	1.06	3.48	6.12	8.68	10.97	13.24	14.46	15.65	16.81	17.73	18.99	19.39	19.91	19.91	19.91
B	5.20	11.00	15.95	19.40	21.88	23.63	25.14	26.57	27.74	29.02	29.89	30.40	30.65	30.65	30.65
CCC	19.79	26.92	31.63	34.97	40.15	41.61	42.64	43.07	44.20	45.10	45.10	45.10	45.10	45.10	45.10

Reprinted by permission of Standard & Poor's

Table 13.2 A Transition Matrix Based on Average One-Year Transition Rates

	AAA	AA	A	BBB	BB	B	CCC	D
Initial Rating								
AAA	88.72	8.14	0.66	0.06	0.12	0.00	0.00	0.00
AA	0.68	88.31	7.59	0.62	0.06	0.14	0.02	0.00
A	0.09	2.19	87.74	5.32	0.71	0.25	0.01	0.06
BBB	0.02	0.31	5.61	81.95	5.00	1.10	0.11	0.18
BB	0.03	0.13	0.61	7.03	73.27	8.04	0.91	1.06
B	0.00	0.10	0.21	0.38	5.66	72.91	3.56	5.20
CCC	0.18	0.00	0.18	1.07	1.96	9.27	53.48	19.79

Reprinted by permission of Standard & Poor's

4. WHAT CREDITMETRICS COULD OFFER TO SENIOR MANAGEMENT

RiskMetrics seeks to assess the returns on a portfolio of assets (loans, bonds, and derivatives) by analyzing the probabilistic behavior of the individual assets, coupled with their mutual correlations. CreditMetrics focuses on counterparty risks which are evaluated by means of a transition matrix of probabilities like those we saw in Tables 13.1 and 13.2 on the assumption that a given credit's rating will change.[2]

The model calculates the expected change in market value for each possible ratings transition, including default. The change in value is given by the recovery rate, with the individual value distributions combined by means of correlations between the credits. This helps in generating a loss distribution for the portfolio as a whole. The algorithmic solution

- Largely reflects on probabilities of ratings transitions and correlations of likelihood,
- Proceeds by means of a simulation-based portfolio evaluation, and
- Necessitates steady mining of a rich database to produce results.

The careful reader will recall what was said in Chapter 12 about operating characteristics curves. While OC curves as such are not directly employed, CreditMetrics does plot the probability that the bank's loans will all turn sour at the same time.

- The default probability will be higher, and capital requirements should be greater, in the case of concentrated risks.
- A bank with a well-diversified portfolio would need less capital than others because its risks are spread.

---

[2] See D.N. Chorafas, *Statistical Processes and Reliability Engineering,* D. Van Nostrand Co., Princeton, NJ, 1960.

As with CreditRisk+ (see section 6) and other models, the computational result is a skewed loss distribution which can lead to the estimation of expected losses and unexpected losses (see Chapter 12) or capital at risk. The model addresses systematic credit risk in a loan portfolio, distinguishing between two credit states (default and nondefault) and handling nondefault states at multiple levels (full-state).

The contribution of CreditMetrics is the consolidation of credit risk across the organization by means of a statement of value at risk expressed as a function of credit quality. The model integrates a number of instruments including

- Personal loans,
- Loans to businesses,
- Other loan-type commitments,
- Commercial credits and receivables,
- Fixed income instruments, and
- Forwards, swaps, and other derivatives.

Under the full-state approach, CreditMetrics compares the portfolio payoff distribution with the corresponding normal distribution based on the hypothesis that all borrowers were uncorrelated. The Morgan Bank is the first to state that

- This use of normal distribution poorly approximates value at risk, and
- While the two-state model provides a better estimate, there are still important discrepancies.

An applications example helps to explain how CreditMetrics works. In connection to fixed-income instruments, for instance, it calculates the probability that a bond's current rating will shift to a different rating within a projected time frame. The outcome of a shift is an estimated change in value computed by the model. Such estimate is based on historical credit spread data and recovery rates in case of default.

A primary objective is to adequately address and quantify *concentration risk*—that is, additional portfolio risk resulting from increased exposure to a counterparty, or a group of counterparties, related by means of

- Belonging to the same holding,
- Falling into the same rating category,
- Working in the same industry,
- Trading in the same financial instrument, or
- Being in the same geographical location.

Cognizant bankers appreciate that underpinning these constraints is the fact that diversification is the best way to mitigate concentration risk. Besides this, banks put limits to each of the classes in the preceding bullet list. But, as section 3 said, the able utilization of what models offer requires a rigorous methodology including procedures for a credit rating system.

CreditMetrics does not provide a particular credit rating methodology. Instead, it capitalizes on the existence of a scoring system within the bank to further study the aftermath of shifts in credit rating, whatever may be the background factor.

- Each value resulting from a shift in credit rating is weighted by its likelihood to create a spectrum of values across a given credit state.
- An asset's expected value and associated volatility are calculated from this distribution which, as shown in Figure 13.1, is not normal but resembles the chi-square distribution for small samples (see Chapter 12).

Many of the algorithms in CreditMetrics are different from those in RiskMetrics, J.P. Morgan's earlier model for computing market risk (see section 2). But the two releases can work in synergy, which is important because it is necessary to have a steady and accurate revaluation of positions concerning financial instruments.

The steady evaluation of the value of exposed positions at a given risk horizon is complicated by the interaction between credit

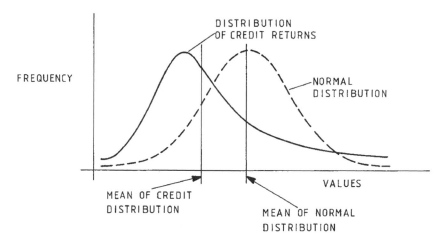

FIGURE 13.1 THE DISTRIBUTION OF CREDIT RETURNS CANNOT BE
APPROXIMATED THROUGH THE NORMAL DISTRIBUTION.

and market risk, leading to an inherent optionality which derives
from the fact that, particularly with derivatives, a credit loss can
occur only if the position is at the money when the counterparty
undergoes a credit rate shift. When the position is out of the money,
the holder has a market risk, but not necessarily a credit risk.

To account for this coupling and its effects, CreditMetrics considers expected exposures at the risk horizon. These are derived
from volatilities and market rates that can be computed through
RiskMetrics. The reader should, however, appreciate that this exercise requires paying attention to default thresholds.

5. CreditMetrics AND DEFAULT THRESHOLDS

One of the competitive advantages of CreditMetrics is a simulator
permitting the user to estimate the distribution of a credit portfolio.
The model can be extended to include rating changes that result in
crossing *default thresholds*. In my judgment, while this facility is
interesting in itself, it should be improved through the implementation of quality control charts.

Assuming that default likelihood is given by the credit rating, it is possible to work backwards to thresholds in asset values delimiting default. Based on Standard & Poor's and Moody's ratings, CreditMetrics utilizes transition matrices that include historically estimated one-year default metrics. The drivers of the model are default likelihood and probability of credit rating migration.

Both Moody's and S&P publish a one-year transition matrix, which is fairly similar to the transition probabilities we have seen in Table 13.2. In Moody's case this ranges from Aaa to Caa and default. In S&P's, it ranges from AAA to CCC and default.

CreditMetrics works on the hypothesis that default correlations actually exist, and investigates the possibility of modeling joint rating changes through changed data regarding historical ratings. Actual rating and default correlations can be derived from rating agency information. This provides an objective measure reflecting actual experience, but the application usually suffers from sparse sample sets.

Alternatively, a financial institute can employ bond spread correlations that give a fairly objective measure of actual correlation in bond values and, by extension, credit quality. These, however, suffer from data quality problems, particularly in connection with low-quality issuers.

A third alternative is equity price correlations. Equity prices offer forward-looking, efficient market information as well as the advantage of good time series. The disadvantage is that they require much computing time to yield reliable information about likely credit quality correlations, and the correlations are not necessarily high.

To model credit correlations, CreditMetrics assumes that transition occurs in discrete ratings, and the change in grades is the result of migration propelled by underlying factors. It is further assumed that (1) the underlying process is a good estimator of distance from default and (2) the default distance can be transformed into a normalized risk score with a unit-normal distribution.

These are comforting references, but they also point to the fact that the developers have felt the need for trade-offs. Simplicity and relative speed of calculation are associated with a uniform constant correlation assumption. This helps to highlight significant overconcentrations but it is not a precise approach. Therefore, it limits the analysis of concentrations and correlations.

CreditMetrics provides correlation data using uniform constant correlation and it can also be extended to equity price correlations to map each counterparty to the industries and countries most likely to determine portfolio performance. To follow this path, the asset manager must attribute industry and country weights to each counterparty.

Weighting is also important because CreditMetrics follows a set of scenarios in connection to counterparties. For instance, the rule for specific risk is that the smaller the obligor, the more idiosyncratic may be its behavior. The system classifies each counterparty for a combination "industry- and country-specific risk." Firms can be related to one another through their common sensitivity to an industry sector and country of origin.

This reduces the size of each axis of the required correlation matrix from the number of names in terms of counterparties, to the level of countries and industries being involved. It is also possible to calculate correlations for firms that have illiquid equity issues or that are not traded in exchanges.

Institutions using the system will be well advised to develop value-added routines permitting examinations counterparty by counterparty. This will not be necessary for all clients, but for major clients it's a must, given the associated amount of exposure.

The software supporting CreditMetrics tracks several statistical references to describe the shape of the portfolio distribution during simulation. The model uses not only the first two moments of the portfolio (mean and standard deviation) but also the next two moments of the distribution: skewness and kurtosis. It also handles percentile levels.

J.P. Morgan continues to work on CreditMetrics with the goal of establishing a methodology for the whole market. The further-out aim is to generalize this model for the calculation of capital requirements connected to counterparty risk, as everybody expects that the 1998 Capital Accord will be subject to a major overhaul during the next few years.

6. CREDITRISK+ AND ITS COMPARISON TO CREDITMETRICS

Developed by Credit Suisse Financial Products (CSFP), CreditRisk+ utilizes a different quantitative approach to credit risk measurement than CreditMetrics, but with the same goal of providing an analytical tool that could render the credit markets more transparent. An advantage of CreditRisk+ is that it can be implemented through a spreadsheet.

CSFP may well be the first institution to come up with a model based on an actuarial rather than statistical approach, that owes more to insurance than to banking—just like Swiss Bank Corporation has been the first player to use the actuarial approach in redesigning J.P. Morgan's CreditMetrics model. With CSFP's CreditRisk+:

- The number of default events over a specified time horizon is approximated by a Poisson distribution.
- The variable might represent mean default rate, exposure from an individual borrower, or some other factor.

In terms of methodology, in an approach similar to the CreditMetrics consortium, CSFP hopes that a constructive public debate over credit risk modeling will convince regulators that for banks able to compute mathematically their credit risk, the 8 percent capital requirement of the 1988 Capital Accord should be relaxed. For regulators, this will be tantamount to recognizing internal models as the basis of capital adequacy and risk capital allocation.

The common ground of both CreditRisk+ and CreditMetrics is that of generating skewed distributions for calculation of expected loss, unexpected loss, and risk capital. The target is to measure credit risks across a wide range of assets, including loans, loan commitments, bonds, and derivatives.

CreditRisk+ is a modified version of the methodology Credit Suisse has used to set loan loss provisions since December 1996. Over time, it has evolved as a way to assess risk capital requirements in a data-poor environment. In such an environment most assets are held to maturity and the only credit event that really counts is whether the lender gets repaid at maturity.

The CSFB model enjoys endorsements from Moody's Investor Services, Standard & Poor's, Fitch IBCA, and the Japanese Bond Research Institute as well as three of the Big Six public accounting firms. The analytical portfolio approach closely follows default rates associated with ratings and the volatility of such rates.

CreditRisk+ proponents point out that this model is more subtle than CreditMetrics because information about correlation is embedded in the default rates and their volatilities. By contrast, CreditMetrics is too dependent on valid data, even if it is difficult to find all necessary data and filter it. This argument tries to bypass the problem of the quality of data without really solving it. As with all models, the effective use of CreditRisk+ can be inhibited by poor data. Also, the scarcity of data makes it difficult to test the hypotheses being made.

The CreditRisk+ approach has been to borrow, to a large extent, the mathematics used in the insurance industry for low-frequency extreme events. But Credit Suisse Financial Products also used its own experience with counterparty risk. This background shows in some of the differences between the two constructs, CreditMetrics and CreditRisk+, particularly when it comes to estimating probabilities of default. CreditMetrics estimates the correlation of default probabilities, while, as already stated, CreditRisk+ utilizes the average default rates.

The CSFB model also incorporates the volatilities associated with each level of the score curves generated by credit-rating agencies. Other differences concern the methodology underpinning each construct.

- CreditMetrics is based on portfolio theory, aiming to mark credit to market. It looks to the far more liquid bond market and the bond-driven credit derivatives market, where fairly extensive price and ratings data are on hand.

- CreditRisk+ is more focused on setting loan loss provisions. This is consistent with its goal to assess risk capital requirements in a rather illiquid environment where loans are held to maturity and the major event is a default (see also Chapter 12's discussion of ACRA).

Unlike CreditMetrics, CreditRisk+ considers only the average default rates associated with each grade of a credit rating, whether published by a rating agency or an internal score. It also incorporates the volatilities of those rates. This assists us in constructing a continuous distribution of default risk probabilities that could be combined with the exposure profile of the instruments concerned.

The output of this approach is a loss distribution and associated risk capital estimates, not unlike those generated by CreditMetrics. Furthermore, CreditRisk+ and CreditMetrics take a similar view of the credit problem.

Both estimate the losses on a portfolio of credit exposures by making judgments about how individual assets correlate with each other and how they will behave. Then, they develop and use a matrix based on transition probabilities of credit rating changes among the assets, a concept that is by now familiar to the reader.

Let me once again emphasize that transition probabilities do require a data-rich environment because published tables may not be applicable to *our* bank's case. The need for data mining remains even if Standard & Poor's and Moody's have made their credit databases available to the general public. For instance, CreditPro, S&P's CD-ROM application, covers the transition and default behavior of some 6,000 companies in 12 industry sectors, including 5,000 transition and default matrices.

CHAPTER 14

Risk Adjusted Return on Capital, CreditPortfolioView, and the Loan Analysis System

1. INTRODUCTION

Developed in the late 1980s by Bankers Trust and based on an earlier model that dates back to the late 1970s, Risk Adjusted Return on Capital (RAROC) is today the most common approach to valuing credit-risk–based performance. Since its introduction to the market, several banks have experimented both with RAROC and with variants. Judging by the feedback I get, RAROC carries the day.

Risk-adjusted return on capital is fundamentally a top-down procedure to align management loans and trade objectives with those of prudential risk control. The aim is to distribute down to products, business units, customers, and individual loans the cost of risk computed by the institution's finance function.

RAROC uses funds transfer pricing and capital allocation in apportioning aggregate risk. "The management of risk, for ourselves and for our customers, is our business. RAROC is a philosophy, a culture, and a discipline. With this intense focus on risk, we expect to remain the industry leader in our business," Bankers Trust stated in a press release December 17, 1993.

A year later, in 1994, the flexibility and functionality of its information system enabled Bankers Trust to develop a comprehensive global Risk Management Application (RMA) that goes beyond RAROC. RMA receives real-time information from trading systems around the world, and it supports an environment that can provide credit risk and market risk exposures for top management. It does so trade by trade and across all business lines.

As both RAROC and RMA demonstrate, the design of a valid risk management system has to be based on the premise that risks take many forms. There are credit risks, interest rate risks, currency risks, country risks, legal risks, settlement risks, operational risks, security risks, technology risks, and many other risks—hence the need for an analytical but comprehensive approach to risk control.

The second model included in this chapter is McKinsey's CreditPortfolioView; the third is KPMG's Loan Analysis System (LAS). Both could be seen as new-generation RAROC, coming onstream 10 years after the original. They are improved versions that fit well the requirements of credit derivatives in terms of analytics.

CreditPortfolioView is macroeconomics-oriented. LAS uses net present value, which serves not only to tune observed spreads and provide for risk compensation, but also to estimate if the cost of carry has been properly priced. In loan securitization, it is always wise to distinguish between market risk and cost of carry, particularly if the institution wishes to experiment with optimization.

2. MANAGEMENT DISCIPLINE AND THE MODELING OF CREDIT RISK

To my knowledge, Bankers Trust has been the first financial institution on record to develop a risk management solution based on computers, networks, and databases, with the objective of earning an adequate return for the risks being taken. It has also been the first to introduce into loans pricing sequential sampling concepts, which have been extensively used by the manufacturing industry.

One of the goals RAROC has targeted through sequential sampling is the sensitization to the fact that credit risk is scaleable. Parallel goals are to delineate management responsibility, assure adequate risk diversification, and maintain strong central risk oversight in partnership with operations anywhere in the world, for any product, at any time.

Knowledgeable bankers appreciate that this policy requires a disciplined practice of risk management throughout the bank. Methodology implies discipline, which is particularly important in terms of

- The things management chooses to do,
- Those it chooses to avoid, and
- The risks it decides to take.

Chapter 13 focused on the issue of methodology. At the time it developed and implemented RAROC, Bankers Trust emphasized the need for a rigorous methodology able to lead to management discipline. This was characterized as a culture to be applied to all aspects of the institution's work:

- The choice of markets it pursues,
- The selection of financial instruments,
- The screening of counterparties,
- The financial transactions it chooses to execute, and
- The technological support it provides to itself and to its clients.

In this comprehensive application of the term, the control of exposure is a thought process that forces us (1) to consider the risks and rewards whenever we are making a significant decision and (2) to carefully and fully explore the potential exposure, reflecting on its financial impact and relating this view to the reward being anticipated. RAROC and RMA consider each disaggregated type of risk in the portfolio (market risk, credit risk, and so on) and, for each risk element, they compute the worst-case scenario or largest potential loss.

As a common unit of measurement, capital permits us to aggregate the various sorts of risk to a total capital requirement for the transaction or the portfolio. This is compared with the anticipated revenue, computed as net present value, to create the risk-adjusted return on capital.

At Bankers Trust, this basic formula was developed at a time when the bank was already at the frontier of sophisticated portfolio risk and performance measurement. Management policy saw to it that each business line and foreign subsidiary was required to monitor and manage its own risk positions:

- Within a business line, risk control must take place at the trading desk itself as well as at one or more levels of the hierarchy.
- Centrally, global risk management was charged with setting business line limits and risk control policy.

The bet has been that global risk management can create a comprehensive and common language for discussing risk, continually refining the formal definitions underlying the comprehensive calculation of exposure. Among its missions are to monitor risk and report to senior management daily on the bank's and each unit's risk profile.

In the case of panics or, generally, crisis situations, this policy enables the bank to respond quickly and precisely because it knows its exposure both in detail and globally. Quantification and real-time reporting also permit effective communication about the possible impact of any contemplated action.

From the time of its original implementation, RAROC has benefited from advanced computer support which made feasible its steady evolution. In the beginning, the model evaluated single deals and small portfolios on a one-off basis. Then, it operated on a quarterly cycle assessing RAROC ratios for all major business portfolios.

Over the years, the scope and frequency of use have grown, as the bank moved from monitoring RAROC on a daily basis for most business portfolios to monitoring as frequently as every 15 minutes. In 1994, a new Risk Management System came online that permits the bank to monitor risk in general, and RAROC in particular, in real time across a broad spectrum of business activities.

The reader should be aware of the fact that the bank's ability to implement RAROC on a global scale with a high degree of timeliness across a variety of product lines derives from the underlying technological infrastructure. This has made feasible not only intraday reporting but also a consistent structuring of business applications based on a proprietary Global Assets Application Architecture.

3. TACTICAL AND STRATEGIC IMPACT OF RISK-ADJUSTED RETURN ON CAPITAL (RAROC)

Risk-adjusted return on capital is a good example of metrics an internal accounting management system must be able to feed to the board and to senior management. But it is also a new way of looking at customer relationships. Typically, when a borrower (company or individual) goes to a bank for a loan, a binary decision is made: "Qualify/not qualify." Risk-adjusted approaches are not binary.

- They stratify according to credit quality and
- They put a *risk premium* by risk threshold.

Traditionally in banking, *risk assessment* aims to quantify dangers so that responsible loan officers can decide if a particular risk is worth running. In my postgraduate years at UCLA, however, I had a professor of banking who taught his students that a loan officer who had no bad loans was as ineffectual as one who had many bad loans because the former threw away applications from good clients.

The difference sequential sampling makes is that it introduces computed layers of risk covered by appropriate premiums. These permit us to expand lending and securities trading activities, further building up and marketing financial services. But they also require

- The ability to measure risk and price the product accordingly,
- Steadily enhancing the quality of risk control services, and
- Developing new information processing solutions to sustain new goals.

The trick is helping management to decide where to draw the line given the level of risk a certain transaction represents. In information systems terms it needs immediate online access to individual and total committed positions, by credit line, client, and type of product. It also requires capital exposure data and the availability of interactive profitability analyses.

There should be no geographic limitations and no time-zone constraints. Within this reference framework, RAROC uses management principles in order to reset risk premiums and it ties a borrower's overall need for capital to counterparty risk and hence to solvency.

- The evaluation process starts with an estimated credit rating translated into an annual default rate.
- Then it proceeds by increasing the interest rate, as if a reinsurance is bought.

In one out of several implementations, which give RAROC an added flavor, this computed annual default rate gets converted into a capital requirement. After analyzing the shape of the projected loss distribution, the loan officer can conclude that, to limit annual default risk, the bank needs enough equity to cover X standard deviations of an annual loss event.

This method is interesting because it can be easily expanded to cover outliers. To the careful reader, this reference will bring to mind the expected risk, unexpected risk, and supercatastrophe curve we examined in Chapters 11 and 12 in connection to ACRA. He or she will also recall its asymptotic shape in the curve's right side.

- The total of debt plus equity capital might amount to, say, six standard deviations.
- RAROC distributes this amount of capital based on each activity's marginal contribution to an annual loss.

Models of this type permit us, when we evaluate the return on our investments, to give due consideration to exposure factors, adjusting by so much—which essentially means downsizing—the benefits that we are projecting. This is another way of looking into the issue of accumulating reserves.

Bankers, treasurers, and investors should be most sensitive to this need to downsize projected gains from current transactions for reinsurance reasons. As RAROC shows, much can be learned from what leading banks and industrial firms have done in this domain. Under risk-adjusted return on capital, every loan or other financial transaction is assigned a portion of the bank's capital, depending on the level of the activity's risk. But the activity's risk also has a premium the officer must cover out of his expected gains. This premium is dynamically adjustable using statistical tools (see Chapter 12 on operating characteristics curves).

Promotion and compensation must support this system. At Bankers Trust, each officer is judged by the earnings he produces in relation to the capital attributed to this activity and the risk factors. Some adjustment is made for officers who are in charge of new and developing businesses that are not expected to produce high returns immediately.

While many of these methods are no different than the ways other banks operate, the novelty lies in the fact that risk becomes an integral part of P&L calculations, and is being tracked in a constant manner. This contrasts with what happens in other institutions where the digging is slow, but the spending is fast. RAROC and real-time tracking see to it that such aberration does not take place.

4. RAROC AND CAPITAL AT RISK

When we consolidate the statements of the operating account and capital account, the cash flows aggregate into a pool of loan cash flows with an expected net present value (NPV). The lender's risk-adjusted return on capital is the return on capital at risk (CAR) implied by these cash flows. In the context of a risk-adjusted return on capital analysis, the spread is set to cover

- Dealer costs,
- Expected and unexpected losses, and
- The cost of risk capital.

In RAROC, the term *risk premium* applies to the expense the lender incurs to rent the risk capital that he allocates to the loan as a reserve against unexpected loss. However, while the risk component is evaluated and the greater risk is compensated by a higher interest rate, in terms of revenue it is difficult to (1) capture the importance of a single business activity or specific transaction and (2) do so in the context of an overall business activity or client relationship.

In a net present value analysis, risk premium denotes the component that compensates the lender for credit loss in excess of expectations. If a bank calibrates to the market, market prices determine the risk premiums that a lender needs to incorporate into the loan valuation. If it calibrates to capital rules of risk and return dictated by bank policy, then those policies will determine the risk premiums.

The capital at risk concept is important because RAROC charges for risk by allocating capital and by calculating the needed return, but also the model charges money for reinsurance. Higher-risk ventures receive a greater return, but also pay more in insurance. A profitable business must generate annual income exceeding the amount needed to pay a basic rate of return on the assigned capital—computed, for instance, on the basis of risk-free Treasury bonds.

The selection of the risk-free basis of reference is not uniform in the banking industry. While some institutions take the Treasury bonds as a basic rate, others set the basic rate at the estimated combined cost of debt and equity capital for the loan. This way, they derive

- The capital allocation rules from a target rating such as AA,
- The associated one-year loss rate, which implies a standard deviation, and
- A correlation coefficient applicable to this trade.

The correlation coefficient measures the rate at which risk at the unit level contributes to the overall business, but critics say that the quantification of this effect is not clear-cut.

The flexibility associated to the choice of reference values should also be given a premium. For instance, a flexible model will accept alternative decisions by senior management for a basic rate and then supply in real time the results.

This is the case with an improved version of RAROC that provides for a risk adjustment technique. It does not analytically address the deal structure, but it ties capital costs to the avoidance of bankruptcy, seeing to it that correlations with the bank's own portfolio get senior management attention.

Critics say that RAROC stays remote from current market information on risk. This is not an accurate critique because market pricing is dynamic, reflecting changing expectations about inflation and overall business volatility. It is, however, true that market prices can fluctuate more than the current rather static RAROC framework is able to accommodate. This particular criticism is correct (see also Chapter 16).

Other market pricing models have a different emphasis, focusing on the risk of losing some, but not all, equity. One significant improvement to RAROC would be an experimentation module that permits us to evaluate alternatives and optimize complex conditions.

Let me explain this through an example. In the leveraged buyout of Avis Europe by Avis USA, General Motors, and a Belgian holding company, the investment bank was Lazard Brothers. Lazard analysts noted that each of the 12 countries where Avis Europe operated had a different set of laws governing (1) how much debt can be assumed by a local subsidiary and (2) how much interest can be deduced from corporate taxes.

To optimize the Avis transaction, Lazard Brothers designed a computer model to figure out the best placement of the debt to minimize taxes; experiment with and maximize the effect of lower interest rates; and avoid running afoul of corporate laws on currency and dividend outflows.

From Bankers Trust to Lazard Brothers, this is the landscape in which cognizant investors, corporate treasurers, investment bankers, and rocket scientists should collaborate. They must develop knowledge-enriched computer models[1] for automated analysis to optimize

---

[1] See D.N. Chorafas and Heinrich Steinmann, *Expert Systems in Banking*, Macmillan, London, 1991.

transactions, measure exposure, apply a reinsurance policy, and provide a better-structured risk-and-return landscape—which makes the best usage of capital at risk.

5. CreditPortfolioView

The pillars on which rests CreditPortfolioView (CPV) by McKinsey are three concepts credit professionals typically use for risk measurement. Two of them, credit cycles and the behavior of industry sectors within these cycles, are macroeconomic. The third is a borderline case between macroeconomic and microeconomic analysis. This concerns credit migrations and counterparty defaults.

The emphasis on macroeconomics is a strength and a weakness at the same time. Critics say that the model does not pay enough attention to microeconomic factors that are market movers.

From a macroeconomic point of view, knowledge of credit cycles is important inasmuch as defaults tend to increase as the gross domestic product (GDP) declines and, in some cases, as unemployment rates increase. But within this credit cycle different industry sectors behave differently in reaction to the ups and downs of the market.

Credit migrations and defaults correlate both among themselves and with the economy. The Systematic Risk Model of CPV targets such relationships, using historical default as well as implied asset volatility information. Then it proceeds by means of Monte Carlo simulation.

A great deal depends on transparency of risks and rewards connected to the bank's credit business. The model computes a discrete loss distribution, making feasible an estimate of large exposure premiums for risk-adjusted capital. This is particularly important for nondiversified portfolios. The cumulative conditional default probability is computed as a function of rating and maturity.

Based on simulated default rates the model computes parameters such as maximum possible default probability and the expected conditional default probability. The probability of default beyond the expected value can be computed at the 99 percent level of confidence.

The model requires marking to market bonds and those loans that are liquid. It recognizes the economic impact of credit migrations and defaults, and uses a multiperiod default approach for those positions that are not liquid. To use CPV, the bank needs both rating and exposure data at the transaction level and for the whole portfolio.

Basic information includes exposure patterns, liquidation periods, recovery classes, and so on. The method CPV uses differs from other approaches because of the association of macroeconomic criteria and of the fact that the model does not assume a normal distribution and does not use mean-variance approximation.

The goal is to assist in bringing management's attention to the implications of credit decisions. CPV serves this purpose by providing institutions with a framework for addressing specific issues connected to loans and to the handling of debt securities. It does so by

- Directly addressing liquid, traded loans and securities,
- Handling nonliquid loans through a risk-reporting framework, and
- Tabulating the resulting loss distribution for a credit portfolio.

Visualization helps us to appreciate the risk profile of a portfolio containing both liquid and illiquid exposures. The model also permits us to recognize the probable timing and impact of defaults with a nonconstant exposure profile. Time is divided into discrete periods, which are indexed.

Portfolios with nonconstant exposures can be found in trading books, particularly those containing derivative financial instruments. Assets with liquid credit risk positions consist of some types of loans and secondary market debt. Commercial loans and trading lines are usually illiquid. Short of securitization, commercial loans are classically held to maturity.

CreditPortfolioView provides the user with a Risk Adjusted Capital (RAC) report which shows the portfolio's credit loss distribution, including risk capital and expected losses. Another document, the Marginal Risk Capital report, focuses on the marginal risk contribution of business units or individual counterparties.

6. THE LOAN ANALYSIS SYSTEM (LAS)

Developed by KPMG, the Loan Analysis System (LAS) addresses valuation problems arising because of the optionality of loan instruments. Its goal is to provide decision support for valuing loans by means of quantifying them in a framework that accounts for market values. LAS is well structured and in all likelihood it can extend into credit derivatives applications.

In this chapter I have discussed RAROC, CreditPortfolioView, and LAS because these solutions have many parallels. I see the LAS model as an improved RAROC that accounts for the difference between internal and external valuation criteria. Such a difference can be significant for a number of reasons:

- Wanting portfolio management,
- Failure to account for prepayment options,
- Lack of market liquidity for the securitization of corporate loans,
- Lack of sensitivity to changes to the borrower's rating,
- Scarcity of information on the rating of loans, and so on.

LAS capitalizes on the fact that since 1995, Standard & Poor has rated some 500 leveraged loans. However, only recently ratings account for individual loans security features rather than for only borrower (counterparty) dependability. This value-added service by S&P matches the consideration of security features (which is already a practice with bonds) and it greatly improves the analytical chores.

In a way similar to the one we saw in section 4, LAS is a net present value model addressing credit pricing, targeting the total loan package, and reflecting current market prices. Compared to other credit risk models in the off-the-shelf class, this is a significant improvement.

The approach chosen by LAS rests on two pillars: cash flows and elements of structure. Cash flows are examined in terms of positive and negative effects, as shown in Table 14.1. The elements of structure include loan type (term, revolver, line of credit, other), fixed or floating interest rate, interest rate caps, floors, and collars as well as

- Fees (up-front and periodic),
- Principal repayment,
- Grid pricing,
- Prepayment,
- Call protection,
- Collateral,
- Debt seniority,
- Financial covenants, and
- Exercise of options.

One of the LAS designers' goals is to address the many dimensions of banking loans in a way allowing for pricing a loan's structure as well as reflecting dynamic credit risk. The chosen approach quantifies the effect of structure on value, dealing with embedded options and accounting for the migration in credit risk.

Based on market prices or on the bank's internal standards, LAS computes values for a variety of differently structured loans. Using net present value, the model evaluates a loan in regard to its expected future cash flows.

Table 14.1 Cash Flow Criteria of LAS Model

Positive Effects	Negative Effects
1. Up-front fee	1. Loan principal
2. Periodic fees facility	2. Cost of funds
3. Interest payments (base rate + spread)	3. Origination and underwriting costs
4. Principal repayments	4. Cost of carry (administration and monitoring)
5. Prepayment penalty	5. Loss in the event of default

- It starts with estimating the cash flows, and
- It considers public or internal credit ratings.

For commercial loans, for example, the cash flow depends not only on spreads and fees but also on embedded options and their exercise strategies. When the lender exercises certain options like covenants, this leads to repricing or restructuring, which must be reflected in the computational procedure.

It is also possible that the borrower will exercise other types of options affecting the transaction—for instance, prepayment, drawn amount, or choice of base rates. All these borrower options can have a significant contribution to value so they should be taken into full account.

LAS uses a decision tree framework to characterize risk as well as to reflect on borrower and lender options. It models dynamic credit risk using transition probabilities (see Chapter 13); assesses the value of loan structures, including embedded options; and evaluates unexpected losses through market-based credit risk premiums. It also incorporates loan origination and carrying costs.

The model's designers have also tried to derive risk analysis benefits through what-if experimentation. Risk rating transition probabilities have been combined with the analysis of net present value. Influenced by ratings and their transition, cash flow determinants include

- Borrower prepayment,
- Revolver usage, and
- Pricing grids.

Through NPV, the model deduces a dollar value for grid pricing, also known as performance pricing, or step-up step-down pricing. For publicly rated companies, ratings changes often trigger repricing under a grid but the lender can distinguish between grids providing value to the bank and grids that subtract economic value.

LAS applies a value to risk capital reflecting observed market risk premiums and a selected interest rate. A hurdle spread equal to the hurdle rate less risk-free rate is multiplied by risk capital. This equals the overall risk premium calculated for the loan. The risk premium quantifies risk, and the hurdle spread measures the amount of risk borne by each unit of capital.

Credit spreads can be derived either from the lender's capital rules or from the market. The measures being used apply both to new loans and to the inventory of loans in the portfolio. As the loans in the banking book age, migrations in counterparty risk rating, changes in interest rates, variations in principal outstanding, and changes in durations make the reevaluation and repricing of inventoried loans mandatory.

7. WHY ANALYTICAL SYSTEMS SERVE SENIOR MANAGEMENT

Bankers Trust, J.P. Morgan, and Credit Suisse have begun voluntarily to include value-at-risk analysis (see Chapter 15) in their annual reports. Other banks have followed suit. But to disclose, the institution must have the information on hand, which means having sophisticated risk management systems and ensuring that they work in a dependable manner.

Banks that have been ahead of the curve in information technology appreciate that no solution can keep market supremacy forever, because new ones come up and take leadership. The example we saw in this chapter with LAS, CreditPortfolioView, and RAROC shows what I just stated. A bank has to run fast to keep its leadership.

The same is true of models. The solution we are using must evolve over time. From an initiative started in the late 1970s, Bankers Trust implemented groupwide risk management through RAROC in 1987 and added value to it in the 1990s. The common thread of these ventures is that

- The desirability of each transaction is judged according to risk and reward, not friendships, and
- The balance sheet is managed as a group of risk portfolios whose return changes with market whims.

Can we learn a lesson from the experiences shown in this chapter and in the preceding three? Yes, we can. The first basic rule for serious bankers is that in all their decisions and actions they must aim to understand the risk component. They must measure exposure in a valid and uniform manner, and assign economic value to each risk.

Because capital is crucial to ensure financial staying power, the second rule can be found in the belief that the risk(s) of a transaction and of a portfolio should be supported by current assets—regardless of their specific accounting definition. In this simple sentence lies the whole concept of risk-adjusted return on capital, no matter which model is used.

The third basic rule is that developing or buying a tool like RAROC, LAS, RiskMetrics, CreditRisk+, or any other is just one step in adopting analytical approaches. Once the bank has the culture of model usage and also understands the risks associated with models, it should generate more sophisticated approaches of its own—the eigenmodels. (See also Chapter 16 on rocket scientists.)

Chances are that these eigenmodels will be more sophisticated than the first-generation models. An example is the Risk Appetite Index by J.P. Morgan. To help in estimating investors' tolerance of risk and how it changes over time, the Morgan Bank has developed what it calls an index for the inclination of taking risks.

- The risk appetite index helps to prove that while investors are rarely indifferent to risk, over time their risk appetite can change.
- The algorithm is based on the correlation between the rank of a currency's performance over the past month and the rank of its historical volatility.

An example is provided by the performance of European currencies. If currencies are ranked according to their performance against, for instance, the German mark (from strongest to weakest) and they are also sorted according to their volatility (from lowest to highest), then the two rankings seem to correlate.

- A value of –1 in this exercise implies full risk aversion.
- A value of +1 means that investors are risk seekers or at least tolerant of risk.

Another financial institution has designed a risk evaluator enriched through knowledge engineering artifacts. Specialized databases are explored online through *agents*[2] activated by other agents who respond to ad hoc interactive queries by end users.

One of the agents is an environment assessor, focusing on market forecasts, industry trends, and the prevailing business climate. Another is a strategy analyst, whose task is to investigate the fit between a group of transactions to be performed and the strategic objectives of the bank.

A financial analyst agent investigates the strengths and weaknesses of a business partner as well as its financial staying power. A borrower assessor studies the nonfinancial strengths and weaknesses of the corporate client, and a profit analyst agent has the mission to determine gains and losses connected to the projected transaction.

These and similar examples help to show that no matter how good a model is at this point in time, it is always possible to do better through added value. Managers and professionals worth their salt will appreciate that the artifacts we have studied in Chapters 11 through 14 are only "assistants to"—they are not substitutes for judgment. Personal judgment and the accountability that goes with it are always necessary because there is no telling what will happen next in highly volatile and risky financial markets.

---

[2] D.N. Chorafas, *Agent Technology Handbook,* McGraw-Hill, New York, 1998.

CHAPTER 15

Value at Risk

1. INTRODUCTION

Long-term exposure is an important indicator of financial health. Accountability for such exposure lies with the board and with senior management. The board members in Orange Country who lost $1.7 billion with inverse floaters and other derivatives would have probably reacted quite differently if they had known that there existed a 5 percent chance of having more than a billion-dollar loss.

This chance of a loss can be computed using the current structure and content of the bank's trading book (see Chapter 2) through value-at-risk (VAR) models. The 1996 Market Risk Amendment by the Basle Committee on Banking Supervision[1] offered two choices to institutions: netting and VAR. A significant number of banks have opted for VAR.

The most significant change induced by the 1996 Market Risk Amendment and the adoption of VAR is cultural. Banks that would have never ventured into using models bought one and launched themselves into a new era of risk management. After VAR, the most

[1] D.N. Chorafas, *The Market Risk Amendment: Understanding Marking-to-Model and Value-at-Risk,* McGraw-Hill/Irwin, Burr Ridge, IL, 1998.

technologically advanced institutions migrated toward the use of models for the control of credit risk.

Through practice over a short period of time, the banking industry found that the use of value at risk presents a number of advantages. Gone are practices where institutions usually measured the risks in individual parts of their trading book separately, and then had difficulty in putting these figures together in a compound estimate of exposure.

By moving toward a whole trading book approach through VAR, bankers, treasurers, and investors aim to calculate on a fairly consistent basis the likely loss they might experience on their whole trading book at the 99 percent level of confidence. This allows them to do more focused trades and better hedges between and within different markets.

Apart from reporting exposure to the supervisors, VAR models are used to assess (1) likely price changes of financial instruments in individual markets and (2) the extent to which prices in one market vary in relation to those in other markets. The results are approximate but accurate enough. Therefore, under a rigorous risk management methodology they serve a purpose.

The careful reader will notice that both VAR for market risk and its variant for credit risk have limitations. A case in point is the difficulty making valid predictions regarding volatility, which is not even included in the model; or correlating datasets that are frequently scant or simply nonexistent in the bank's databases.

Other major limitations of VAR and Credit VAR result from less than commendable banking practices—for instance, the vagaries of repayment and the exceptional treatment afforded to some favored customers by credit institutions. These are ad hoc subjective factors, and like anything subjective, they are hard to factor into the model.

2. A BIRD'S-EYE VIEW OF VALUE AT RISK

Value at risk is a probability-weighted aggregation of current results in gains and losses embedded in a trading portfolio, under various market scenarios. VAR typically assumes that no trading occurs during the pricing exercise. In other terms, at least on an instantaneous basis there is zero liquidity in the market.

The daily estimate of value at risk can take the form of a revenues-and-exposures graph as well as of a holding period over 10 days with no risk-reducing trades. The computation should be made at the 99 percent confidence level to be consistent with the 1998 Market Risk Amendment by the Basle Committee.

As seen in Figure 15.1, the calculation of value at risk assumes a normal distribution of exposures, which is evidently an approximation, whether we talk of individual instruments or of the contents of the whole trading book. A positive aftermath of this approximation is that we can use the concept underpinning the operating characteristics curve (lower part of Figure 15.1) to estimate the 99 per-

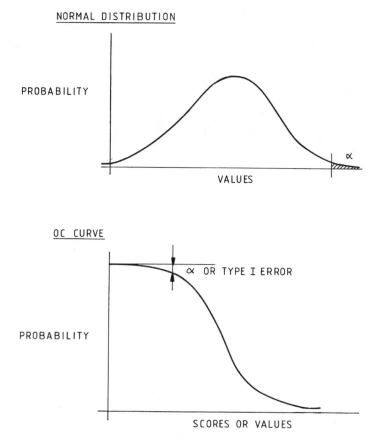

FIGURE 15.1 VALUE AT RISK ASSUMES A NORMAL DISTRIBUTION OF EXPOSURE, WHICH IS AN APPROXIMATION.

cent probability that the worst case will not exceed the value derived from our computation.

The reader knowledgeable in mathematical statistics will appreciate that this 99 percent level of confidence corresponds to a *Type I* error, on the OC curve, of 1 percent. This is known as α. In the long run, in 1 percent of cases the VAR estimate will not cover the worst case.

In the computation of VAR there may be other errors too that are not statistical in nature, but depend on our assumptions and on the correlations that we admit. Empirically derived correlations are used for aggregation within each of three basic risk classes: currency exchange, interest rates, and equities.

Other classes, too, can be distinguished depending on the business of the bank. Across risk classes, cumulative exposure is computed assuming zero correlation among highly defined risk classes. This is, of course, another approximation reflecting the diversification that might or might not exist in a universal bank's business areas. Hence, depending on the institution and its trading habits, this hypothesis may be weak or outright false.

From a statistical viewpoint, VAR is a scalar *estimate* of an unknown parameter of the loss distribution. Sampling errors can affect the accuracy of point estimates so institutions using VAR must be careful with the hypotheses that they make and the way these hypotheses influence the outcome.

Confidence intervals for the VAR can be derived through a parametric or nonparametric approach taken in connection with a portfolio structure and its distributed returns. Some analysts prefer to compute VAR through interval estimates and choose the use of asymptotic confidence intervals, but the basic methods for VAR calculation are two:

- Parametric (VAR/P) based on the assumption of a normal distribution of asset and liability prices.
- Nonparametric or simulation (VAR/S), which uses Monte Carlo[2] and can lead to stress analysis.

---

[2] See D.N. Chorafas, *Chaos Theory in the Financial Markets,* Probus, Chicago, 1994.

Practical applications of VAR include the measurement of and report on exposure, which is demanded by regulators, as well as the management of market risk. VAR extensions now target credit risk. Senior management can benefit from VAR if it has taken care to appropriately define capital at risk (see Chapter 14). This has two aspects:

- What's the level of capitalization—essentially the entrepreneurial capital—that is required by the market?
- What is the capital at risk—i.e., the economic capital—*our* bank can afford to put on the block?

Because VAR provides a basis for experimentation, the visibility senior management is after will be achieved iteratively between these two poles of reference. Sophisticated experimental approaches, however, require handling nonlinear distributions for daily changes in market variables; using Monte Carlo simulation; and employing Taylor Series expansion to calculate VAR when distributions are non-normal.

Senior management finds these issues awfully technical. Yet, they are crucial in defining and measuring market risk in an accurate way. Just as important is that the board and senior management understand the role of *backtesting* for tuning the parameters of VAR calculations, as well as the importance of using *stress scenarios* for measurement of catastrophic market risk.

Backtesting is required by the 1996 Market Risk Amendment, and institutions have to present the results to the regulators. The results essentially consist of how well the VAR model has prognosticated the real-life exposure. Depending on these results, the prognostication falls in the green, yellow, or red zone. The green zone is the best.

A study done by the Bank of England suggests that other things being equal, in regard to the classification of the results required by the Basle Committee, VAR/P tends to push into the yellow zone. For this reason, big British banks are now moving to VAR/S.

Stress testing is not required at present by the Basle Committee, but institutions are well advised to learn how to do it.

The study of catastrophic scenarios is an added value to VAR. Rigorous models can help in distinguishing levels of exposure (see also Chapter 11) in terms of expected business risk, unexpected risk, and catastrophic risk.

These differ in both their measurement and management; therefore, they require appropriate solutions to testing and reporting. In an information technology sense, typical business risks can be served through "pull" software (the classical approach where the user asks to be informed on results), while "push" software supported by agents is needed for catastrophic and near-catastrophic risks.

3. SATISFYING REGULATORY AND MANAGERIAL REQUIREMENTS

The 1996 Market Risk Amendment outlines regulatory specifications for VAR. These are the 99 percent confidence interval (see also section 6); a 10-day holding period; a historical observation period of at least one year; a minimum three-month frequency for the update of data sets; and the recognition of correlations across broad risk factors categories: interest rate, currency exchange, equities, and commodities. Another regulatory requirement is a scaling factor for VAR results.

For internal management accounting reasons the bank may also follow another list of "musts." Chapter 13 reported that many institutions have started to internally differentiate between value at risk and capital at risk. Also, for internal management control purposes VAR has started to be endowed with delta/gamma hedging[3] to calculate risk based on a one-day holding period, exponential moving average volatilities, and correlations within risk factors.

This enlarges the implementation horizon of value at risk, and the use of estimates of potential losses in the bank's portfolio for a predetermined probability and holding period. Attention must be paid to the methodology employed to capture all significant risks and meet or exceed industry standards in terms of accuracy and timeliness.

---

[3] See D.N. Chorafas, *Advanced Financial Analysis, with Derivatives Trades,* Euromoney, London, 1994.

The careful reader should understand that there are a number of weaknesses connected to VAR. I have already made reference to the fact that in real life rates, risks, and returns are not normally distributed—as it is assumed. When markets are calm the bell-shaped distribution may be acceptable, but in nervous markets it leads to implementation flaws:

- VAR models are particularly weak at the edges, because of extreme movements, and
- Outliers occur much more frequently than suggested by the normal distribution.

A second issue that I find the management of institutions does not particularly appreciate is that VAR incorporates a significant probability of financial disaster—particularly if the 95 percent level of confidence is used, as many banks do, instead of the regulatory 99 percent.

The most technically inclined reader will also understand that VAR fails to account for fat tails. Yet, leptokyrtotic distributions very commonly appear with financial time series. The discarding of extreme or repetitive values weakens the benefits obtained from the model.

These remarks are not written to discourage bankers, treasurers, traders, and investors from using VAR. Their objective is to make readers aware that models (like people) have weaknesses and if one is not aware of them, he or she can fall in a trap. One major weakness with the *method* (but not necessarily with the model) is the use of meager databases, which leads to meaningless if not outright misleading results.

- Whether for regulatory or for internal management reasons, banks with rich databases employ up to 10 years of statistics for computation.
- But in other institutions, two years of underlying data is all that is used to derive the market movements for VAR calculation—an inadequate practice.

High technology banks have the policy of recalculating VAR weekly; very few, except the leaders, do so daily. Other banks recalculate VAR monthly; still others do so on a quarterly basis—which is also inadequate even if some banks review VAR after renewed market turbulence.

One question I am often asked in my seminars is "In arriving at aggregate VAR, is it advisable to consider offsets between different markets, currencies, and risks to reflect relationships and account for the impact of diversification?" Banks use a number of approaches to calculate risk offsets, trying to find sufficiently stable empirical relationships that can be demonstrated, but few are doing so in a convincing manner.

Generally, only a limited use is made of correlation models for netting, because correlation coefficients may be extremely unstable over short time periods. This is particularly true at times of significant extreme market volatility. (Remember that VAR does not account for extreme events.)

In several financial institutions risk offset is primarily directed at netting between currencies within each risk type, in a way consistent with the manner in which risk is managed and monitored against limits. When offsets are done, they are calculated under the methodology suggested by the Basle Capital Accord.

In conclusion, we can say that value at risk denotes what will be the likely losses at a 99 percent level of confidence if the market movements during the historical data period, whose statistical effects have been calculated, were all to take place

- At this time and
- In the same direction.

This is computed on the hypothesis that if the actual positions currently held were not changed during the holding period, then losses incurred by the bank are likely to be greater than the value at risk in only 1 percent of the cases. What I have added to this reference is that institutions must be aware, and beware, of extreme values that might turn this estimate on its head.

Neither the parametric VAR nor the simulation VAR say anything about extreme values: precisely what might happen in the "other" 1 percent, beyond the 99 percent confidence limit. UBS found out that in the case of LTCM's near-bankruptcy this other 1 percent showed a loss of $1.36 billion. Banks should be very careful with extreme events.

4. APPLICATIONS EXAMPLES USING VALUE AT RISK

Let me start with a real-life reference. In its 1996 Annual Report, Credit Suisse points out that the relationship between daily trading revenue and daily VAR calculated under the Full Offset Basle Method has been tracked over the course of that same year.

- The average daily trading revenue in 1996 was $4.1 million (versus $3.4 million for 1995), and
- The maximum level of daily trading revenue was $18.9 million.

The average daily VAR estimate was $22.5 million (versus $18.3 million for 1995), and the maximum level was $ 31.2 million. A comparison of daily trading revenue and daily VAR showed that the daily trading revenue was never larger than the corresponding VAR figures. If one generalizes based on these statistics,

- The average daily trading revenue is about 18 percent of the daily VAR,
- But the maximum daily trading revenue is 60 percent of the daily VAR.

This frame of reference can be valuable to senior management. Let's now examine what VAR could contribute on the trading floor. A dealer may hold an overnight $/£ position, being short on sterling 50 million, equivalent to $78 million at the prevailing spot rate of 1.56. The average level of historical £/$ daily price changes is

- Mean £/$ 1.5245,
- Standard deviation 0.035 (which is the daily volatility),

- Mean +2.34 standard deviations = £/$ 1.6054 (99 percent level of confidence, one-sided), and
- Mean +1.65 standard deviations = £/$ 1.5822 (95 percent level of confidence, one-sided).

If the bank assumes that historical volatility will hold over the next 24 hours, it can be estimated at the 99 percent level of confidence that the value of the position will not deteriorate by more than $2,269,000—which the trader's position will need to pay to cover his being short in sterling.

In other terms, the bank does not expect the position to lose more than $2,269,000 with a 99 percent degree of confidence. For this trader alone, this amount is the value at risk. However, 1 percent of the time—which roughly represents three days in the year—the expected loss will exceed the VAR level.

Notice that if the 95 percent level of confidence had been chosen, then in the estimated worst case the loss would have been less, equal to $1,109,000. But in the longer run, in 5 percent of all cases (or 15 days per year) this loss would be exceeded.

The trader was short on sterling because he expected the dollar to rise in the currency exchange market. The value at risk in the preceding example regards the possibility that, contrary to expectations, the dollar will fall against the sterling. In other terms, the market will move contrary to the trader's best judgment.

Say, as an alternative, that the trader, rather than being short on sterling, was long on sterling. In this case, if everything else in the preceding example is kept the same, he will make a profit. But we should also consider the case where the dollar rises against sterling, which essentially means the other end of the distribution.

If the trader is long on sterling and sterling falls against the dollar, the value at risk at 99 percent and 95 percent intervals will be those we have already examined but for the opposite reasons. In other words, we will still be dealing with a one-tailed distribution, but our concern will be the left tail rather than the right.

A different way of saying this is that the actual gain or loss to be realized will depend not only on whether the $/£ movement is up or down but also on the nature of the bet: going long or short.

In either case, the greater the confidence level chosen, the greater the VAR that results—and the less the likelihood that it will be exceeded.

The focal point of this example has been a snapshot evaluation of risk. A more complete approach would consider the holding period, which impacts the calculation. Let me explain the method in a few words. To find how the holding period affects the VAR estimate, it is first necessary to use the standard deviation appropriate to the time window. If we consider a holding period of one day, and liquid assets, then estimates of daily standard deviation are enough.

For a longer-term investment in illiquid assets, a holding period of at least a month—or even a year—will be appropriate. Correspondingly, volatility calculations should be done on monthly (or yearly) price data, since adjusting daily volatility data does not necessarily give dependable results.

5. CHALLENGES WITH THE TEST OF HYPOTHESES USED IN THE MODEL

Banks with experience in modeling, and in the computation of credit risk and market risk, have evidence that mapping the market into the computer and doing a rigorous experimentation allows diversification. This brings up a number of other issues relating to management culture, skills requirements, the hypotheses being made, and technological leadership.

A basic but not always appreciated policy is that, in principle, the more diversified are the trading book and the banking book, the lower the corresponding capital requirements will be. There are regulatory measures, however, that do not permit this flexibility; neither are the available eigenmodels able to serve reliably all sorts of diversification moves.

Beyond the pricing models and the risk models for derivatives, an institution also needs optimization models that address the contents of the trading book and banking book for diversification reasons. Since the algorithms being used most often rest on the normal distribution and its confidence intervals, one of the concerns is the existence of correlations, outliers, and spike volatilities.

Usually spike patterns see to it that data are not normally distributed. Therefore, our hypotheses are not substantiated by market facts. Furthermore, because the way to bet is that every distribution has outliers, one of the critical questions is how well our model will cope with them.

- Is it really sensitive to extreme events?
- Will such events upset its behavior?

As Dr. Paul Embrechts suggests, we want to have methods for estimating conditional probabilities that account for fat tails. An institution may incur a loss beyond VAR; but how far can it expect it to go?[4]

- The study of extreme events can be done through extreme value theory.
- Because extreme events matter, in all likelihood this theory will become an important part of a bank's methodology.

The best way to judge models is by what they deliver; therefore, the preceding bulleted items are most relevant. Sometime down the line the current linear models based on the normal distribution will become inaccurate. Then they will become unacceptable, if we have not been careful enough to test for outliers in a dual sense: as predictors and as deviators of model behavior.

A similar point can be made about correlations. Usually the algorithms we develop are based on a hypothesis of independent events. This rarely happens in real life, and if we have not been careful about the existence of correlations or their neutralization, our model will give inadequate results.

The opposite is also true. Fairly frequently the assumption of the existence of correlations is made without the appropriate study and associated tests. It is, for instance, often assumed that the G-10

---

[4] See also P. Embrechts, S. Resnick, and G. Samorodnitsky, "Living on the Edge," *Risk,* London, January 1998.

stock markets move in synergy and that they highly correlate because of globalization.

Yet, a recent study by the Bank of England documents that from 1988 onward the market behaviors of the London Stock Exchange and of the Tokyo Stock Exchange don't positively correlate in any significant manner. Indeed, if intraday statistics are considered, then sometimes the correlation is negative.

Such findings invalidate the hypotheses we sometimes make. They also impact model behavior, and for this reason they should be kept in perspective. Other issues, too, influence the choice of value-at-risk algorithms to be used.

6. IS THE VAR OUTPUT COMPARABLE FROM BANK TO BANK?

Frequently in my seminars, I am asked an intriguing question, "Is VAR output comparable from bank to bank?" The answer to this query is not linear, because institutions have the habit of improving upon a model—and every time one hears, "My model is better than yours," it means the two are incompatible.

Few commercial and investment bankers appreciate that value-at-risk estimates are not necessarily comparable among different financial institutions. To become comparable, major underlying assumptions and parameters have to be comprehensively disclosed—for example, information on the portfolios covered by the model and model parameters such as holding period, confidence level, observation period, and aggregation method.

To obtain comparable, homogeneous results from VAR, the Basle Committee rules must always be observed. This is not presently the case. The 1996 Market Risk Amendment specifies that in calculating value at risk, a 99 percent one-tailed confidence interval must be used. But many banks use 98 percent, 97.5 percent, or 95 percent confidence levels, as shown in Table 15.1. These statistics come from one of the European regulatory authorities.

The specs by the Basle Committee also say that in calculating value at risk, a 10-day holding period must be used. However, the range used by different financial institutions in one country goes

Table 15.1 Major Assumptions and Associated Differences Underlying Value-at-Risk Estimates Presented in Annual Reports to One of the European Regulatory Authorities

	Bank A	Bank B	Bank C	Bank D	Bank E	Bank F	Bank G	Bank H	Bank I	Bank J
Confidence Interval	99%	99%	99%	99%	99%	98%	97.7%	97.5%	95%	95%
Holding Period	10 days	10 days	10 days	10 days	30 days	1 day	1 day	30 days	1 day	1 day
Aggregation Method	Corre-lation	Simu-lation	No corr.	NA	Corre-lation	Simu-lation	Corre-lation	Corre-lation	Corre-lation	No corr.
Maximum Daily VAR	471	121	80	NA	118	47	30	1090	21	6.9
Minimum Daily VAR	389	64	20	NA	63	19	10	366	4	3.2
Average Daily VAR	415	81	NA	280	100	34	23	NA	10	4.4

NA = not available

from 1 day to 30 days. Table 15.1 also identifies other differences such as the use of correlation, simulation, or other method.

Normalization is important because only then does an analysis of the portfolio through VAR show where risks are concentrated, and raise warning flags to even unsophisticated users. The results are not comparable if the factors being employed diverge, and this brings prejudice not only to the concept of regulation but also to the internal prudential management of an institution. Another signal that I picked up from a meeting with a regulatory authority is that senior management does not clearly appreciate that

- The 99 percent level of confidence does not provide full assurance of maximum possible loss.
- Few top managers understand that the remaining 1 percent exception could be catastrophic to the bank.

In fact, to remedy potential weaknesses of the model, the 1996 Market Risk Amendment by the Basle Committee specifies a multiplier to the VAR output. The factor varies from 3 to 4 depending on the performance of the model in terms of green or yellow classification, while falling into the red zone means that the model does not work. But while a multiplier of 3 may be high for a good model, a multiplier of 4 would not correct the output of a flawed algorithm.

Moreover, senior management is not always aware that formal statistical procedures for the computation of VAR should include a steady assessment of the model's accuracy. Performance-based verification tests should go beyond comparing estimates of one-day potential losses with one-day actual data. They should do so *intraday.*

The message is that while this daily test is necessary, it is not enough. Even more important is the dynamic test over time, which gives both a *microseasonal* and a *macro* dimension of the VAR model's output. This involves

- *Intraday* exposure changes, which follow intraday market values and can be significant to the bank's management for operational reasons and for test purposes.

- *Longer-term* verification tests performed to analyze the model's accuracy over time as well as to evaluate alternative hypotheses and characteristic factors.

Furthermore, while models are not made to—and cannot— provide 100 percent assurance, they can be instrumental in reinforcing the qualitative approaches taken by the board and senior management as well as by supervisors. The focal point of my idea is internal control.

Senior management should watch that models don't give loan officers, traders, and other professionals an incentive to tailor their risk computation to meet internal and external supervisory requirements while concealing exposure growth. This happens sometimes, and it is the wrong practice.

VAR is made to enhance transparency. It should not be used to manipulate or hide financial results.

Finally, the model that we use has to capture the nonlinear price characteristics of the bank's positions. For instance, a full 10-day price shock has to be applied to the options positions or positions that display optionlike characteristics. The model has also to have a set of risk factors that capture kappa (vega) risk. All these are basic issues that impact the model's output, helping to define how accurate and how sophisticated it can get.

Let me close this chapter by bringing the board's and senior management's attention to the fact that models can be awfully mismanaged, sometimes by the same people to whom they are entrusted. To show the manipulation of VAR models and their emasculation, I will take once more as an example the case of LTCM-UBS.

In this particular incident of a highly geared hedge fund and its unfortunate investor, the mismanagement of risk seems to have been so advanced that UBS received only piecemeal information on exposure from LTCM regarding its more than $1 billion investment. Precisely:

- An announcement about the "inner worth" of LTCM, a kind of guestimated stock value.

- This secretive information came to UBS at the incredible frequency of *once-per-month.*

Yet, with such a highly unreliable and obsolete number, UBS updated its *daily VAR model,* when it calculated its consolidated exposure. No attention was paid to the fact that *quality of output* directly depends on *quality of input.* This is not a one-tantum phenomenon. It is widespread among financial institutions, with the result that *the value of VAR has become 0.0.* Few boards care about this VAR emasculation and even fewer do something about it. The reason is that board members don't understand what VAR is all about in the first place.

In an interview with Zurich's *CASH* magazine, the chief risk management officer of UBS gave some other interesting information on the unreliability of VAR's input/output.[5] He said that LTCM's data, received once per month and fed into the bank's *daily* VAR calculations, was complemented with "artificial data," computed by UBS itself. In terms of the value of the output, the CRMO added: "The [VAR] model only shows which maximal loss in the next 10 days will not be surpassed, with 99 percent confidence level. If, however, an event happens in the remaining risk of 1 percent, the system does not tell how big the maximal loss will be." With LTCM's near-bankruptcy as an extreme event, the maximal loss to UBS happened to be $1.36 billion.

---

[5] October 2, 1998.

CHAPTER 16

Rocket Scientists

1. INTRODUCTION

We live in an age in which knowledge holds the key to our future. Today in the banking industry, research and development (R&D) and technological leadership determine who wins the next round of global competition. The knowledge quotient we put into financial products is instrumental in propelling a bank's profits in an age in which events move very rapidly.

In a modern bank, over 50 percent of the profits and about 30 percent of the business come from products that did not exist two to three years earlier. Interestingly enough, we find a parallel in the communications, computer, and software industries where some 70 percent of the revenues come from products that did not exist two years ago.

Securities trading at large, and derivatives in particular, is an area where there has been significant change in the way the bank looks at its future. The cultural change ranges from the design of new products to the control of risk—and for all practical purposes this process is still in an early phase.

The development of credit derivatives has given banks the incentive to focus more on the mathematical analysis underpinning product research and market competition. It also underlines the need to manage more closely the institution's risk profile.

The dual requirement for pricing financial instruments and for controlling exposure has led to more sophisticated in-house systems. This has been helped by cross-fertilization from science and technology through the employment of rocket scientists.[1]

The term *rocket scientist* comes from the fact that earlier in their careers many of the physicists, engineers, and mathematicians who today work in the financial industry were employed in aerospace and nuclear engineering. More recently, their skills have been instrumental in bringing service institutions into the 21st century. Bankers appreciate this contribution.

2. THE USE OF ROCKET SCIENCE IN BANKING

Traditionally, security analysis and trading have attracted some of the best minds in any marketplace: in the city, Wall Street, or elsewhere. The job demands good stock-picking ability grounded in rock-solid analytic skills and a flair for salesmanship. Derivative financial instruments magnify the need for these qualities.

A successful *financial analyst* is a person with a multiple personality: one-part pragmatic researcher; another part fortune-teller; still another either academician or salesperson. While not everything he or she says is analytical, the advice he or she gives must be properly researched and well founded. This requires a lot of investigative field work, database mining, and mathematical modeling.

As this job gets to be increasingly more complex, banks and securities houses orient their recruitment of financial analysts to postgraduates with experience in science and technology and a sharp investigative mind.

In 1998 I asked a senior German banker whether his institution is using rocket scientists to model exposure. His answer would have been unheard of five years earlier in continental Europe: "In all

---

[1] See D.N. Chorafas, *Rocket Scientists in Banking,* Lafferty Publications, London and Dublin, 1996.

areas related to risk modeling—on both the business and the control side—the bank employs staff with exceptional knowledge in mathematics, physics, financial engineering, and other related fields. These are MBAs and PhDs."

"The people we meet in risk management are to a very substantial extent engineers, mathematicians, physicists, and oceanographers," said the Securities and Exchange Commission in New York. "Both the investment banks and ourselves have adapted to what happens in the industry: modeling, pricing formulas, and experimentation."

Other regulators in the United States and in Europe commented similarly, though many among them lamented the difficulty in keeping up with the rapid developments in the banking industry. Modeling and pricing formulas exceed many regulators' classical accounting backgrounds—but they do see that they need to challenge the bank's model if they find something that does not add up during an examination.

The idea of cross-fertilization between physicists, engineers, mathematicians, and accountants is good, and many of the results obtained so far have been first-class. But the collaboration between bankers and rocket scientists can really be fruitful only when the former appreciate the nature of the work done by the latter and when the rocket scientists understand the secrets of banking (see section 6). Today, neither of these two preconditions is fulfilled. In the majority of cases there is a gap between the two professions.

Yet, the processes underpinning prognostication, evaluation, new product design, and risk management are of equally great interest to bankers and rocket scientists alike. For both professions, the threshold of knowledge is broken practically every day because technology develops so fast. "Five years ago nobody had value-at-risk experience," said one of the European regulators with whom I met. "Now VAR models come into credit risk."

Correctly, both commercial and investment bankers and their regulators run fast to catch up with developments in the industry. But this is hard not only because of the market's and technology's fast paces, but also because solutions must hit a moving target in two different directions at the same time: improving business opportunity and steadily controlling exposure.

Added to this is the need to operate successfully in a global sense but at low cost. These factors describe the magnitude of the task. Yet, the market is a relentless judge who increasingly differentiates a well-managed bank from one whose qualities of management and rocket science are wanting.

Board members and senior managers need to understand the new processes of analysis and their terminology, not only in order to take advantage of them in a business sense, but also to help themselves document their investment decisions. A great deal of equity research done today by rocket scientists filters down the line to the bankers and brokers who serve individual customers—and earn an income by giving advice.

The new forms of financial analysis no longer focus only on "buy," "hold," or "sell" but also, if not primarily, on "swaps." Swaps provide a more accurate definition of trading and investing because, as the word *swap* suggests, the investor does something else with the proceeds of the sale—while classically financial analysts and investment advisors did not make a lot of friends issuing "sell" recommendations.

During the last five years, many senior bankers have asked me what's the difference between the nontraditional financial perspectives opened up by rocket science and the traditional financial research. This text has been born out of answering this query—explaining something that is not so obvious in terms professional bankers can understand.

3. WHAT THE ROCKET SCIENTISTS DO

Where are the rocket scientists working? The answers I received when asking this question divide into two groups: Some are working on trading, developing, and pricing new financial products; others concentrate on risk management, analyzing exposure, and producing risk profiles.

In Zurich, Bank Leu said that rocket scientists are at Group level (Credit Suisse). In London, Barclays reminded me that since the early 1990s, it has had a financial engineering team (originally associated with BZW). For one of the central banks, the people doing in-depth financial analysis are mainly statisticians, but other central banks (especially supervisory authorities) employ rocket scientists.

If a general statement was to be made regarding rocket scientists in the banking industry, it would be that the demand for them has accelerated. While tier-1 institutions have been employing mathematicians, physicists, and engineers since the mid-1980s, it is essentially the 1996 Market Risk Amendment that brought to senior management's attention the need to have people able to do in-depth quantitative analysis and modeling.

Still, few banks are really ahead in this domain. One of the reasons is that top management does not quite understand the rocket science culture. A more fundamental reason is that the real price to be paid for the skill an institution requires for complex financial operations does not lend itself easily to calculation.

Putting together the answers I got during my research meetings regarding major projects in which rocket scientists contribute their skills and time, I came up with two areas where human resources are primarily allocated, as shown in Table 16.1. Implementation roughly represents 80 percent of the rocket scientist's time; applied research accounts for the other 20 percent.

The management of institutions with experience in rocket science work has suggested this field attracts a different kind of thinker than classical financial analysis. The traditional business administration major with some exposure to statistics cannot do the rocket scientist's work. The new quantitative professionals (also known as *quants*) think algorithmically but at the same time they are especially good at dealing with situations where different rules apply than those that characterized banking for a couple of centuries. The new professionals can thrive with paradigm shifts.

Several cognizant banking executives suggested that people able to perform rigorous mathematical studies in finance can rapidly change the levels of abstraction they are using, simultaneously seeing things in the large and in the small.

This is important because the new form of financial analysis requires different levels of abstractions in order to deal with increasingly complex problems. It also calls for intellectual tools to assist in

Table 16.1   The Jobs Rocket Scientists Do

---

1. Implementation

Assistance to traders in new product development

Assistance to salesmen in client support

Beta, delta, gamma, theta, kappa, rho, and liquidity studies

New or improved risk management models

Comprehensive risk management procedures

Real-time simulation

---

2. Applied Research

Advanced financial analysis

Research requested by clients

New simulation and optimization models

Pricing functions, particularly for derivatives

Breaking the algorithmic insufficiency (fuzzy engineering, genetic algorithms, and so on)

---

conceiving, reasoning about, designing, and programming new financial instruments.

The development of *pricing functions* is an example. A feasible value for a new financial product is a value for which market response will be positive. But the feasibility of a product's price value is not necessarily stable. Hence the adjunct need to study price fluctuation by simulating market behavior and doing real-life testing in an effective manner.

Some senior bankers lamented that the typical rocket scientist is very young and has no trading experience. As a result, he or she makes assumptions without understanding the implications of these assumptions. Alternatively, he or she may leave out of the equation some of the outliers.

An example where lack of trading experience leads to the wrong hypotheses is the aftermath of inflation which should be integrated into the model as one of its important scenarios. Other examples are the negative rates applied in the 1970s by the Swiss to protect the franc, and Japan's near-zero interest rate over a long stretch of the 1990s.

Said a former president of the New York Federal Reserve Board, "I was in a meeting on advanced methods for financial analysis, with no economists in it—but physicists, engineers, and mathematicians priding themselves on knowing nothing of economics." Another senior banker was worried that—from an academic viewpoint—fledgling economists cannot get tenure at major universities without proving theoretical virtuosity, even if they have to abandon relevance along the way. Yet,

- The making of models is not a goal but a means for better perception, leading to focused investment or trading decisions.
- We should never lose sight of the fact that financial modeling is an interdisciplinary art; it is not a science.

In fact, one of the major contributions of rocket scientists is that of interdisciplinary migrants and therefore cross-fertilizers. Financial analysis and modeling will not become a science until we return to the fundamentals. This is a role financial particle physics might be able to fulfill.[2]

4. ADDING VALUE TO MODELS ALREADY IN USE: ACRA AND CREDITMETRICS

As Chapters 11 through 15 demonstrated, it is not easy to develop a model that accurately represents market movements or computes the bank's exposure, but it is feasible. The forecast of future market action is what traders, bankers, investors, and speculators are continually trying to do through their hypotheses and assumptions. What the rocket scientists are being asked to contribute is to cast these hypotheses into an algorithmic form.

---

[2] D.N. Chorafas, *How to Understand and Use Mathematics for Derivatives,* Volume 1, *Understanding the Behavior of Markets*, Euromoney, London, 1995.

It would be incorrect to assume that future market behavior will follow the same pattern as it did in the past. Therefore, the scientific approach is to gather and analyze information that permits us to make an objective estimate of future risks and rewards. The aim is to *quantify uncertainty.*

- A serious approach starts with the acceptance that we cannot accurately predict the future.
- What we usually do is to massage historical data and make them reveal a pattern of market movements.

As with all human activities, neither is modeling perfect nor does perfection characterize its implementation. Like the assumptions traders and investors make, modeling is approximate. But the successful use of models depends more on the implementation of rigorous systems and procedures than on precision.

- If there was a case of making a choice between precision in modeling on one side and systems, procedures, and databases on the other, then the better solution by far would be an approximate model but first-class systems and rich databases mined ad hoc in real time.

It is also better to have an approximate model that is understood by its users who appreciate it, because it helps them in amplifying their experience—rather than have a perfect model in the hands of people who don't understand it, don't really care to use it, or even are scared of it.

For these reasons, one of the most significant contributions rocket scientists can make to the institution for which they are working is to improve the model currently in use.

- Rarely, if ever, will the first release of a simulator, knowledge engineering construct, or any other artifact be perfect at the time of its first release.
- It probably will be wanting, and there will be a learning period during which rocket scientists will be called on to improve the model.

Figure 16.1 shows in a nutshell the learning curve with any system. In many financial institutions the use of VAR has followed this type of learning curve. Notice that the use of any new tool or device takes time to penetrate down into the organization. The difficulty that will be presented with VAR when it becomes old hat will be low, but by then new tools will come on-stream to which people will find it difficult to adapt.

The need for adding value to existing models and sometimes for significantly improving them or replacing them altogether may not be visible immediately, but the test of real life invariably shows the ugly side of the model. Alternatively, after the first wave of admiration of the model goes by, contrarians will point out that there are cracks.

The ACRA model, which we examined in Chapters 11 and 12, is an example. Its major contribution as it currently stands is the attempt to legitimize the extraordinary reserves necessary to face unexpected risks and a supercatastrophe. But as we have seen, in

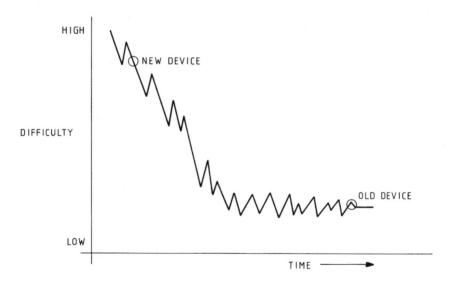

FIGURE 16.1 LEARNING CURVE SHOWING LEVEL OF USER DIFFICULTY
WITH NEW SYSTEMS, EQUIPMENT, AND PROCESSING TOOLS

many countries, including the United States, regulators and the tax authorities don't look kindly at secret reserves.

Secret reserves are also an anathema to GAAP. Companies that wish to be listed on the New York Stock Exchange, as many big firms do, have to depart with this time-honored method of providing a good financial cushion. ACRA could, however, become a predictive tool

- If it is improved to make transparent the bank's credit risk over time and
- If it proves useful in assisting the board and senior management in perceiving the evolution of credit risk in a three-dimensional frame of reference.

A model that in its current state does not go far enough should be the point of attention of rocket scientists, who must be able to perceive that ACRA and CreditMetrics, as they now stand, fail to appropriately map the lifetime of loans. Figure 16.2 corrects this failure by introducing the dimension of time. The careful reader will notice that I have incorporated a 10-year time frame. This is only an example.

- The life span should be scaleable to reflect the number of years of the bank's commitments.
- The board and senior management should be able to visualize at a glance the whole landscape, including the spikes in the plane of losses versus time.

Investors in credit derivatives should demand this three-D picture of every securitized pool of corporates, like in the mid- to late-1980s with mortgage-backed financing they demanded option-adjusted spread (OAS). To answer the call for OAS, investment banks that securitized mortgages had to learn to do Monte Carlo. Today, they have to do three-D visualization of the frequency/size of losses/time plane.

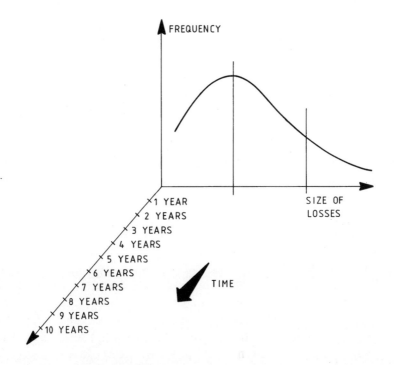

FIGURE 16.2 ACRA and CreditMetrics Need a Third Dimension
to Be Meaningful Tools.

5. WHO DECIDES ON THE WORK ROCKET SCIENTISTS DO?

During my research I asked who decides on the projects rocket scientists should do. The answers were not homogeneous. Therefore, let me start with one of the best examples that I have seen when the whole business of rigorous analytical and mathematical studies in finance started gaining momentum.

In the late 1980s, Morgan Stanley put together its human and technological resources in rocket science, creating a new independent business unit, Advanced Systems Group (ASG). This unit became very market sensitive and profitable to the parent firm.

With the exception of internal applied research (see section 3) the projects that it undertook had sponsors. Some of the sponsors were from Morgan Stanley, which needed models to keep competitive. But many of the sponsors were from other Wall Street firms and from commercial banks that required assistance.

This way, ASG kept on being a profitable business unit of Morgan Stanley, hitting two birds with one well-placed stone. It provided the parent firm with expertise in rocket science and also contributed to its investment banking fame—and year after year it came up with good profits as its appeal to the market widened.

Very few institutions follow this path. Most keep their rocket scientists in-house, though they may give away some of their models for relationship banking reasons (RiskMetrics, CreditMetrics) or sell them to competitors and other firms (RAROC, CreditRisk+). By contrast, ASG was a profit center.

When the rocket scientists are kept in-house, who decides on the projects they undertake? Who writes the specifications? Who says if they answer these specifications and if they fit the objectives? Who pays for them, essentially supporting through his budget the work being done? There is no unique answer to these queries.

Usually requests for models come from the trading desks, which react to demands by clients or else feel they themselves need assistance. Rarely is top management involved in writing specifications for models or even defining what should be done. Yet, this is a good approach because it brings a strategic perspective into the work rocket scientists do.

The second major channel for projects in interactive computational finance is risk management (see section 6), which usually has its own group of rocket scientists.

In talks during my research there was much debate regarding who has the better rocket scientists: trading or risk management? If it is the former (which often happens), then those in risk management would have great difficulty in controlling the models the traders' analysts create as well as in challenging the correctness of financial instruments' pricing.

The rocket scientists of both the traders and the risk managers are working to ensure that the results are positive. But they do so from two totally different viewpoints since the job of the latter is to control the former.

Usually, the traders' rocket scientists work with microeconomic models, with macroeconomic models an exception. Usually, macroeconomic models come from academia and aim to identify the factors that cause crises or predict trouble ahead.

Some investment banks, too, work in this field. An example is the "Currency Jump Probability" measure by Lehman Brothers. In the general case, the results are rather mixed. With a few exceptions, like the macroeconomic model of the Italian economy Dr. Franco Modigliani developed in the early 1970s for the governor of the Bank of Italy, I would not make a case about the fit of macroeconomic models used by banks.

Designed primarily for emerging markets, some current macroeconomic models in the banking industry are meant to help investment bankers and their clients to work out whether and when a country's currency will crash. How well did they work in connection to the 1997 crisis in East-Asia? Not so well.

There is no evidence that these models improved on what investors classically use: a careful but informal analysis of a country's circumstances. The crucial question is not whether models are successful at predicting past crises. This they do since they are calculated on the basis of historical statistics and with the benefit of hindsight. The real-life test is whether they are capable of predicting crises that occur well after the period from which their equations were derived.

In other words, are they good predictors of future turmoil in the financial markets? As Figure 16.3 documents, for one of them the answer is not at all convincing, while for another it is on the edge.

I would like to know how the sponsors of one of these models reacted when the results came in. Also, regarding the other model, which was nearly accurate, what kind of measures did the board and senior management take to heed the warning about exposure in East-Asia? Forewarned about what was coming, has the Morgan Bank positioned itself to profit from the meltdown in East-Asia?

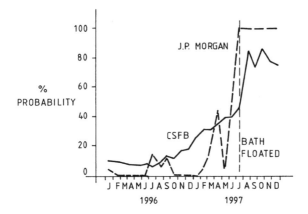

FIGURE 16.3 THAILAND'S CRISIS PROBABILITY ESTIMATED BY DIFFERENT
MODELS

6. ROCKET SCIENTISTS, A STRATEGIC PLAN, AND THE BOARD

VAR, which Chapter 15 addressed, is a market risk model. By contrast, ACRA, CreditMetrics, and CreditRisk+—as their name implies—are models designed to gauge credit exposure. We have also spoken of the need to integrate market risk and credit risk, as well as to address other domains that are not currently covered by quantitative approaches. What has not yet been said is that there is a risk in this expansion when it is not part of a plan—specifically, when the model *is* the plan. Today most financial institutions are faced with the requirement to extend their current market risk and credit risk models to all areas of securities trading and to other types of exposure—for instance, operations risk.

If there is no strategic plan to govern the introduction and implementation of quantitative solutions, the issue of how best to police the institution's activities in the different model-making projects remains unanswered. This issue concerns not only commercial and investment bankers but also the regulators, the shareholders, and the bank's clients.

Only after the strategic perspective has been established, comes the issue of the discipline that should characterize the tactical approach(es). Analysts active in risk management appreciate that in tactical solutions first and foremost it is important to develop the ability to break down risk into fine-grained factors that can be studied both individually and in synergy with one another. Procedures and tools are necessary to tear an option apart, ripping out, for instance, credit risk, foreign exchange risk, liquidity risk, and volatility risk.[3]

This needs to be done across the board with instruments able to assist in making accurate estimates, then recompiling the individual risk factors in order to permit a strategy of offsetting those risks, implementing limits, assuring the observance of these limits, and controlling whether appropriate action has been taken.

Because many derivative financial instruments are not liquid, models are needed for an objective pricing done in a way that also furthers risk management. One of the added advantages of marking to model is that it follows the central idea that the amount of capital a bank needs is related to the riskiness of its business. It is measured by the volatility of its income, the volume and type of trades it undertakes, and its accumulated past exposure.

This example helps to define the polyvalent type of work rocket scientists must do and therefore the requirements concerning their background. But models should not make senior management forget that the control of exposure requires much more than algorithms.

Like internal control, risk management is not the personal responsibility of rocket scientists. It is the personal responsibility of every member of the board and of senior management. Therefore, an institution's reporting structure should be revamped into a tool for translating and visualizing financial data for risk analysis, preferably in a three-dimensional frame of reference.

Designing the proper reporting structure for senior management is not the rocket scientists' job, but that of the information

---

[3] See D.N. Chorafas, *Understanding Volatility and Liquidity in Financial Markets,* Euromoney, London, 1998.

technologists and of the organization department. The rocket scientist's job is the analytics. The reporting structure should help the bank's executives not only to perceive opportunities and risks but also to proceed with a factual and documented corrective action. No model will take this responsibility away from them.

While the coming years are likely to see continued expansion of capital markets worldwide, increasing the size and diversity of issuers, high-risk, low-quality investing will by all probability decline. Belatedly investors start appreciating the ancient truth that *money is credit*. The answer to the query "Where else can money go?" is that it can disappear if credit is doubtful, investors run for cover, and banks don't lend.

More than ever, rigorous analytical solutions are necessary because during the mid- to late-1990s, and as far as we can see in the new millennium, the big problems are mainly revolving around geared debt markets rather than the equity markets. Credit derivatives are a prime example on this debt markets reference. Risks are arising partially because of leverage and partially because of the unknowns connected to the business opportunity presented by new financial instruments. Better and better analytics are the tools that permit dealing with unintended consequences.

Index